GUINNESS
CRICKET FIRSTS

GUINNESS CRICKET FIRSTS

Robert Brooke and Peter Matthews

Robert Brooke is a freelance cricket writer and researcher. He was sole author of the Collins *Who's Who of First-Class Cricketers* (1985) and *The Cricketer Book of Cricket Milestones* (1987). He contributes a monthly 'Milestones' column to *The Cricketer* magazine, for whom he also looks after the 'Obituaries' page. He is a regular member of the team which annually produces *Wisden Cricketers Almanack*, and a contributor to numerous books and magazines, both in England and elsewhere. Robert Brooke also keeps the records for Warwickshire, his native county, of which he is a long-standing member and supporter.

Peter Matthews, a sports consultant to *The Guinness Book of Records*, is an athletics commentator for ITV and also editor of the *International Athletics Annual.* Previous works include: *Track & Field Athletics: The Records* (1986) and the *Guinness Encyclopaedia of Sports Records & Results* (1987). He has collected cricket statistics and records from boyhood.

Editor: Beatrice Frei
Picture Editor: Alex Goldberg
Design and Layout: Michael Morey

© Robert Brooke, Peter Matthews and Guinness Publishing Ltd, 1988

Published in Great Britain by Guinness Publishing Ltd, 33 London Road, Enfield, Middlesex

Typeset in Century Schoolbook by Ace Filmsetting Ltd, Frome, Somerset
Printed and bound in Great Britain by Hazell Watson and Viney Ltd, Aylesbury, Bucks

'Guinness' is a registered trade mark of Guinness Superlatives Ltd
British Library Cataloguing in Publication Data

Matthews, Peter, 1945–
    Guinness cricket firsts.
    1. Cricket—Encyclopaedias
    I. Title   II. Brooke, Robert
    796.35'8

ISBN 0–85112–365–1

ACKNOWLEDGEMENTS

Those to whom thanks are due include:
John Goulstone—especially for help with early cricket.
Anandji Dossa (India)
Peter Sichel (South Africa)
Vic Isaacs
Marion Collin, Women's Cricket Association

ABBREVIATIONS

Aus	Australia
Eng	England
Ind	India
NZ	New Zealand
Pak	Pakistan
SA	South Africa
SL	Sri Lanka
WI	West Indies
Zim	Zimbabwe
ICC	International (Imperial) Cricket Conference
MCC	Marylebone Cricket Club
WSC	World Series Cricket

CONTENTS

INTRODUCTION

When the idea of compiling a *Cricket Firsts* book was suggested to me by Guinness in the Spring of 1987, my first thought was to seek the assistance of Robert Brooke, one of the very few people whose breadth of cricket knowledge could help probe the depths of the subject.

We started from the milestones in the history of cricket and the firsts established in the development of the game and its records. For each major cricket playing country we have surveyed the firsts from the first clubs and matches of any sort to the start of first-class and Test cricket, proceeding to cover their major championships. In each category we have documented firsts to such cricketing achievements as first century, double, triple and quadruple centuries; five wickets in an innings, ten wickets in a match, hat tricks, five catches in an innings and so on. Then we have listed those men to have been the first to achieve significant season's or career targets in such competitions as the County Championship, Sheffield Shield, Ranji Trophy, Shell Shield and the more recently established limited-overs competitions in each country.

With such a core structure we have then added many miscellaneous firsts that may have been important or which simply caught our attention. From the first player to be out 'handled the ball', to the first riot at a cricket match, the first flood-lit game, or the first cricketers to be killed mountaineering or in a motoring accident.

We have looked at the Test playing nations and, more briefly, at cricket elsewhere, in the USA, Canada, Denmark and the Netherlands for instance.

We are grateful to Marion Collin for her assistance in the chapter on women's cricket, and to John Goulstone for essential information for the equipment and grounds section.

Then we have added various miscellaneous sections, such as a survey of the first cricketers to achieve prominence at other sports or in politics, the arts or the church. Overall we have tried to include a wide-ranging collection of as many firsts as we could within the confines of the size of book.

It is hoped that a further selection of miscellaneous firsts might be included in any future edition, so the authors would be delighted to hear any suggestions for new items or corrections to the current text.

Peter Matthews

ENGLAND

MILESTONES

The earliest **certain reference to cricket** was in 1598 in the Guildford Guild Merchants' Book, Guildford, Surrey. The book quotes a 59-year-old court witness that 'when a scholar in the free school of Guildeford he and diverse of his fellows did runne and play there at crickett and other plaies'. The implication is that when this witness was a schoolboy (i.e. in the late 1550s) cricket was a game played fairly frequently among children.

The first **match in which two teams are named** took place in *c.* 1610. This was only recorded in 1640 when one Robert Spilstedd, taking an action for trespass in the King's Bench on 12 May that year mentions that on a parcel of land named in the case '. . . about 30 years since (i.e. about 1610) (there had been) a Cricketting between the Weald & Upland and this Chalkehill (i.e. North Downs) distinguished'. Despite the quaint language, this surely proves that cricket had been played on the land in question —near Sevenoaks in Kent—around 1610.

The first known case of **cricketers being in trouble for playing on the Sabbath**: It was reported that on Easter Sunday, 24 Mar 1611, Richard Latter and Bartholomew Wyatt of Sidlesham, Sussex, played 'crickett' together instead of attending divine service in their parish church. After being arraigned by the churchwardens they were tried in Chichester Cathedral, found guilty, and fined one shilling each (which seems an amazingly severe punishment!).

Henry Cuffin, curate of Ruckinge, Kent, was 'presented' in 1629 at the local archdeaconry court for having played cricket after evening prayer with 'boys, and other mean and base persons'. Cuffin, who admitted the charge of playing cricket but claimed his fellow players were 'persons of repute and fashion', was educated at King's College, Cambridge, and was **the first recorded cricketer from a university**.

The earliest known Oxford University cricketer was Thomas Harlackenden, who, with Samuel Filmer, both members of prominent Kentish royalist families, beat four Maidstone men, Walter Francklyn, Richard Marsh, Robert Sanders and William Cooper, in a 'game of cricket' held on Coxheath, an open common near Maidstone, Kent, on 29 May 1646. This was **the first match in which all the players were named, and the result recorded**.

The first documented wager on cricket was made the day before the match when William Wood, possibly a woollen draper of Maidstone, had a bet on the result with one Nicholas Hunt, promising to deliver to Hunt one dozen candles should Harlackenden and Filmer win the match. The referee was Robert Brooke, a Maidstone blacksmith. Wood reneged on the bet.

The first reference to **cricket being played abroad** was in 1676, when at least 40 English residents of Aleppo (Syria) journeyed to a valley 4 miles outside the city and there '. . . had several pastimes and sports, as duck-shooting, fishing, shooting, hand-ball, krickett . . .'.

According to a report in the *Foreign Post* of 7 July 1697 '. . . a great match at cricket was played in Sussex, they were eleven of a side and they played for fifty guineas apiece'. This was the first **mention of eleven players in a side**.

The first known **cricket advertisement** appeared in *The Post Boy* on 30 Mar 1700 '. . . to inform gentlemen, or others, who delight in cricket playing, that a match at cricket, of ten gentlemen on each side, will be play'd on Clapham Common . . . on Easter Monday'.

The first **publications devoted to cricket** were published in 1712. These were two tracts attacking Sunday cricket, *The Devil and the Peers*, 'being a true account of a famous cricket match between the Duke of M . . ., another Lord, and two boys . . . in Windsor Forest' and *The Sabbath-Breakers*, or *Young Man's Dreadful Warning Piece*, 'being a very dismal account of four young-men who made a match to play cricket . . . in a meadow near Maiden Head Thicket'. (The 'Duke of M . . .' was the famous Duke of Marlborough.)

The first **record of cricket by a club side** was when the Rochester Punch Club Society played London in the White Conduit Fields, Islington, London, on 1 Sep 1718. The game was left unfinished, the earliest recorded instance of

Cricket played at White Conduit House in 1787.

'rain stopped play' as the Rochester men claimed that through 'the rains, which fell so heavy, it was impossible to continue the game'. However, after a trial at the Guildhall, presided over by the Lord Chief Justice, it was ordered to be completed the following season. The match was for £60, yet the legal costs, it was said, amounted to nearly £200—considerable sums for those days.

The first recorded **innings victory** was reported in the diary of Thomas Marchant of Hurst, Sussex, in 1721: 'a cricket match in ye Sandfield between Stenning and our parish, the latter won at one innings'.

A detailed list of Rules and Regulations ('Articles of Agreement') was drawn up in 1727 for two matches in Sussex and Surrey between teams 'got up' by the 2nd Duke of Richmond and Alan Brodrick, later Viscount Midleton. Such questions as catches, run outs, players' residential qualifications, substitutes and umpires were dealt with; it would appear that these regulations were supplementary to an existing Code of Laws about which nothing is now known.

A code of cricket laws was drawn up in London in 1744. This was subsequently printed in the *New Universal Magazine* in 1752 as 'the game at cricket, as settled by the cricket-club, in 1744, and play'd at the Artillery-ground, London'. According to a later edition, advertised in the *Reading Mercury* in 1767 they had been 'settled in the year 1744 by the Society of Noblemen and Gentlemen at the Star & Garter in Pall Mall'.

The first known **team total recorded** was 52 by Kent v Sussex in Penshurst Park in late July or early August 1728.

The first known **three-figure innings total** was 119 for Mr Chambers' XI v The Duke of Richmond's XI, on Richmond Green, Surrey, on 23 Aug 1731.

Cricket was known to have been **commemorated on an inn-sign** for the first time in 1735. 'YE 11 CRICKETERS' beside the green at Meopham, Kent, was kept by a sister of Valentine Romney, 'allowed to have been the best cricket-player in the world'. The inn-sign was later transferred to a nearby house, which

Opposite *Print of Lord's first ground, the match was between teams got up by the Earls of Winchilsea and Darnley for 1000 guineas on 20–21 June 1793. Curiously, the wickets show only two stumps, whereas the 1785 version of The Laws provided for three stumps.*

remains the headquarters of the present Meopham Cricket Club.

The first documented **case of a batsman being injured by a 'bouncer'** was in 1736. During a match on Kennington Common in June a breast-high ball deflected off this unnamed man's bat, broke his nose, 'hurt his eye, and bruised his face in a most sad manner'. In consequence the game had to be postponed for a fortnight. The earliest known instance of a batsman actually being knocked out by a ball occurred a year later, again on Kennington Common, when the striker received 'so smart a blow by the ball that he was knocked down and lay stupid for a long time'.

The first recorded tie match was a three-a-side contest in August 1736 in Lamb's Conduit Fields, London: London 5 and 18 v Richmond, Fulham & Barnes 17 and 6.

The first known **cricket picture** issued was an engraving by the French artist Hubert Gravelot in 1739 for a small book of children's games, showing a number of small boys playing an informal game with bat, ball and rudimentary wicket. There are, however, several much earlier, medieval depictions which may represent an older form of cricket. Perhaps the most convincing are a boy with a ball and curved stick portrayed in a window in the north east transept of Canterbury Cathedral, dating from the late 12th century, and the picture of a man with a curved stick and ball in the east—'Crécy'—window of Gloucester Cathedral dating from the mid-14th century. This is illustrated as plate I opposite page 28 in *The Art of Cricket*, by Robin Simon and Alistair Smart.

An England 'national' team (the first) played Kent on Bromley Common on 9 July 1739. In one account the match is styled 'eleven gentlemen from any part of England, exclusive of Kent'; an alternative version has it 'eleven gamesters picked out of all England'.

The earliest surviving **score-sheet** is for a trial match on London's Artillery ground on 2 June 1744. It gave total runs by each batsman and byes for both innings.

The first full match score preserved which in any way resembles a modern score-card is for England v Kent at the Artillery ground on 18 June 1744.

The earliest known **'hat-trick'** was by an unnamed bowler for Addington (Surrey) v Dartford on the Dartford ground on 17 July 1750. 'Dartford had five men bowled and caught out in five succeeding bowls the last hands', ran the report. In those days, 4-ball overs were normal for more important matches, so one of the Addington bowlers must have taken three or four wickets in consecutive balls.

The first known **fifty partnership between two batsmen** was 51 for the first wicket for England in the second innings of their match with Kent at the Artillery ground on 21 May 1751. According to *Kent Cricket Matches* one of the partners was 'Harding, the Thursley bowler', the other is unknown, other than that he, too, came from Thursley. Stephen Harding, in scoring precisely 50, made the first authenticated **half century**, 'sending one of the balls out of the ground against a house in Bunhill-Row, for which he was allowed (as is customary) four notches'.

The first recorded **university team**, Cambridge, played the Old Etonians at Cambridge in 1754. The match was regarded as an annual one by 1755.

The first recorded **hit for six** was made by Stephen Harding, batting for Chertsey against Richmond on Richmond Green in September 1765.

The first mention of **cricket played on ice** was on 18 Jan 1766. A correspondent from Newcastle-on-Tyne wrote: 'We hear from Hexham that the frost was so severe there, and the River Tyne so strongly frozen over that a sheep was roasted on it, and sold for 12d per pound to a numerous company, who afterwards played at cricket, while others danced.'

The first **century recorded on ice** was 162 by Henry Sampson for Sheffield Wednesday v Sheffield Skaters at Sheffield in February 1841.

The first documented **century partnership** was 192 added in 3½ hours by 'two new hands from Hampshire' for the Hambledon Club against Caterham Club near Croydon in October 1767. Neither the names nor individual scores of the batsmen were reported but the feat was

described as 'the greatest thing ever known'. While it is probable that one of the players scored a century, the first documented **individual century** was scored by John Minchen or Minshull, who made 107 out of an innings total of 236 for His Grace The Duke of Dorset's XI v Wrotham on Sevenoaks Vine, Kent, on 31 Aug 1769.

The first **century in an unarguably 'great' match** was probably scored by Thomas White for Kent & Surrey v Middlesex & Hampshire on Sevenoaks Vine, probably during July 1771. He was later stated to have made 197 runs in the match, though no contemporary reference has ever been found. If this was so, he almost certainly scored a century, but the first definite century in an undeniably first-class or 'great' match was scored by John Small, Snr, for Hampshire v Surrey at Broadhalfpenny Down, Hambledon, on 13–15 July 1775. Small's unbeaten 136 was almost certainly the first instance of a **batsman carrying his bat** through an innings. Small's runs came in an innings total of 357, leaving Surrey to make 375 runs to win. The game went on until 8 p.m. on the third day when Surrey, having scored 78–3, gave up the game.

In July 1769 a **double-tie** was reported near Godalming, Surrey, 'esteemed very extraordinary'. The only instance of a **triple-tie** occurred at Chelsfield, Kent, on 29 July 1840, in a three innings-a-side game between the Revd. Tarleton's staff at Chelsfield Rectory and the staff of J. Berens Esq. at Kevington. Both teams totalled 42, 64 and 115.

The first report of a **knock-out cup competition** was in 1770, organised during Whit Week at Thame, Oxfordshire, and the prize was a silver cup valued at 2 guineas, competed for by four teams, all of which were 'required to play the game'.

The earliest known use of an **'attacking field'** was by England v Hampshire at Sevenoaks Vine on 28–29 June 1773. One of the England fieldsmen, Richard Simmons, was placed deliberately close to the bat and thereby 'greatly intimidated the Hampshire gentlemen'. England won by an innings and 51 runs.

The county retaliated by attempting similar tactics in a return match on Laleham Burway near Chertsey on 13 July, when the Duke of Dorset ran a large number of runs for England, to a great extent from 'off strokes'. 'The Hampshire people very unpolitely swarmed round his bat so close as to impede his making a full stroke.' After pointing out their danger 'he, with proper spirit made full play at a ball and in so doing brought one of the gentlemen to the ground'. England again won the match.

The first known **innings total of more than 300** was 307 all out by Hampshire v England on Broadhalfpenny Down, Hambledon, on 21–23 June 1774. Hampshire also obtained **the first recorded total over 400**, 403 v England at Sevenoaks Vine on 18–20 June 1777. James Aylward scored 167, the first **individual score of over 150 in a 'Great' match**. The left-handed Aylward went in at 5 o'clock on the first day of the match, and was dismissed after 3 o'clock on day three. Hampshire won by an innings and 168 runs. Note that contemporary sources referred to Hampshire, while *Scores and Biographies* later referred to Hambledon.

The first recorded **tie in an important or 'Great' match** was when Hampshire scored 140 and 62 against Kent's 111 and 91 at Windmill Down, Hambledon, 8–9 July 1783. It was later discovered that one of the scorers had made an error which meant that Kent had in reality won by one run but the other scorer could not, or would not, produce his version.

Thomas Sueter was dismissed **'hit the ball twice'** 3—the first on record—playing for Hampshire against Kent on Windmill Down, 13–15 July 1786.

The first **overseas touring team** was organised in 1789. During a period of anti-British agitations, following the outbreak of the French Revolution, the British Government arranged for a cricket team to play in Paris as a goodwill gesture towards the newly-formed National Assembly. From Chertsey the team travelled as far as Dover where on *c.* 15 August it was met by the British Ambassador fleeing from renewed violence in France. In view of the situation the tour was abandoned—undoubtedly a wise decision.

The first recorded match at Lord's was played on 21 May 1787, between 'Eleven Noblemen of the White Conduit Club and Eleven Gentlemen of the County of Middlesex, with two men given'. It was played for £500 a side. The advertisement in the *Morning Herald* for 19 May stated that the wickets were to be pitched at 10 o'clock and the match would be played out.

Nottingham Old Club fielded the first recorded **'second eleven'** and beat Beeston by 41 runs on 29–30 Oct 1792.

The first recorded **cricket match on horseback** was played in Linstead Park, Kent, on 6 May 1794 by 'the Gentlemen of the Hill and the Gentlemen of the Dale, for one guinea a man, the whole to be performed on horseback'. Special long-handled bats were made for the occasion.

The earliest known **inter-school match** was Charterhouse v Westminster at Lord's (Dorset Square) on 5 Aug 1794. The match was played for 500 guineas, and the result was Charterhouse 42 and 24; Westminster 171 (Henry Comyn 37). For Westminster Charles Lewis Atterbury bowled down five wickets in the two innings while for Charterhouse Edward Kempe bowled down six wickets.

In the first innings of a match at Moulsey Hurst, between Thirteen of England and Surrey, played on 12–15 Aug 1795, the Hon. John Tufton became the first known **victim of 'leg before wicket'** when dismissed by John Wells. Going in no. 3 for the England team, Tufton scored 3 runs. In Britcher's scorebook Tufton is put down as 'bowled', with the leg before wicket added in a note. In fact the leg before wicket rule appeared in the revised Laws published in 1774 but this is the first case of such a dismissal actually being identified in a score.

The first cricket **coaching manual** was published *c.* 1800: *Rules and instructions for playing at the game of cricket, as practised by the most eminent players; to which is subjoined the laws and regulations of cricketters* (sic) *as revised by the Cricket Club at Mary-Le-Bone*, compiled by Thomas Boxall and printed by Harrild & Billing of Russell Street, Bermondsey, London. The contents were serialised in *Cricket—A Weekly Record of the Game* for 1891, and printed in volume XIV of *MCC Cricket Scores & Biographies*.

In 1802 the first **teams left the shores of England to play cricket**, in what was described as a 'celebrated match' on the Goodwin Sands. It lasted at least two days, on one of which the 'Duchess of Devonshire and a host of female fashion were present'.

The first known reference **to round-arm bowling** was in the match between 23 of Kent and 13 of England on Penenden Heath, Kent, 20–22 July 1807. *The Sporting Magazine* recorded

THE NEW, OR OVER-HAND SYSTEM,

DEMONSTRATED AT LORD'S GROUNDS, 1842

On Monday an interesting match took place at Lord's Grounds, wherein the relative merits of the fast and slow systems of bowling were tried by eight gentlemen and players, with three bowlers on the new system and the same number with three slow bowlers. The same event has been contested on four previous occasions and the match excited considerable interest. The fast bowlers were Alfred Mynn, Esq., Redgate, and Dean, with E. Bayley, William Felix, R. W. Keate and F. Thackeray, Esqrs., Box, Butler, Dorrington, and Guy, against Lillywhite, Hillier, and Nixon, with the Hon. R. Grimston, R. Kynaston, and Anson, Esqrs., with G. Lee, Hammond, Pilch, and Wenman, on the old systems. The first innings only was completed on each side, when the wickets were struck – the result being in favour of the fast bowlers by 115 runs to 89. Of the players of the swift bowling side, Box secured 35 runs, and W. Felix, Esq., 23; while the Hon. R. Grimston scored 41 runs, and carried his bat out, at the conclusion of the opposing party. The match was concluded on Tuesday, the fast bowlers coming off victorious by a majority of 47 runs on the two innings. The numbers scored by the players on the new, or over-hand system, was 194, while their opponents scored only 147. PICTORIAL TIMES, 1842

Reintroduction of night cricket in England—August 1980, West Indies v Essex at Chelsea AFC ground.

that 'In this match the straight arm bowling introduced by John Willes Esq. was generally practised, and fully proved an obstacle in getting runs, in comparison with what might have been got by the straightforward bowling'. In the match John Hammond obtained 12 stumpings and 4 catches in the two Kent innings, but whether this was partly, or mainly, due to the new sort of bowling is impossible to say.

Over-arm bowling was said to have been employed for the first time in 'first-class' cricket, by Sussex against Epsom at Brighton on 7–9 Aug 1815.

The first **reference to cricket being played by an animal**—a dog named Drake who assisted James Bridger in a single wicket match against J. Cock and W. Wetherell at Holt Pound cricket ground near Farnham, Surrey—was on 16 Aug 1813. After the first innings—scores, Bridger 50, Drake 0, total 50; Cock 6, Wetherell 0, total 6— the two humans conceded defeat. Drake, who did all the fielding for his side but did not bat or bowl, was accorded the honour of having his por-

trait published in *The Sporting Magazine*. Details of his birth and death are not known.

In the first important **match played at the new (present) Lord's ground**, MCC (161) defeated Hertfordshire (79 and 55) by an innings and 27 runs on 22 June 1814. Thomas Lord, whose third ground this was, had advertised the ground as being '. . . completely ready for playing on' in the *Morning Post* for 7 May.

The first recorded **score of 0 all out** was when Walsingham and Fakenham were dismissed by Litcham, Dunham and Brisley, at Hampton Green in 1815.

The first **cricket match to be played under artificial lights** was played by candlelight at Sedley Green, Bexhill, Sussex, on 19 Aug 1816. It was described as 'Beaching v Thomas', which suggests a single wicket game. Press reports stated that the candles were placed in lanterns around the ground. Night cricket, using the somewhat more sophisticated electric **flood-lighting**, was reintroduced more than 150 years later. Several floodlit matches were played in

Australia under the auspices of Kerry Packer, commencing on 14 Dec 1977, and a floodlit tournament was run, with little spectator interest, for the first-class counties in England in 1981. An inter-province floodlit tournament has been run very successfully in South Africa, under the sponsorship of Benson & Hedges, since 1982.

William Lambert became the first batsman to score a **century in both innings of a match**, with 107 not out, out of 292, and 157 out of 445 for Sussex v Epsom at Lord's on 2–6 July 1817. The feat was not repeated until W. G. Grace scored 130 and 102 not out for South v North at Canterbury in 1868, and was not again achieved at Lord's until 1893, when Andrew Stoddart scored 195 not out and 124 for Middlesex v Nottinghamshire. The match aggregate of 1047 runs was the first ever **over 1000**.

William Ward became the first scorer of **a double century** when, on 24–26 July 1820, he obtained 278 in the first innings of 473 for MCC v Norfolk at Lord's. MCC won the match in four days by 417 runs. Ward is reported to have been dropped from an easy chance when 30, otherwise the innings was without a real blemish. There is disagreement about the exact length of Ward's innings. He definitely commenced early on 24 July, batted the whole of the next day, and into the third day (26 July) as the match was completed on 27 July. Ward's score was not beaten in a first-class match until 1876, when W. G. Grace scored 344 for MCC v Kent at Canterbury. It remained the record for Lord's until 1925, when Percy Holmes of Yorkshire scored 315 not out against Middlesex.

BOWLING FIRSTS IN NON-FIRST-CLASS MATCHES

John Kirwan became the first bowler to be recorded as having taken **all ten wickets in an innings**, all bowled, for Eton, who had much the worse of a drawn game with the MCC at Eton on 9 July 1835. The first such instance for **0 runs** was by A. Dartnell for Broad Green v Thornton Heath at Norbury in 1867.

Heathfield Harman Stephenson achieved the **hat-trick** of taking three wickets with three successive balls, playing for the All-England XI v 22 of Hallam and Staveley at Hyde Park, Sheffield, on 8 Sep 1858. This was the earliest recorded instance of a hat actually being presented for this feat. His victims are thought to have been H. Champion, caught for 2, W. Hopkinson, bowled for 0, and J. Dawes, caught for 0. The feat was described as 'a hat' in 1863, 'earning the hat' in 1868 and 'the hat-trick' in 1877.

The first recorded instance of a bowler taking a **wicket with every ball of a 4-ball over** was by Beaumont for Shrewsbury v Liverpool in 1859.

J. Walker, for Ashcombe Park v Tunstall at Leek in 1882, became the first bowler to take **eight wickets with successive balls**.

BOWLING FIRSTS

The first 'all-ten' in a first-class match was by Edmund Hinkly, a fast left-armed round-arm leg break bowler, in England's second innings for Kent at Lord's on 10–11 July 1848. His innings analysis is not known, but five of his victims were bowled, three caught and two stumped and he had taken six wickets in the first innings. England were all out for 72 but eventually won the match by 55 runs.

John Wisden became **the first and only cricketer to take all ten wickets** in a first-class innings, **all bowled**. This feat, for which no analysis has been discovered, was for North in South's 76 at Lord's on 15 July 1850.

For Sussex v Kent at the Royal Cricket Ground, Brighton, on 12–13 Sep 1836, William Lillywhite, slow round arm, and George Millyard, slightly faster round arm, **bowled throughout both innings**, the first time this had been done in a first-class or 'great' match. It is not recorded how many wickets each man took, nor what runs were conceded, but Sussex won by seven wickets. In 1837 Lillywhite became the first bowler to take more than **100 wickets in a season** in 'important' matches, and he had been the first to take 16 wickets in a 'great' match, playing for Sussex v Hampshire and Surrey at Bramshill Park, Hampshire, on 7 Aug 1826. He took seven wickets in the first innings and nine in the second; seven were stumped by W. Broadbridge, five were bowled and four caught.

John Wisden once bowled down all ten wickets in an innings. The Almanack *he started in 1864 is his lasting memorial.*

The first bowler to take **17 wickets** in a 'great' match was Francis Fenner, later known for laying out the ground at Cambridge which bears his name. For Cambridge Town v Cambridge University at Parker's Piece on 21–22 May 1844 he took eight wickets in the first innings and nine in the second; nine of his victims were bowled and eight caught.

Henry Arkwright was the first to take **18 wickets** in a first-class match, bowling for an all-amateur MCC team against a similar Kent team in a 12-a-side match at Canterbury on 14–16 Aug 1861. His analyses were 9–43 and 9–53, each in 24 4-ball overs. He was the first first-class cricketer to be **killed mountaineering**, in a fall on Mont Blanc in 1866.

Four wickets in four balls were taken for the first time in a first-class match by Joseph Wells, the father of novelist H. G. Wells, for Kent v Sussex at Box's (Royal Brunswick) Ground, Hove, on 26 June 1862. The victims, all bowled, were James Dean, Jnr, Spencer Leigh, Charles Ellis and Richard Fillery. Kent won by ten wickets despite a first innings lead of only 8 runs.

BATTING FIRSTS

The Hon. Frederick Ponsonby, later the 6th Earl of Bessborough, was the first batsman known to have scored **nine runs from one ball** in first-class cricket, while playing for MCC v Cambridge University on Parker's Piece, Cambridge, 19–21 May 1842. **Ten runs** were first scored by Lancashire's A. N. 'Monkey' Hornby at The Oval on 14 July 1873 off a delivery from James Street of Surrey.

On 21 Aug 1866, the second day of the Middlesex–Surrey match at The Oval, John Sewell, the Middlesex opener, took his overnight score of 29 not out to 166 before being dismissed, the first recorded instance of a batsman scoring **100 runs in a pre-lunch session** in first-class cricket. It was his only first-class hundred.

Playing for Gloucestershire v Yorkshire at Bradford on 23–25 July 1900, Gilbert Jessop scored a **century in each innings** and in both cases started and finished his innings **before lunch**, 104 on the second day, 139 on the third. Despite this Yorkshire won the match.

Between 16 August and 12 September 1901 Charles Fry became the first batsman to score **six successive centuries** in first-class cricket, in fact the first to obtain more than three. He started with five for Sussex: 106 v Hampshire at Portsmouth, 209 v Yorkshire at Hove, 149 v Middlesex at Hove, 105 v Surrey at The Oval and 140 v Kent at Hove, and then made 105 for Rest of England v Yorkshire at Lord's. His next first-class innings came at the beginning of the 1902 season when he scored 82 for London County v Surrey before being caught by Ernest Nice off Hugh Dolbey. His last innings prior to this sequence was 88 in the first innings v Hampshire. Fry's feat has been equalled by Don Bradman in Australia in 1938–39 and Mike Procter in South Africa in 1970–71.

For the Indians v Surrey at The Oval, 11–14 May 1946, in a first innings score of 454, Chandrasekhar Sarwate (124*) and Sarbindu Banerjee (121) became the first **nos. 10 and 11**

Opposite The all-conquering Australian tour of 1948 gets under way as Arthur Morris clips Worcestershire paceman Reg Perks to leg, watched by partner Sid Barnes. Bob Wyatt is at slip and Laddie Outschoorn in the gully. Three years later wicket-keeper Hugo Yarnold achieved a record six stumpings against a somewhat less awesome Scotland team.

both to score centuries in a first-class innings, as they added 249 together, still the record last wicket partnership in England.

BATTING FIRSTS IN NON-FIRST-CLASS MATCHES

The first known **triple (or quadruple) century** was 404 not out by Edward Tylecote, 14 years later an England player, for Classical v Modern at Clifton College ending 26 May 1868. The first **over 500** was also made in a house match at this school, and it remains the highest score ever made in a bona fide cricket match, 628 not out by Arthur Collins in 6 hr 50 min in the Clarke's House score of 836 v North Town over five afternoons on 22–23, 26–28 June 1899.

Frank Crawford, with 218 in 160 minutes, was the first to hit **200 runs in a pre-lunch session**, for Surrey Amateurs v Professionals at The Oval in 1896.

William Hyman was the first batsman to hit **30 or more sixes in an innings**, 32 during his 359 not out for Bath Association v Thornbury at Alveston in 1902.

ALL-ROUND FIRSTS

V. E. Walker became the first player to score a **century and take all ten wickets in an innings** in the same first-class match. Captaining England v Surrey at The Oval on 21–23 July 1859, he took 10–74 in 43 4-ball overs, with 17 maidens, in Surrey's first innings and made 108, going in at no. 8 in England's second innings. Walker had made 20 not out in the first innings and rounded off his feat with 4–21 in 5 overs in the second innings.

WICKET-KEEPING FIRSTS

Edward Pooley became the first keeper to **dismiss ten batsmen** in a first-class match, for Surrey v Sussex at The Oval, 6–7 July 1868. He caught five and stumped one in the first innings, and in the second caught and stumped three for a match total of **12** dismissals.

Keeping wicket for Worcestershire v Scotland at Broughty Ferry, Dundee, on 2 July 1951, Hugo Yarnold **stumped six** Scottish batsmen in their second innings, a performance which remains unique. Four were off leg-spinner Roly Jenkins, two off left-armer Michael Bradley.

In non-first-class matches, H. W. P. Middleton was the first to take **nine dismissals in an innings**, one caught and eight stumped, Priory v Mitre house match at Repton School in 1930.

TEAM SCORING

Firsts for non-first-class team scores over:

500: An Oxford XI 546 v Purton at Purton 22 June 1859.

600: Classical 630 v Modern at Clifton College ending 26 May 1868.

700: Royal Engineers 724–8 v I Zingari at Chatham 20–21 Aug 1875.

800/900: Orleans Club 920 v Rickling Green at Rickling Green on 4–5 Aug 1882, when Arthur Trevor 338 and George Vernon 259 added 603 runs for the second wicket, the first ever **stand of over 500**.

The first case of over **100 extras in an innings** was 106 (58 byes, 48 wides) in MCC's 372 v Royal Artillery at Lord's on 14 July 1842.

In first-class cricket England were all out for 503 v Surrey at The Oval on 25–27 Aug 1862, the first score of **500 or more**. The first **over 800** in England was 843, then a record, by the Australians v Oxford and Cambridge Universities Past & Present at Portsmouth, 31 July–2 Aug 1893.

Cambridge University were the first team to achieve a target of over **500 runs in a fourth innings**. At Lord's on 27 June 1896, after being 98–2 overnight, they passed the requisite 507 for the loss of seven wickets. Norman Druce made 146, and Harold Marriott 146 not out, adding 118 for the eighth wicket with Edward Bray in 75 minutes.

On the first day of their match against Essex at Southend on 15 May 1948 the Australians scored 721 all out, the only occasion on which **700 runs have been made in one day** of first-class cricket. There were four century makers: Bill Brown 153, Don Bradman (captain) 187, Sam Loxton 120 and Ron Saggers 104 not out, and the innings lasted 6 hours, with four bowlers conceding over 125 runs. Essex collapsed twice, for 83 and 187, next day and lost by an innings and 451 runs.

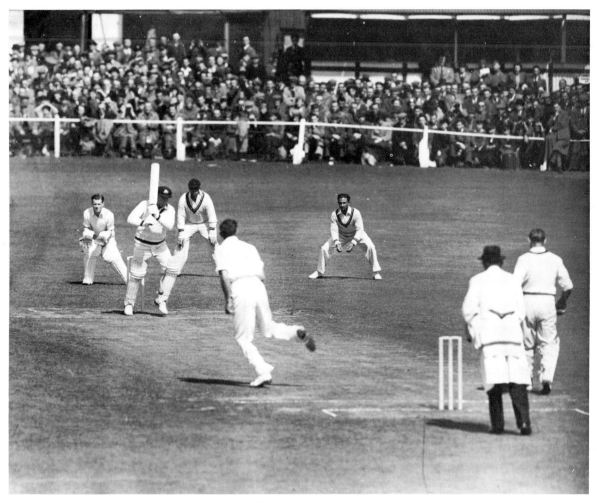

METHODS OF DISMISSAL IN FIRST-CLASS MATCHES

James Grundy was the first to be dismissed **'handled the ball'**, when he had scored 15 for MCC v Kent at Lord's in 1857. Henry Bull, for MCC v Oxford University at Lord's, was the first to be dismissed **'hit the ball twice'**, in the second innings on 10 June 1864 after scoring 29, and Charles Absolom was the first to be given out **'obstructing the field'**, after scoring 38 for Cambridge University v Surrey at The Oval on 19 June 1868. A return from a fielder after overthrows hit Absolom's bat and the umpire believed that to be deliberate.

W. G. GRACE

Dr William Gilbert Grace, the great 'W.G.', a legend in his own lifetime, set numerous 'firsts' in his brilliant career. His first first-class match was for the Gentlemen of the South v Players of the South in 1865, his last in 1908 for the Gentlemen of England v Surrey, both at The Oval.

On 11 Aug 1869, at Canterbury, W.G. opened for the MCC v Kent and by luncheon had taken his score to 116 not out. This is the first recorded case of a batsman scoring a **century on the first morning** of a first-class match. He was eventually dismissed for 127. In 1871 he became the first batsman to score more than **2000 runs** and **ten centuries** in first-class matches in a season; 2739 runs av. 78.25 in 39 innings (4 not outs). In eleven innings in August he scored 1024 runs av. 93.09, the first instance of a player scoring **1000 runs in first-class cricket in a calendar month**. In 1895 W.G. became the first batsman to score **1000 first-class runs in the month of May**. His innings were: 13 & 103, 18 & 25, 288, 52, 257 & 73*, 18, 169 for a total of 1016 runs av. 112.88 in seven innings (one not out). The 288, for Gloucestershire v Somerset at Bristol on 18 May, was his **100th first-class hundred**, by far the first man to achieve that figure.

Grace's runs totals and averages were usually far ahead of his contemporaries. After first scor-

Opposite *W. G. Grace—ready for anything, c. 1890.*

Dinner menu to celebrate W.G.'s 100th hundred. The list contains entries rejected by some statistical zealots 90 years later.

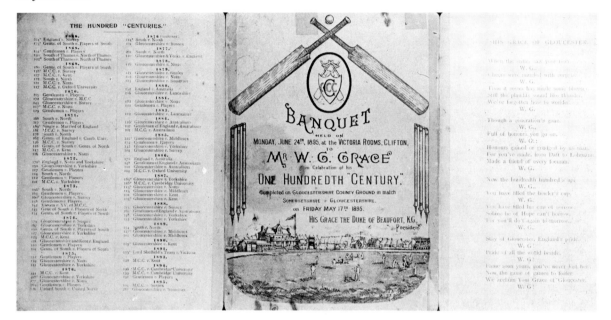

ing 2000 runs in 1871, he did so again in 1876 (2622 av. 62.42) and 1887 (2062 av. 54.26), before William Gunn became the next man to achieve this feat in 1893. Grace did so again in 1895 and 1986. An aggregate of over 2000 runs was exceeded every year from 1895 to 1973, but now, partly due to the reduction in first-class fixtures, the figure is rarely achieved. In 1874 W.G. achieved the first **double of 1000 runs and 100 wickets** in first-class cricket: 1664 runs av. 52.00 and 140 wickets av. 12.71, and he went on to be the first to 2000/100 in 1876, with 2622 runs av. 62.42 and 130 wickets av. 12.71.

On 11–12 Aug 1876 W.G. scored the first **triple century** in first-class cricket, 344 in an innings total of 557–9 for MCC v Kent at Canterbury. His innings commenced at 4.55 p.m. on the second day of the match, MCC following on 329 runs behind on first innings. By close of play he had scored 133 out of 217–4 and by the time he was dismissed on the third afternoon he had been at the wicket for about 6¼ hours and had saved the match for his side. He hit 51 fours, 8 threes, 20 twos and 76 singles. In his first-class career Grace was the first to achieve all **career totals** from **20 000 to 50 000 runs** and the first to take **2000 wickets**.

FIRST-CLASS SEASONAL FIRSTS

The first batsman to score **3000 runs** in first-class cricket **in a season** was Kumar Shri Ranjitsinhji, with 3159 in 58 innings (8 not out) for an average of 63.18 in 1899. 'Ranji', who played for Sussex and England, repeated the feat in 1900 and it has now been achieved 28 times, with a peak of 3816 av. 90.85 by Denis Compton in his *annus mirabilis* of 1947. The last to do so was Bill Alley of Somerset in 1961; the subsequent reduction in the English first-class programme is partially responsible for the demise of this feat.

The first bowler to take over **200 wickets in first-class matches** was James Southerton of Surrey in 1870 when his 210 in 27 matches cost him 14.63 runs apiece. The first to take more than **250** was Charles Turner for the visiting Australians in 1888, when his innings by innings record was as follows: 5–58 & 4–32, 6–44 & 3–57, 4–47 & 3–24, 4–37 & 4–34, 2–48 & 6–67, 6–161, 4–94 & 0–3, 3–90 & 0–15, 2–91 & 2–74, 3–89 & 6–59, 4–30 & 7–29, 4–60 & 5–44, 1–31 & 6–52, 3–66 & 1–66, 4–35 & 8–29, 5–40 & 6–36, 9–15 & 4–33, 5–27 & 5–36, 5–36 & 5–35, 4–56 & 0–8, 5–23 &

5–23, 5–52, 8–13 & 9–37, 4–41 & 6–28, 6–112, 0–75, 4–82 & 1–23, 6–56 & 4–42, 6–85 & 3–14, 5–86, 5–63 & 5–51, 4–48 & 8–74, 2–52 & 3–34, 6–72 & 0–13, 4–59 & 4–42, 3–77 & 4–42; a total of 283 wickets for 3307 runs av. 11.68 in 36 matches.

In 1906 George Hirst achieved the unique feat of a **double double** with 2385 runs av. 45.86 and 208 wickets av. 16.50.

Alfred 'Tich' Freeman of Kent and England achieved the unique feat of taking **300 wickets in a season** in 1928. In 1976.1 6-ball overs of leg-spin he took 304 wickets for 5489 runs, av. 18.05. The nearest approach to this was his own 298 in 1933, and previously Tom Richardson had taken 290 in 1895.

Fred Huish of Kent became, in 1911, the first wicket-keeper to obtain a **hundred dismissals in a season**. His 101 comprised 62 catches and 39 stumpings. He did the feat again in 1913 and to date it has been done on 12 occasions by a total of eight men, of whom the first to achieve the **wicket-keepers' double** with 1000 runs as well was Les Ames of Kent in 1928, when he scored 1919 runs av. 33.53 and took 121 dismissals, a total only once exceeded, by Ames with 129 the following year, when he also scored 1795 runs.

The first **fielder to take 50 catches in a season** was Hugh Trumble, who caught 52 for the Australian tourists in 29 matches in 1893. John Tunnicliffe was the first over **60**, 65 in 32 matches in 1895, and **70** in 35 matches in 1901.

TOURING TEAMS

The first **visit to England** by a cricket team from overseas was when the Phoenix Park Club of Dublin was beaten by the Liverpool Club on Liverpool's ground at Wavertree Road on 29 July 1839. In the return in Dublin on 5 August, the first match played overseas by an English club, the home team won by an innings. The earliest recorded fixture between an English team and one from outside the British Isles was River Club v Calais, played near Dover, Kent, on 9–10 June 1840, with a return at Calais on 29 June. The Calais team consisted wholly of Nottinghamshire weavers resident in France.

The first **professional touring side**, the All-England XI, was organised by the Nottinghamshire captain William Clarke. Its inaugural match was played v 20 of Sheffield at Hyde Park, Sheffield, starting on 31 Aug 1846. According to a contemporary source it 'soon caused cricket to increase vastly all over England, as being the means . . . of discovering many fine players who would never have been brought out had they not had the opportunity of first distinguishing themselves against the England Elevens in their visits to their various part'.

Opposite Famous English Cricketers, 1880.

The first full **tour of England by an overseas team** was in 1868 by 14 Australian Aborigines, captained by Charles Lawrence, who played for Surrey and Middlesex before emigrating to Australia as a cricket coach. The team played 47 matches between May and October, winning 14, losing 14 and drawing the rest. The first tour of England by a representative Australian side was in 1878.

MISCELLANY

The question of cricket was first raised in **Parliament** in 1843 after seven boys had been fined 3 shillings (15p) plus about 12 shillings (60p) costs for playing on their village green at Hurley, Berkshire. Previously cricket had been referred to in passing in the Commons by William Pitt in 1803, when he introduced his Defence Act and specified a maximum distance of six miles between place of residence and assembly, 'not more than people are in the habit of going when led to a cricket match'. Cricket was also mentioned in 1834 by speakers responding to a bill aimed at curbing public activities on the Sabbath.

A **Board of Control** to administer Test cricket in England was established in 1898. It became part of the Test and County Cricket Board in 1969.

William Pitt—Prime Minister 1783–1801; 1804–06. He mentioned cricket in the House of Commons whilst in opposition.

COUNTY CRICKET

The first mention of a **fixture between two counties** was announced by the *Postman* newspaper on 29 June 1709: '. . . a famous match of cricket for £50, by Kent and Surrey', to be played on Dartford Brent.

The earliest recorded **county club** was probably the 'Essex Cricket Club' which met at the Green Man, Navestock, every other Monday from 3 May to 23 Aug 1790. There was reference to 'Oxfordshire Cricket Club' in an engraving of a man in late-18th-century costume holding a bat and ball inscribed 1788. However, the existence of another copy of the print bearing the handwritten date 23 Nov 1825 tends to cast a degree of doubt over its authenticity.

The earliest known reference to a **county match to decide the Championship** was when Kent defeated Nottinghamshire by nine wickets at Town Malling on 27–28 July 1837. Prior to the game the *Maidstone Journal* stated: '. . . the approaching match may be considered as a contest for the Championship'.

The MCC initiated a **county knock-out cup** in 1873. Six counties were scheduled to take part, but Gloucestershire, Middlesex, Nottinghamshire and Yorkshire withdrew for various reasons, so just one match was played. On what was described as 'perhaps the worst wicket ever seen at Lord's', Kent beat Sussex by 52 runs on 9–10 June. Since it had been arranged that no cup be offered during this first experimental season, their victory was not commemorated and the competition collapsed. However, as a direct result of this event, proper and binding rules for county qualification were drawn up for the first time at a meeting of county representatives at The Oval on 9 June 1873. It was not to be until 1962 that an inter-county knock-out competition was re-established.

THE COUNTY CHAMPIONSHIP

County cricket had been played for many years, and a 'Champion county' selected by the press for a number of years, but it was not until 1890 that the counties officially recognised the **County Championship**. This survey therefore starts with that year (which is not to decry or ignore county cricket played earlier).

FIRST SEASON – 1890 – FIRSTS

Wisden for 1891 stated: 'The points in the now officially recognised competition were reckoned in the manner adopted by the county secretaries in December 1889, the losses being deducted from the victories, and drawn games being altogether ignored.' This left no doubt that Surrey were **champions**, nine wins and three defeats gave them six points, two more than Lancashire. Surrey had ensured the title by beating Middlesex at Lord's on 14–15 August, so defeat in two of their last three matches made no difference. The first **wooden spoonists** were Sussex, who hit the bottom in July and withstood all subsequent challenges with great dedication and success. Even Middlesex's six defeats in their last seven matches could not dislodge Sussex.

The **first match** played that year was at Bristol on 12–14 May. The first over, a maiden, was faced by none other than Dr W. G. Grace, captain of Gloucestershire and the greatest cricketer who had ever lived, and bowled for Yorkshire by England left-arm Bobby Peel. W.G.'s elder brother, Dr E. M. Grace, then faced the bowling of the amateur William Whitwell, and fell almost immediately for the first 'duck', caught by the Yorkshire skipper, Lord Hawke. Later in that over Octavius Radcliffe scored the first run and later that day Jimmie Cranston made the first

century, 101 including 6 fours in 3 hours. Yorkshire, for whom George Ulyett (107 in 200 minutes) was the first professional to score a century in the Championship, achieved the first win, by eight wickets on the third afternoon.

Nottinghamshire stalwart Arthur Shrewsbury scored a monumental 267 in 535 minutes for Notts v Sussex at Trent Bridge on 15–17 May, the first **double century** and the first time a batsman had **batted throughout the day** in the Championship. He was joined by William Gunn after the first Notts wicket had fallen for 26 early on the first day. In mid-afternoon they became the first pair to add **200** together and shortly before the close took their **stand** past **300**. They finally added 398 in 360 minutes, then the highest stand for any wicket in first-class cricket. It remained a Championship second wicket record until 1974 and remains a Notts record for any wicket. Gunn's share was 196. During the Notts score of 590, the first of **over 500** in the Championship, Jesse Hide was the first bowler to deliver **300 balls in an innings**, 0–135 in 65 5-ball overs. C. Aubrey Smith bowled 61 overs, taking 1–130, and they were the first to **concede 100 runs** in an innings. Notts achieved the first **innings victory**, with 266 runs to spare.

Hide, an all-rounder who had played for South Australia from 1880–81 to 1882–83 while on a coaching engagement, was one of two men who made their Championship debut in matches played on these days, having **previously played first-class cricket for Australian teams**. The other was James Phillips, an Australian-born player of uncertain age who had played for Victoria since 1885–86, for Middlesex v Kent at Lord's. In this match Middlesex won the toss and became the first to insert the opposition. They skittled Kent on the first day for 98, the first **total under 100**, with their slow bowler George Burton achieving the first **seven wickets in an innings**, 7–46 in 50.2 overs. With 5–62 in the second innings, Burton was the first to take **12 in a match**. Neither of these records lasted the match, however, for the Kent left-armer Walter Wright followed 5–53 with 8–53 in 39 overs in the second innings, for a match analysis of **13 wickets** for 106, enabling Kent to win by 39 runs.

The first bowler to take **14 wickets in a match** was John Sharpe, the Surrey pace bowler, 6–60 in 45 overs and 8–27 in 27 overs v Gloucestershire at The Oval, 29–31 May. In this match H. W. Brown (Gloucestershire) conceded 155 runs while taking six wickets in Surrey's only innings, the first **concession of over 150**. Sharpe (4–27 and 3–23) and George Lohmann (6–23 and 7–21) for Surrey v Lancashire at Old Trafford, 9–10 June, were the first **pair to bowl unchanged throughout a match**.

The first bowler to take **nine wickets in an innings** was fast bowler Arthur Mold 9–41 in 31.1 overs for Lancashire v Yorkshire at Huddersfield, 17–19 July.

For Gloucestershire v Kent at Maidstone, 22–24 May, W. G. Grace opened the match by **carrying his bat** for 109 not out in a total of 231. Kent replied and took their overnight score of 69–2 to 277–4 before lunch on the second day, the first time **200 runs had been scored in the first session**, and eventually won the match by five wickets.

For Yorkshire v Sussex at Bradford, 2–4 June, George Ulyett became the first player to **open batting and bowling in both innings**. He scored 69 and 19, and had bowling figures of 5–72 and 1–32 as Yorkshire won by six wickets.

The Lancashire all-rounder Johnnie Briggs was the first to **score a century and take ten wickets in a match**, as his team beat Sussex by an innings and 187 runs at Old Trafford, 30 June–2 July. He scored 129 not out in 160 minutes and, bowling unchanged, 5–25 and 5–16.

The first **innings total of less than 50** was Kent's first innings 46 v Yorkshire at York on 9 June. Three batsmen, Walter Hearne, Stanley Christopherson and William Spottiswoode were unable to bat due to erroneous instructions by their management.

BATTING FIRSTS

George Bean, opening for Sussex v Nottinghamshire at Hove, 9–11 July 1891, took his score from 45 not out to 145 not out on the second day of the match, the first case of a batsman scoring **100 before lunch** on any day of a Championship match. He carried his bat through an innings of 246 and scored 92 in the second innings, but Sussex lost the match. The first batsman to score a

Robert Peel, left-handed Yorkshire all-rounder with more than 1700 wickets and 12000 runs. Notorious for taking the field when drunk, leading to his removal and dismissal by his captain, Lord Hawke.

century before lunch on the first day of a Championship match was Andrew Stoddart, 101 not out for Middlesex v Nottinghamshire at Lord's on 5 June 1893. He eventually carried his bat for 195 not out in a total of 327 in 215 minutes.

Gilbert Jessop scored a **century in each innings** for Gloucestershire v Yorkshire at Bradford, 23–25 July 1900, in both cases starting and finishing his innings **before lunch**, 104 on the second day and 139 on the third.

On 16 July 1901 Somerset began their second innings v Yorkshire at Headingley with a first wicket stand of 222 between Len Braund and Lionel Palairet. The stand was broken when Braund was out for 107, when Palairet was 112 not out. This was the first time in the Championship that **both openers had scored a century before lunch**. Palairet went on to 173 in Somerset's 630 as they won an amazing victory over the

champions by 279 runs.

Archie McLaren scored 424 in 470 minutes for Lancashire v Somerset at Taunton, 15–17 July 1895. He had reached 289 at the close of the first day out of 555–3, and in all hit 1 six and 62 fours. This remained the only score over 400 in English first-class cricket until 1988. It was both the first **triple and quadruple century**, and Lancashire's total of 801 was the first **over 800**, in the Championship. They won easily by dismissing Somerset for 143 and 206.

This total was improved to 887, still the Championship record, by Yorkshire v Warwickshire at Edgbaston on the first two days of the match, 7–8 May 1896. In this innings there was the first instance in first-class cricket of **four batsmen making centuries**: Bobby Peel 210*, Stanley Jackson 117, Ted Wainwright 126, Lord Hawke 166.

A **century in each innings** of a match was first achieved by George Brann, 105 out of 229 in 175 minutes and 101 out of 223–9 in 170 minutes, for Sussex v Kent at Hove, 22–24 Aug 1892. The first, and so far only, batsman to score **two double centuries** in any first-class match was Arthur Fagg, for Kent v Essex at Colchester on 13–15 July 1938. He made 244 out of 429 in 5 hours and 202 not out in a total of 313–1 dec in 170 minutes, with 58 fours in the two innings.

Jack Brown (300) and John Tunnicliffe (243) put on 554 together for the first wicket for Yorkshire v Derbyshire, who replied with 118 and 157 at Chesterfield on 18–20 Aug 1898, for Yorkshire to win by an innings and 387 runs. This was the first ever **stand over 400** in first-class cricket.

Late on the first day of the Glamorgan/Nottinghamshire match at Swansea, 31 Aug 1968, Gary Sobers, the Notts captain, became the first batsman in first-class cricket to **hit every ball of a 6-ball over for six**. The unfortunate bowler was left-arm Malcolm Nash. The ball was twice hit out of the ground, on the second occasion not being found until the next day. Notts won by 166 runs. Ravi Shastri equalled this feat off Tilak Raj for Bombay v Baroda at Bombay, India on 10 Jan 1985 during his 200 not out in 113 min off 123 balls.

Alfred Shaw bowled the first ball in Test cricket. The accuracy and meanness of his slow medium round arm was legendary; he bowled more overs than he conceded runs.

BOWLING FIRSTS

Arthur Mold became the first to take **15 wickets in a match**, 7–59 in 22.1 overs and 8–72 in 29.2 overs for Lancashire v Somerset at Taunton, 9–10 July 1891, and he also became the first to take **16**, 7–49 in 24.1 overs and 9–62 in 29.4 overs for Lancashire v Kent at Old Trafford, 6–8 June 1895.

The first **hat-trick** was achieved by William Best, an occasional amateur right-arm spinner for Kent, as he dismissed George Nichols, Sammy Woods and Edwin Tyler of Somerset at Taunton on 31 July 1891. **Four wickets with successive balls** was first achieved by pace bowler Frank Shacklock of Nottinghamshire, when he dismissed Somerset batsmen R. P. Spurway, A. E. Newton, W. Trask and J. A. Gibbs at Trent Bridge on 3 June 1893.

Alfred Shaw, at the age of 52, bowled 100.1 5-ball overs (501 balls) for Sussex against his old county, Nottinghamshire, at Trent Bridge, 16–18 May 1895 in the only instance of over **500 balls bowled in an innings** by a player in the Championship.

Bowling for Essex v Leicestershire in the first innings at Leyton, 3–5 June 1895, pace bowler Harry Pickett became the first to take **ten wickets in an innings**, 10–32 in 27 5-ball overs. Leicestershire were dismissed for 111 but eventually won the match by 75 runs.

Edwin Tyler, the Somerset slow left-arm spinner, was the first to **concede 200 runs in an innings**, with 5–215 in 60.3 5-ball overs during Essex's 692 at Taunton, 11–13 July 1895. Over **300** was conceded for the first time by Johnnie Briggs, who was also the first to **bowl over 600 balls** in a Championship match, when he had figures of 2–174 in 66 5-ball overs and 2–132 in 60 overs, a total of 630 balls and 310 runs, for Lancashire v Sussex at Old Trafford, 15–17 July 1897.

The unique feat in first-class cricket of a bowler taking **two hat-tricks in one innings** was achieved by Albert Trott in his benefit match for Middlesex v Somerset at Lord's on 22 May 1907, indeed the first was four in 4 balls and he ended the innings with figures of 7–20 in 8 overs.

ALL-ROUND FIRSTS

W. G. Grace was the first player to be **on the field throughout a completed match**, for Gloucestershire v Kent at Gravesend on 23–25 May 1895. Kent batted first for 470, the visitors replied with 443 with Grace last out for 257. Kent then scored 76 and Gloucestershire made 106–1 to win, Grace 73 not out.

For Yorkshire v Somerset at Bath on 27–29 Aug 1906 George Hirst scored 111 and 117 not out, 6–70 and 5–45; a unique feat in first-class cricket of a **century in each innings and five wickets twice**.

FIELDING FIRSTS

Frank Tarrant of Middlesex was the first fielder to take **six catches in an innings**, v Essex at Leyton, 30 July–1 Aug 1906. Bill Burns, with four in each innings, was the first to take **eight in a**

The great Walter Hammond; the cigarette is somehow apposite. Bristol, a home of the tobacco industry, saw more of Hammond than any other place.

Opposite Eight members of the 1956 Surrey side which had just won its fifth successive Championship. Back row: Micky Stewart, Roy Swetman and Ken Barrington. Front row: Jim Laker, Stuart Surridge, Peter May, Peter Loader and Tony Lock. Surridge retired as captain, to be succeeded by May, who led the county on to seven titles in a row.

match, for Worcestershire v Yorkshire at Bradford on 19–21 Aug 1907. Frank Huish was the first **wicket-keeper to claim ten dismissals in a match**, for Kent v Surrey at The Oval, 21–23 Aug 1911. He stumped four in the first innings, and five with one caught in the second, for what remains a world record **nine stumpings in a match**. E. J. 'Tiger' Smith, for Warwickshire v Derbyshire at Edgbaston, 31 July–3 Aug 1926, was the first wicket-keeper to dismiss **seven batsmen in an innings** in world first-class cricket. In the Derbyshire first innings he caught four and stumped three. The first to take **eight** in the Championship was David East of Essex, as he caught the first eight Somerset batsmen at Taunton on 27 July 1985, his 26th birthday.

The first wicket-keeper to take **eleven dismissals in a match** had been Arnold Long, all caught for Surrey v Northamptonshire at Northampton, 5–7 June 1957.

The first **fielder to take ten catches** in any first-class match was Walter Hammond for Gloucestershire v Surrey at Cheltenham, 15–17 Aug 1928. He held four in the first innings and six in the second, eight of the ten off the left-arm spinner Charlie Parker. Hammond also scored a century in each innings (139 and 143)!

Micky Stewart was the first fieldsman, other than a wicket-keeper, to take **seven catches in an innings**; six at backward short leg and one in the gully, three off Tony Lock and two each off Alec Bedser and Jim Laker, as Surrey dismissed Northamptonshire for 111 on a rain-affected pitch at Northampton on 7 June 1957. Surrey won the match by ten wickets.

TEAM FIRSTS

Lancashire, who batted first after winning the toss, were bowled out for 92 in 197 balls at Old Trafford on 14 July 1892 by Middlesex, for whom J. T. Hearne took 7–42. This was the first occasion on which a whole **side was dismissed before lunch on the first day**.

The first county **score over 600** was made by Nottinghamshire, 674 (Arthur Shrewsbury 164, William Gunn 156, William Barnes 102) in about 9 hours v Sussex at Hove on the first day and a half of the match, which ended as a draw, 8–10

June 1893. Nottinghamshire were also the first over **700**, totalling 726 when they beat Sussex by an innings and 378 runs at Trent Bridge, 16–18 May 1895. They batted for 510 minutes, with three centuries: William Gunn 219, Dick Howitt 119, Robert Bagguley 110.

Hampshire were the first team to score more than **600 runs in a day** in first-class cricket, taking their score from 63–4 to 672–7 on 21 July 1899 v Somerset at Taunton. Robert Poore scored 304 and Teddy Wynyard 225 and they added 411 together, then a world record for the 6th wicket. Hampshire declared at that total and won the match by an innings and 151 runs.

All eleven players bowled, but only three took wickets, for Hampshire at The Oval, 9–11 Aug 1897, in Surrey's 579.

SEASON'S FIRSTS IN CHAMPIONSHIP MATCHES

Arthur Shrewsbury of Nottinghamshire became the first to score **1000 runs in a season** in the Championship, reaching that during an innings of 69 v Yorkshire at Trent Bridge on 7 Aug 1890. In all he scored 1082 runs av. 49.18 in 14 matches,

the only batsman to exceed 1000 in that first season. The only bowlers to take **100 wickets** that year were the Surrey pair, first the medium-pacer George Lohmann, whose 100th victim was Yorkshire's George Ulyett at The Oval on 22 August, then his team-mate John Sharpe the next day.

The first bowler to take **200 wickets** in a season was Tom Richardson of Surrey. His 200th victim, in his 22nd match, was Edwin Tyler of Somerset at Taunton, 22–24 Aug 1895. His total that year was 239 wickets av. 13.78 in 25 matches.

The first to score **2000 runs** was K. S. Ranjitsinhji, reaching that seasonal total in his 17th match for Sussex v Lancashire at Hove, 21–23 Aug 1899. He ended the year with 2285 runs av. 76.16 in 20 matches. Later that month Bobbie Abel of Surrey also completed 2000 runs.

Charles Townsend, left-handed batsman and off-spin bowler, became at 21 the first to achieve the **double of 1000 runs and 100 wickets** for Gloucestershire in 1898. He completed this v Surrey at Clifton during the final match to take his final figures to 1072 runs av. 38.28 and 130 wickets av. 19.96 in 20 matches.

The mightily built, yet agile, Mordecai Sherwin was among the best wicket-keepers in the 1880s. He sometimes turned his hand to bowling and in winter kept goal for Notts County.

The first county team to go through a **season** in the Championship **undefeated** was Yorkshire in 1900, when of 28 matches, they won 16 and drew 12. The first to go **without a win** was Derbyshire in 1897, when they lost 9 and drew 7 of their 16 matches. No county has lost every match in a season, but Derbyshire came uncomfortably close in 1920 when they lost 17 of their 18 matches, and the other, against Nottinghamshire, was abandoned without a ball being bowled.

MISCELLANY

John Rawlin was the first player to appear in the Championship as both **player and umpire** in 1890. Unusually, his first match was as umpire, Middlesex/Yorkshire at Lord's on 12–14 June, before making his playing debut for Middlesex v Lancashire at Old Trafford, 14–16 July. A month later he played for Middlesex v Surrey at Lord's, two months after umpiring a Championship match there, a unique happening.

Yorkshire were the first team in the Championship to be **captained by a professional**, Louis Hall in his benefit match, v Surrey at Bramall Lane, Sheffield, on 30 June–2 July 1890.

They were also the first to field a **team of eleven pros**, when they beat Hampshire by an innings and 271 runs at Hull, 21–23 June 1900: J. T. Brown, Snr, J. Tunnicliffe, D. Denton, E. Wainwright, G. H. Hirst, W. A. I. Washington, S. Haigh, L. Whitehead, W. Rhodes, H. Riley and D. Hunter.

George Watts, selected to keep wicket for Surrey at The Oval, 28–29 Aug 1890, removed his pads for a while in Kent's first innings and bowled 11 overs for 21 runs, but no wickets. It is believed that Bill Lockwood took over behind the stumps. The first **wicket-keeper to come on to bowl and take wickets** was Mordecai Sherwin, when Nottinghamshire needed to take five wickets in the last 30 minutes of play to defeat Middlesex at Lord's on 22 June 1892. He took 2–9 in 7 overs, regular bowler William Attewell three and Nottinghamshire won with about 4 minutes remaining.

The game arranged to take place at Liverpool between Lancashire and Kent on 4–6 June 1891, was completely **rained off**, the first time in the Championship.

When Arthur Sellers, for Yorkshire v Lancashire at Old Trafford, 30 July–1 Aug 1891, was taken ill while fielding Samuel Jackson was brought on as **substitute** and **batted in both innings**, scoring 9 and 0. An amateur from Sheffield, Jackson never again played first-class cricket.

The first **overseas Test player** to play in the Championship was the former Australian bowler John Ferris, who had his debut, having qualified by residence, for Gloucestershire v Surrey at The Oval on 27–29 June 1892. He was dismissed by the first ball of the match!

Pace bowler Frank Gutteridge became the first player to **appear for two counties** in the Championship when he made his Sussex debut v Lancashire at Old Trafford, 19–20 May 1892, having played for Nottinghamshire in 1890.

Bill Scotton, former England batsman, who played for Nottinghamshire in 1890, died by his own hand at the age of 37 in London on 9 July 1893, and is believed to be the first **player** who participated in the official County Championship **to die**.

The Middlesex team group of 1981 includes the eleven who made up the first all-Test player county side. Back: D. Bennett (Coach), R. Maru, R. Butcher (Eng), N. Cowans, J. Thomson (Aust), W. Merry, A. Smith,

K. James, P. Downton (Eng), W. Slack, K. Tomlins, Miller (Physio). Front: J. Emburey, G. Barlow, C. Radley, M. Brearley, P. Edmonds, M. Selvey, M. Gatting (all Eng), W. Daniel (WI).

In 1919 an experiment was tried with **two-day matches** starting on Monday, Wednesday and Friday, with extended playing hours for each day. The first such game was a draw between Middlesex and Northamptonshire at Lord's, 16–17 May 1919. Due mainly to the long hours and travelling difficulties the experiment was abandoned after this one season.

The first **Sunday play** in a Championship match was on 15 May 1966, the second day of Essex v Somerset at Ilford. No admission fee could be charged according to the law, but nearly £500 was taken from about 6000 spectators through the sales of scorecards, seats and collections.

The first county team to field a **full team of Test players** was that by Middlesex at Lord's on 6–8 May 1981. Ironically, Middlesex (153 and 116-5) had the worst of a drawn game with Essex (250-8 dec) who had just four Test players. The top score in the Middlesex first innings was 35 by no. 10 Jeff Thomson, on his debut for the county. The team with the number of Tests played by that date was:

Mike Brearley	Eng	35
Paul Downton	Eng	3
Clive Radley	Eng	8
Mike Gatting	Eng	8
Roland Butcher	Eng	3
Graham Barlow	Eng	3
John Emburey	Eng	14
Phil Edmonds	Eng	18
Mike Selvey	Eng	3
Jeff Thomson	Aus	34
Wayne Daniel	WI	5

The first man to be **awarded his cap by three counties** was slow left-arm bowler Bob Berry. His first was from Lancashire in 1950, in which year he played twice for England v West Indies, and he followed with Worcestershire in 1957 and Derbyshire in 1961.

The first player to play first-class cricket for **four counties** was fast-medium bowler Allan Jones, Sussex in 1966–69, Somerset 1970–75, Middlesex 1976–79, Glamorgan 1980–81, being capped by Somerset and Middlesex. This much-travelled man also played for two South African

Gentlemanly Jack Hobbs—'The Master'—the first professional to be knighted. Still alone in exceeding 60 000 runs in first-class cricket.

sides: Northern Transvaal and Orange Free State. James Southerton had been the first to play for **three counties** (in pre-Championship days), indeed he played for Sussex, Hampshire and Surrey all in the same season, 1867, but that was before a rule was introduced in 1873 to prevent a player appearing for more than one county in any one year.

Four-day County Championship matches were introduced in 1988, when the counties played a mixture of three- and four-day games. The first set of fixtures were played on 21–23, 25 April, when the Essex–Kent match at Chelmsford produced the first instance in the Championship of a **match aggregate of over 1500**. Kent made 400–7 dec (Mark Benson 110, Neil Taylor 95) and 384 (Graham Cowdrey 145, Steven Marsh 120) but lost by eight wickets to Essex. Their first innings score of 616 was the first over 500 in a four-day county match and Graham Gooch (275) made the first double century, aided by Derek Pringle 125. Gooch made 73 in their second innings 170–2, with Allan Border 55 not out. The match aggregate of 1570 surpassed the previous championship record of 1475—Northamptonshire v Surrey at Northampton in 1920.

The first **triple** or **quadruple century** in a four-day match was Graeme Hick's 405 not out for Worcestershire v Somerset at Taunton on 5–6 May 1988. Scored off 469 balls and out of 550 runs made while he was at the wicket in the Worcester total of 628–7 dec, Hick's score was the second highest ever in England, beaten only by MacLaren's 424 in 1895.

FAMILIES

The Graces in the first match had been the first **brothers** to play together in the Championship; the first **father and son** were the Dafts for Nottinghamshire v Surrey at The Oval, 3–5 Aug 1891. Harry Daft, a professional and regular member of the side, was joined by his father Richard, an amateur who had played for the county many years before.

CAREER FIRSTS

Bobbie Abel of Surrey reached **10000 runs** during an innings of 219 v Kent at The Oval, 15–17 Aug 1898, in his 173rd Championship match and his 63rd innings. It gave him an interim career record of 10056 runs av. 41.21.

Tom Hayward, also of Surrey and England, was the first to **20000**, reached in the second innings of a match v Nottinghamshire at The Oval on 5–7 Aug 1907, when he scored 131 not out to take his career total at that point to 20009 runs av. 41.51 in 346 matches.

For many years it seemed likely that Jack Hobbs would be the first to complete **30000 runs** in the Championship, but Phil Mead of Hampshire overtook him in 1926 and reached the milestone first during a typical innings of 183 in 6¼ hours v Yorkshire at Portsmouth, 22–23 June 1927. *Wisden* described the batting of Mead and George Brown, with whom he added 344, as 'wearisome', but it seems none too slow by modern standards. This was Mead's 421st Championship match and his 705th innings, to take his total to 30078 runs av. 47.21. Mead went on to reach exactly **40000** av. 48.54 during his 572nd match and 952nd innings for Hampshire v Nottinghamshire at Trent Bridge, 14–16 June 1933. His final career total of 46268 runs av. 48.19 is likely to remain the record for all time.

Arthur Mold, whose career ended sadly under a cloud due to doubts about his bowling action, was a most effective county bowler. He was the first to take **1000 wickets**, 1002 av. 16.14 after the Lancashire v Nottinghamshire match at Old Trafford, 30 June–2 July 1898.

George Hirst was the first player to complete the **double of 10000 runs and 1000 wickets**, during the Yorkshire v Kent match at Tunbridge Wells, 13–14 July 1905. After this, his 306th match, his figures were 13260 runs av. 35.54 and 1006 wickets av. 19.35. He became the first to **2000 wickets** and the **double double** with **20000 runs** as well, when he reached 2001 wickets av. 17.70 and 23509 runs av. 35.67 after his 487th match, v Warwickshire at Bramall Lane, Sheffield, on 23–25 June 1913. His final Championship record was 27096 runs av. 35.37 and 2095 wickets av. 18.09.

The young George Hirst became the ideal county all-rounder and, for some, the creator's model for a working Yorkshireman.

Hirst's figures have been matched only by his great friend and team-mate Wilfred Rhodes, who reached 20000/2000 in his 526th match. Yorkshire v Glamorgan at Headingley, 1–4 July 1922, during an innings of 110. His figures then were 20048 runs av. 28.68 and 2410 wickets av. 15.65. Uniquely, he took his **3000th wicket** when, appropriately in a 'Roses' match v Lancashire at Old Trafford, 18–21 May 1929, the victim was the great Tasmanian pace bowler Ted McDonald. Rhodes's career ended in 1930, by when he had played in a record 762 Championship games, scoring 26859 runs av. 30.38 and taking 3112 wickets av. 15.71, unapproachable figures.

FAMOUS MATCH SERIES

CHAMPION COUNTY V THE REST

The first match in the regular series was played in 1903 at The Oval, although two years earlier the Rest of England had beaten Yorkshire by an innings and 115 runs at Lord's. The first champion county win was by Yorkshre in 1905.

GENTLEMEN V PLAYERS

The inaugural match in the long series between amateurs and professionals was staged at Lord's on 7–9 July 1806, won by the Gentlemen by an innings and 14 runs. However, the Gentlemen had two 'given' pros, two of the leading players of the day: William Beldham of Hampshire and Surrey, and William Lambert of Surrey. The series ended with the abolition of the distinction in status after the 1962 season. For many years the Lord's match was a highlight of the season, with the teams selected by the MCC. Of 137 matches, the Players won 68 and the Gentlemen 41. Additional matches were played at The Oval and at the Scarborough Festival and other venues. The first **century** in the series was 113 not out by Thomas Beagley of Hampshire forthe Gentlemen at Lord's in 1821, and the first **double century** 215 by W. G. Grace for the Gentlemen at The Oval in 1870.

Arthur Fielder of Kent was the first to take all **ten wickets in an innings**, 10–90 for the Players at Lord's in 1906.

The first man to **play for both teams** was Teddy Diver of Surrey; Gentlemen 1884, Players 1886. He later joined Warwickshire and again was in the Players team in 1899; all his games were at The Oval. Walter Hammond **captained both teams** to successive wins, the Players in 1937 and the Gentlemen in 1938.

UNIVERSITY MATCH – OXFORD V CAMBRIDGE

The first recorded match between the undergraduates of the two senior universities was played at Lord's on 4 June 1827. Due to rain the match was left drawn with only one innings per side completed. Oxford scored 258 with Rice Price top scorer on 71. Cambridge replied with 92, in which Charles Wordsworth, a nephew of the poet William Wordsworth, took at least **seven wickets** (only those bowled down were credited to the bowler). Cambridge's most successful player was Herbert Jenner, who was later knighted and who changed his name to Jenner-Fust; he scored 47 and took at least five wickets.

The varsity match series is continued to this day, with the game played annually at Lord's, as it has always been with the exception of the war years, and at Oxford in 1829, 1843, 1846, 1848 and 1850 when the Magdalen College ground was used (the 1843 game was started there but moved to Bullingdon Green, Oxford, because of the extreme wetness of the Magdalen ground on Cowley Marsh).

The first **century** was 100 scored by William Yardley of Cambridge in 1870, and he followed that with 130 in 1872. In that 1870 match Frank Cobden took the first **hat-trick** in the series, to gain an astonishing victory for Cambridge, as this was achieved when Oxford needed but 3 runs for victory, with three wickets left in their second innings.

The first, and only, instance of **all ten wickets in an innings** and **15 wickets in a match** was by fast bowler Samuel Butler of Oxford, 10–38 and 5–57 in 1871.

The first **double centuries** came in the match played on 6–8 July 1931. Alan Ratcliffe, opening for Cambridge, scored 201 out of his side's 385 on the first day. The Nawab of Pataudi replied with 238 not out (still the record score) in Oxford's 453–8 dec reply. Cambridge were skittled for 122 in their second innings, and Oxford won by eight wickets.

Robin Boyd-Moss, with 139 and 124 for Cambridge in 1983, was the first player to score **two centuries in a match**. He had scored a century (100) the previous year.

The first player to gain **blues with both teams** was David Jarrett, Oxford 1975 and Cambridge 1976.

LIMITED-OVERS CRICKET IN THE BRITISH ISLES

In the early 1960s with gates, membership and general interest plummeting, the English first-class counties got together to try to suggest ways of stemming the decline. In the meantime a few Midland counties organised the **'Midlands Knock-out'** competition, which was played in May 1962. This was under the sponsorship of Leicestershire, and at the instigation of their secretary, Michael Turner, who may therefore be ranked as the 'father' of limited-overs cricket (and, perhaps, the saviour of the game). This was played on a knock-out basis by Derbyshire, Leicestershire, Northamptonshire and Nottinghamshire. Northamptonshire became the first, and only, winners, beating Leicestershire in the final. The first round was played on a basis of 65 overs per side, with each bowler allowed 15 overs. In the final no limit was put on the number of overs a bowler was allowed, but each side was again allocated 65 overs.

Maurice Hallam had the honour of scoring the first run and the first half-century in county limited-overs matches when opening the Leicestershire batting against Derbyshire. He scored 86, and added 106 for the second wicket with Alan Wharton, the first **century partnership**. Notts pace bowler John Cotton took the first wicket, that of Northants batsman Mike Norman, who achieved the first 'duck'.

The competition was adjudged sufficiently successful for the Board of Control to organise a competition for all the first-class counties, which started in 1963.

THE GILLETTE CUP

The first **inter-county limited-overs competition**, competed for by all the first-class counties, and sponsored by Gillette, started in 1963; the opening match was a preliminary round between Lancashire and Leicestershire at Old Trafford. Scheduled to be played on 1 May, rain delayed the start and the match was completed the following day.

Leicestershire skipper Maurice Hallam won the toss and inserted Lancashire, whose opener Brian Booth scored the first run, in the first over, off the bowling of Terry Spencer. Booth's opening partner Robert Entwistle was the first to lose his wicket in the competition, dismissed 'hit wicket' by Leicestershire seam bowler Rodney Pratt. In their 65 overs Lancashire scored 304 for nine wickets, with Peter Marner scoring 121, the first **century in a major inter-county limited-overs competition**. Marner and the Lancashire skipper Ken Grieves added 136 together for the fourth wicket, the first **century stand**. Leicestershire replied with 203 all out in 53.3 overs; thus Lancashire were the first **team to win a match** in this competition. Hallam (106) became the first losing century scorer, and the first captain to score a century; Brian Statham took 5–28 in 12 overs—the first bowler to take **five wickets in a match**. Statham gained most bowling support from Peter Marner, whose figures of 3–49 in 11.3 overs, added to his century, made him the first winner of the **'man-of-the-match'** gold medal.

The first round proper was played on 22 May, when six of the eight ties were won by the side batting first (against tradition). Two of the winners of the 'man-of-the-match' awards were members of the losing side; Peter Richardson scored 127 for Kent v Sussex at Tonbridge as they lost by 72 runs, while Brian Bolus's unbeaten 100 out of 159 all out for Nottinghamshire v Yorkshire at Middlesbrough won him the gold medal, and was the first case of a batsman **carrying his bat** throughout a complete innings.

The first **final** was played at Lord's on 7 September. In poor conditions Sussex, after winning the toss, were dismissed for 168 in 60.2 overs by Worcestershire, who replied with 154 in 63.2 overs. Thus Sussex, captained by Ted

Fresh-faced Norman Gifford proved slow bowlers had a place in limited-overs cricket for Worcestershire in the 1960s. Still 'keeping it tight' for Warwickshire when approaching his 50th year; christened 'Babe' by his more light-hearted fans.

Dexter, became the inaugural **winners of the first inter-county limited-overs competition**, but the first 'man-of-the-match' was Norman Gifford of Worcestershire, who had bowling figures of 4–33.

Leading minor counties participated for the first time in 1964, when the over limit per innings was reduced from 65 to 60. Ireland first took part in 1980 and Scotland in 1981, when NatWest Bank took over the sponsorship from Gillette.

The first **century in a one-day final at Lord's** was made by Geoffrey Boycott, 146, with 3 sixes and 15 fours, for Yorkshire v Surrey on 4 Sep 1965. In the same match Ray Illingworth became the first bowler to take **five wickets in an innings in a final**: 5–29 in 11.4 overs, as Yorkshire won by 175 runs.

OTHER FIRSTS IN GILLETTE CUP/NATWEST TROPHY

MATCH FIRSTS
300 in 60-overs innings: Warwickshire 307–8 v Hampshire, Edgbaston, 27 May 1964

500 in match: 507, Lancashire 304–9 v Leicestershire 203, Old Trafford, 1–2 May 1963

Total under 50: Sussex 49 in 35.2 overs v Derbyshire, Chesterfield, 30 July 1969

Complete match aggregate under 100: 84, Middlesex 41 v Essex 43–2, Westcliff, 19 July 1972

Double century: Alvin Kallicharran 206, Warwickshire v Oxfordshire, Edgbaston, 4 July 1984

200 partnership: Roy Marshall and Barry Reed, 227 for 1st, Hampshire v Bedfordshire, Goldington, 25 and 27 May 1968

6 wickets by bowler: Jack Flavell 13–4–14–6, Worcestershire v Lancashire, Worcester, 10 July 1963

7 wickets by bowler: Peter Sainsbury 13–3–30–7, Hampshire v Norfolk, Southampton, 1, 3 May 1965

8 wickets by bowler: Derek Underwood 11.1–2–31–8, Kent v Scotland, Edinburgh, 24 June 1987

Hat-trick: David Larter, Northamptonshire v Sussex, Northampton, 10 July 1963

80 runs conceded: Derek Underwood 11–0–87–0, Kent v Sussex, Tunbridge Wells, 22 May 1963

90 runs conceded: Robin Johns 12–0–95–2, Hertfordshire v Essex, Hitchin, 11 July 1981

100 runs conceded: Derek Gallop 12–0–106–2 and Simon Porter 12–0–105–1, Oxfordshire v Warwickshire (record score of 392–5), Edgbaston, 4 July 1984

6 dismissals by wicket-keeper: Bob Taylor (5ct 1st), Derbyshire v Essex, Derby, 19 August 1981

10 wickets victory: Northamptonshire 59–0 beat Leicestershire 56, Leicester, 27 May 1964

CAREER FIRSTS
1000 runs: Brian Luckhurst in 24th match, Kent v Durham, Canterbury, 10 July 1974

50 wickets: Peter Lever in 25th match, Lancashire v Hampshire, Bournemouth, 2 Aug 1972

The first **match decided with scores level**, on fewer wickets, was when Somerset 215–9 beat Nottinghamshire 215 at Taunton on 27 May 1964.

Music-loving Mick Norman—batsman and gifted fielder—was a backbone of the county game during service with Northamptonshire and Leicestershire in the '50s, '60s and '70s.

winners of the Gold Cup were Leicestershire who passed Yorkshire's total of 136 for the loss of five wickets in 46.5 overs at Lord's on 22 July. Chris Balderstone, 41 not out, made the top score for Leicestershire, and became the first **'man of the match'** winner in a B&H final.

MATCH FIRSTS

300 in innings: Leicestershire 327–4 v Warwickshire, Coventry, 13 May 1972

500 in match: 514, Hampshire 321–1 v Minor Counties (South) 193, Amersham, 28 Apr 1973

Century: Colin Cowdrey 107*, Kent v Middlesex, Lord's, 29 Apr and 1 May 1972

Carrying bat through 55 overs: Graham Saville 85*, Essex 181–7 v Middlesex, Lord's, 3 and 5 June 1972

100 partnership: Ron Nicholls and Sadiq Mohammed 120 for 1st, Gloucestershire v Glamorgan, Swansea, 29 Apr and 1–2 May 1972

200 partnership: Michael Norman and Brian Davison 227 for 3rd, Leicestershire v Warwickshire, Coventry, 13 May 1972

5 wickets by bowler: Don Wilson 11–4–26–5, Yorkshire v Lancashire, Bradford, 30 Apr–1 May 1972

6 wickets by bowler: Tony Nicholson 11–3–27–6, Yorkshire v Minor Counties (North), Middlesbrough, 20 May 1972

7 wickets by bowler: Wayne Daniel 11–5–12–7, Middlesex v Minor Counties (East), Ipswich, 22 Apr 1978

Hat-trick: Graham McKenzie, Leicestershire v Worcestershire, Worcester, 3 June 1972

80 runs conceded: Jack Smith 11–0–80–0, Minor Counties (South) v Hampshire, Amersham, 28 Apr 1973

8 dismissals by wicket-keeper: Derek Taylor (all ct), Somerset v Combined Universities, Taunton, 8 May 1982

10 wickets victory: Essex 136–0 beat Middlesex 133, Harlow, 2 June 1973

CAREER FIRSTS

1000 runs: Geoffrey Boycott in 24th match, Yorkshire v Northamptonshire, Middlesbrough, 30 April 1977

2000 runs: Graham Gooch in 44th match, Essex

The first match reduced to a **10-over game** was played at Castleford on 25 May 1967, when Yorkshire 46–4 beat Cambridgeshire 43–8.

The first **minor county victory over a first-class county** was when Durham beat Yorkshire at Harrogate, 30 June 1973.

THE BENSON & HEDGES CUP

This, the third of the regular limited-overs competitions in Britain, was started in 1972, contested by the 17 first-class counties, Minor Counties (North) and (South) and Cambridge University. Oxford and Cambridge alternated each season until 1975, from when they formed a Combined Universities team. Scotland entered in 1980, when the Minor Counties were restricted to one team. Four regional leagues determine two teams from each to go through to quarter-finals of a knock-out competition. Matches are over 55 overs, with bowlers restricted to 11 overs each.

The first matches were commenced on 29 Apr 1972, but none was completed that day. They were extended over the next three days. The first v Minor Counties, Slough, 17 May 1983

3000 runs: Graham Gooch in 69th match, Essex v Combined Universities, Cambridge, 16 May 1987.

50 wickets: Graham McKenzie in 24th match, Leicestershire v Lancashire, Leicester, 4 June 1975

100 wickets: Robin Jackman in 55th match, Surrey v Hampshire, Southampton, 27 May 1982

100 dismissals: David Bairstow in 68th match, Yorkshire v Worcestershire, 17 May 1986

500 runs in a season: Graham Gooch 591 av. 84.42 for Essex in 1979 (133, 66, 83, 2, 138, 49, 120)

The first **score of under 60** was the freak 1–0 declared by Somerset after just one over v Worcestershire at Worcester, when on 24 May 1979 they threw away the match to lose by 10 wickets in order to ensure that they maintained the requisite striking rate which ensured them a place in the quarter-finals. At a TCCB meeting a few days later Somerset were charged with bringing the game into disrepute and became the first **team to be disqualified** from a limited-overs competition.

The **Minor Counties team first beat a first-class county** at Chippenham, Wiltshire, on 22 May 1980, when they scored 212–8 to Gloucestershire's 209.

THE SUNDAY LEAGUE

The John Player League was first contested in 1969. The 17 first-class counties played 40-overs matches on a league basis, the format remaining unchanged until 1988, when a final first decided the championship. New sponsors, Refuge Assurance, took over in 1987.

The first set of matches were played on 27 Apr 1969, and the winners in that first season were Lancashire, by one point from Hampshire.

MATCH FIRSTS

300 in innings: Worcestershire 307–4 (in 38 overs) v Derbyshire, Worcester, 3 Aug 1975

500 in match: 519, Sussex 288 v Middlesex 231, Hove, 31 Aug 1969

600 in match: 600, Essex 299–4 v Warwickshire (first **side to score 300 batting second**) 301–6, Colchester, 22 Aug 1982

Total under 50: Northamptonshire 45 in 28.1 overs v Essex, Ilford, 6 June 1971 (match completed in 2 hr 13 min)

Total under 30: Middlesex 23 in 19.4 overs v Yorkshire, Leeds, 23 June 1974

Century: Greg Chappell 128*, Somerset v Surrey, Brislington, 15 June 1969

150 score: Barry Richards, 155* in 142 balls, Hampshire v Yorkshire, Hull, 7 June 1970

100 partnership: Mike Denness and Brian Luckhurst, 111 for 2nd, Kent v Somerset, Bath, 4 May 1969

200 partnership: Alan Butcher and Geoff Howarth 218 for 1st, Surrey v Gloucestershire, The Oval, 13 June 1976

Carrying bat through 40 overs: Roger Prideaux 68, Northamptonshire 174–4 v Worcestershire, Northampton, 11 May 1969

5 wickets by bowler: Terry Spencer 8–4–13–5, Leicestershire v Somerset, Weston-super-Mare, 27 Apr 1969

6 wickets by bowler: Ray East 8–1–18–6, Essex v Yorkshire, Hull, 22 June 1969

7 wickets by bowler: Richard Hutton 7.4–1–15–7, Yorkshire v Worcestershire, Leeds, 29 June 1969

8 wickets by bowler: Keith Boyce 7.4–0–26–8, Essex v Lancashire, Old Trafford, 30 May 1971

Hat-trick: Alan Ward, 4 wickets in 4 balls, Derbyshire v Sussex, Derby, 7 June 1970

Eight maiden overs: Brian Langford, Somerset v Essex, Yeovil, 27 July 1969

70 runs conceded: Ray East 8–0–79–1, Essex v Glamorgan, Swansea, 31 Aug 1969

80 runs conceded: Anton Ferreira, 8–0–85–0, Warwickshire v Essex, Colchester, 22 Aug 1982

7 dismissals by wicket-keeper: Bob Taylor (6ct 1st), Derbyshire v Lancashire, Old Trafford, 4 May 1975

10 wickets victory: Surrey 87–0 beat Warwickshire 86, Edgbaston, 6 July 1969

CAREER FIRSTS

1000 runs: Harry Pilling in 30th inns, Lanca-

Graham Gooch has had a career of great vicissitudes. Peaks and troughs, but his many outstanding contributions are indicative of character as well as ability.

Glenn Turner was a batsman with great soporific qualities in his early years with Worcestershire and New Zealand. Later metamorphosed to become effective in all situations, scoring 300 in a day, centuries before lunch, and dominating the Sunday League thrash.

Opposite Durham has a longstanding reputation as a supplier of first-class cricketers, though not itself a top county. As long ago as May 1849, an England XI beat 22 of the county in the shadow of the cathedral. This pen and ink drawing by Edward Bradley (d 1867) shows leading statistician Fred Lillywhite's printing tent in the centre of the picture, proving the importance of the match.

shire v Yorkshire, Old Trafford, 30 Aug 1970

2000 runs: Barry Richards in 53rd inns, Hampshire v Worcestershire, Worcester, 27 Aug 1972

3000 runs: Barry Richards in 83rd inns, Hampshire v Nottinghamshire, Southampton, 1 June 1975

4000 runs: Barry Richards in 106th inns, Hampshire v Essex, Southampton, 18 July 1976

5000 runs: Glenn Turner in 137th inns, Worcestershire v Middlesex, Worcester, 18 May 1980

6000 runs: Glenn Turner in 168th inns, Worcestershire v Gloucestershire, Bristol, 23 May 1982

7000 runs: Dennis Amiss in 237th inns, Warwickshire v Worcestershire, Worcester, 5 July 1987

50 wickets: Bob Woolmer in 26th inns, Kent v Gloucestershire, Cheltenham, 16 Aug 1970

100 wickets: Keith Boyce in 50th inns, Essex v Kent, Ilford, 18 June 1972

200 wickets: Stuart Turner in 141st inns, Essex v Middlesex, Lord's, 9 July 1978

300 wickets: John Lever in 214th inns, Essex v Yorkshire, Leeds, 1 July 1984 (just 15 minutes before Derek Underwood of Kent took his 300th)

100 dismissals: Bob Taylor in 80th inns, Derbyshire v Sussex, Derby, 21 July 1974

200 dismissals: Bob Taylor in 164th inns, Derbyshire v Hampshire, Derby, 14 June 1981

500 runs in season: Mike Smith, 517 av. 36.92 for Middlesex, 1969

750 runs in season: Clive Rice, 814 av. 58.14 for Nottinghamshire, 1977

30 wickets in season: Bob Woolmer, 32 av. 16.87 for Kent, 1970

The first county to win **two limited-overs competitions in one year** was Lancashire with the Gillette Cup and John Player League in 1970.

Leicestershire were the first to win the **County Championship and a limited-overs competition in one year**, in 1975 when they won the Benson & Hedges Cup. Middlesex were the first to win both **County Championship and Gillette Cup in the same year**, 1977, when they shared the Championship with Kent. In 1984

Essex became the first county to win the two league competitions, the **County Championship and the John Player League**.

The first **players to have experienced winning all four competitions** now open to the first-class counties were the Kent players who played on the winning side in the 1973 Benson & Hedges Cup Final, who had previously played in the Kent County Championship team in 1970, John Player League in 1972–3 and in the 1967 Gillette Cup Final: Brian Luckhurst, Mike Denness, John Shepherd, Alan Ealham, Derek Underwood and Norman Graham.

OTHER CRICKET IN ENGLAND

MINOR COUNTIES

An unofficial table was first drawn up in 1888 to reflect competition between the 'Second Class Counties', the first winners being Leicestershire. After most of the counties con-

cerned in that compilation were awarded first-class status in 1894, representatives of a number of non-first-class counties assembled in Birmingham in March 1895, and under the inspiration of the Worcestershire secretary formed the Minor Counties Cricket Association. The first Championship was held that year, when any minor county which arranged at least eight matches, home and away, against other minor counties qualified. The championship was determined on the simplest possible method, one point for a win, minus one for a defeat, with draws ignored. The **first title** was shared by Durham, Norfolk and Worcestershire. The latter became the first outright winners the following year and won again in 1897 and 1898, when they were elevated to first-class status. A fairly unsatisfactory facet of the competition in the first few seasons was that matches against minor counties, which did not themselves qualify, were scored in a team's record. For example Norfolk in 1895 had eight games, but four of these were two matches each against Lincolnshire and Cambridgeshire, neither of whom counted in the table.

In 1959 a competition (Gloucestershire were the first winners) was inaugurated for the **2nd XIs of first-class counties**, so many such teams withdrew from the Minor Counties Championship.

From 1983 the Championship has been contested in two divisions, with the divisional winners playing-off to determine the title. In that year also a **one-day limited-overs competition** was introduced, sponsored by English Industrial Estates; the first winners were Cheshire who beat Bedfordshire in the final at Macclesfield by 36 runs.

TEAM FIRSTS

The first **innings total under 30** was 23 by Staffordshire in their second innings to lose by an innings to Worcestershire on 6 Aug 1895. The first **under 20** was Cheshire's 14 v Staffordshire at Stoke-on-Trent, 2–3 Aug 1909.

The first **total over 500** was by Northamptonshire, 517–8 dec v Durham at South Shields, 27–28 July 1900, and the first **over 600** was Surrey II's 621 v Devon at The Oval, 4–5 June 1928.

The first **tie** was that between Berkshire (155 and 80) and Oxfordshire (89 and 146), at Oxford on 5–6 Aug 1903.

BATTING FIRSTS

The first **century** was made by Granville Bromley-Martin for Worcestershire v Staffordshire at Stoke on 8–9 July 1895, and the first **double century** by Herbert Morgan for Glamorgan v Monmouth at Cardiff, 19–20 July 1901, although Arthur Heath had scored 217 for Staffordshire v Lincolnshire at Stoke-on-Trent in 1889 in the pre-championship era.

The first **double century stand** was between C. Y. Adamson (139) and F. Simpson (85) who added 248 for Durham's fourth wicket v Northamptonshire at Northampton, 23–24 July 1897. Charley Walters (220 not out) and Montagu Burrows (151) added the first **triple century stand**, 331 for the second wicket for Oxfordshire v Bedfordshire at Luton, 9–10 July 1924.

Norman Riches of Glamorgan was the first to **carry his bat** through a completed innings, scoring 178 not out in a total of 357 v Northumberland at Cardiff, 26–27 June 1906. He was also the first to score **1000 runs in a season**, with 1015 av. 92.27 in 1911.

BOWLING FIRSTS

Ten wickets in an innings was first achieved by Ted Arnold, 10–54 for Worcestershire v Northamptonshire at Northampton, 9–10 June 1897. Harry White of Hertfordshire was the first bowler to take **16 or 17 wickets in a match**, with figures of 17–74 v Berkshire at St Albans, 16–17 July 1909; and **18 wickets in a match** was achieved by Norman Harding, 9–39 and 9–61, Kent II v Wiltshire at Swindon, 9–10 Aug 1937. George Thompson of Northamptonshire was the first bowler to take **100 wickets** in a season, with 101 av. 13.72 in 1901, when he also scored 558 runs av. 37.20. The previous year he had been the first to **score 500 runs and take 50 wickets in a season**: 502 av. 32.88 and 72 av. 15.49.

The first **hat-trick**, indeed **four wickets in four balls**, was by Matt Wright of Buckinghamshire, enabling his side to beat Norfolk by an innings at Lakenham, 22–23 Aug 1904.

ALL-ROUND FIRSTS

Century and 17 wickets in a match: Sydney Barnes 136 and 9–37 and 8–46, Staffordshire v Durham at South Shields in 1911.

Century and hat-trick in same match: Michael Falcon, 104 and in 7–82 for Norfolk v Buckinghamshire at Ascot, 25–26 July 1928.

IRELAND

Cricket was reputed to have been proscribed by Oliver Cromwell's commissioners in 1656, but the first known reference to an **actual match** in Ireland was in 1792 between The Garrison and All-Ireland at Phoenix Park, Dublin. The Garrison won by an innings and 94 runs with a wager of 1000 guineas on the result.

The first known **century** in Ireland was 160 by Ensign Beckett for Coldstream Guards v 3rd Guard at Kinsale in 1800, and the first **200**, exactly that in 1864 by J. Gilligan for Sandy-

mount v Co. Wicklow, which (in 1835) had been the first **county club** to be formed. The first **triple century** was 313 not out by Captain William Oates for 1st Royal Mounted Fusiliers v Army Service Corps at The Curragh on 12 June 1895. With Private F. Fitzgerald he added 623 for the second wicket, a world record. The innings score of 658–1 was the first **over 600** in Ireland.

John Crawfurd scored 125 not out and took all ten wickets in an innings for Phoenix v Curragh District in Dublin in 1905, the first such **match double** in Ireland.

IRISH INTERNATIONALS AND FIRST-CLASS MATCHES

The first match played by a truly **representative Irish XI** was in 1855, and the first **Ireland v Scotland** match was played in 1888. However, the first Irish team to take part in a match classified as **first-class** by the MCC, to the surprise of the cricketing press of the time as only one of the

home team seemed to have first-class pretensions, was Dublin University v MCC at College Park, Dublin, on 20–22 May 1895, as the home team won by 56 runs.

The first generally recognised first-class match played by **Ireland** was in 1902, when they made a tour of England in which four such matches were contested, the first a win by 238 runs v London County, captained by W. G. Grace, at Crystal Palace, 19–21 May 1902. The Irish captain, Sir Tim O'Brien, who had played five Tests for England, made the first **first-class century for Ireland** in the third match, 167 v Oxford University (and this is still their record score). In the final game of the tour Bill Harrington (7–76 and 4–42) became the first bowler to take **ten wickets in a match** for Ireland.

Ireland's first score of **over 400** was 409–4 dec v Scotland at Hamilton Crescent, Glasgow, in 1911. At the same venue in 1976 Ivan Anderson became the first Irish batsman to score a **century in each innings**, 147 and 103 not out. With Alex O'Riordan he added 222 for the fourth wicket, the first **double century stand** for Ireland.

The first **double century against** Ireland was 239 not out by Norman Riches for Wales at Belfast in 1926.

SCOTLAND

The first known reference to cricket in Scotland was in 1750 by the '45 Garrison troops at Perth. The first definite **match** was on the Earl of Cathcart's estate at Schaw Park, Alloa, on 3 Sep 1785 for 1000 guineas a side when the Duke of Atholl's XI (30 and 21) lost to the Hon. Lord Charles Talbot's XI (83 and 62). The first mention of an actual **club** was Kelso CC in 1820 and the first **county club** formed was Lanarkshire in 1834.

The first known **century** in Scotland was 136 not out by the Hon. Col. Charles Lennox for Gordon Castle v 55th Regiment at Aberdeen on 9 Oct 1789.

Charles Lawrence was the first bowler to take all **ten wickets in an innings** in Scotland, 10–53 for 22 of Scotland v 11 of England in 1849.

The first **double century** was 206 not out in a Glenalmond School match in 1870 and the first **triple century** was 303 not out by W. F. Holms for Blair Lodge School v Campsie Glen at Blair Lodge in 1884.

The first innings in excess of **600** was Edinburgh's 692 v Glasgow at Edinburgh in 1878, and the first over **700** was the 733–6 made by the Australian Imperial Forces XI v Districts of Scotland at Glasgow in 1919.

SCOTTISH INTERNATIONALS AND FIRST-CLASS MATCHES

The first match played by a **representative Scottish XI** was in 1865, but the first match generally accepted as **first-class** was Scotland v Australians at Raeburn Place, Edinburgh, on 30 June, 1–2 July 1905.

From then the first **centuries** were scored for the opposition, by Percy Sherwell (109) and Bert Vogler (103) for the South Africans at Raeburn Place in 1907. **Scotland's first first-class century** did not come until 1922, when Alexander Fergusson made an unbeaten 103 in 2 hr 45 min, despite his team's overwhelming defeat by the MCC at Lord's. The first bowler to take **ten wickets in a match** for Scotland was Walter Ringrose, 8–86 and 4–60 v Nottinghamshire at Raeburn Place in 1908.

Scotland's first score of over **400** was 485 v Ireland at Perth in 1909, and their first **win against an English county** was against Warwickshire in 1959.

MISCELLANEOUS COMPETITIONS

The first **National Village Championship** was staged in 1972 with nearly 800 teams entering the nationwide competition. The inaugural winners of the John Haig Trophy were Troon (170–3) who beat Astwood Bank (165–8) in the final, at Lord's on 9 September by seven wickets. Troon won again in 1973 and 1976 to become the first team to win a hat-trick of victories.

The first **National Club Cricket Championship** was first played for the Derrick Robins Trophy in 1969 when 256 clubs entered. The first winners were Hampstead who beat Pocklington Pixies in the final. The first team to win in successive seasons was Scarborough in 1981–2; they had previously won in 1972, 1976 and 1979, for a record number of wins.

The **Silk Cut Challenge for all-rounders** was first held at Taunton in 1984, when Clive Rice was the winner from Kapil Dev and Ian Botham. Rice won again at Arundel in 1985 and completed three wins in four years by winning the tournament held in Hong Kong in 1987.

AUSTRALIA

MILESTONES

Cricket was first reported played in Australia in 1803–04, during which period Phillip's Common, an area of scrubland in Sydney, which is now part of Hyde Park, was cleared. The *Sydney Gazette and New South Wales Advertiser* for 8 Jan 1804 reported: 'The late intense weather has been very favourable to the amateurs of cricket who scarce have lost a day for the past month.' This paper for 28 Apr 1810 made the first mention of a **cricket ground**: 'Monday last being Easter Monday, a fair commenced on the Cricket Ground, to which a sort of popular acquiescence has given the appellation of St George's Fields.' This ground was on Phillip's Common, and later that year a larger area of open ground, of which this was a part, was named Hyde Park, as it continues to be known. The first mention of the present Sydney Cricket Ground was on 5 Oct 1811, when the *Sydney Gazette* published an order outlining the boundaries of 'Sydney Common'. Part of this, Moore Park, became known variously as

Bottom of page *A match in the historic Hyde Park, Sydney c. 1842.*

Sydney Domain and Garrison Ground and was taken over by Sydney Cricket Association in 1877 to become known as the 'Association Ground' and eventually Sydney Cricket Ground.

The first reference to **cricket in Tasmania** was in 1815, when the Revd. Robert Knopwood observed in his diary that 'crickett' was a popular pastime in Hobart in the sort of hot weather they had endured the previous December. The first mention of an actual match was one organised in 1825 by Joseph Bowden, a Hobart publican, between teams representing the Hobart Garrison and the Free Settlers. The Military won by 15 runs, but no further details have been traced.

The first intimation that cricket was played at **school** in Australia was in 1821 when Governor Macquarie ordered some bats and balls for his son Lachlan, then a pupil at the Revd. Thomas Reddall's School (at Macquarie Fields) in Sydney. The Governor stated that after his son left the school the articles should be for the school's use.

The first known **cricket club** in Australia was the Military Cricket Club, established in Sydney

in 1826 by and for military personnel. Later that year was formed the Australian Club, the first club for native-born civilians.

The first **match for which team totals survive** was played on Hyde Park, Sydney, immediately adjacent to the present St Mary's Cathedral on 26 Feb 1830. Scores: Civilians 76 and 136 beat 57th Regiment 101 and 87 by 24 runs. The stakes were £20 per side, and a press report stated that at one time there were 'upwards on 100 spectators on the ground'—the first mention of the number of spectators.

John Richard Hardy, a former Charterhouse schoolboy, who had played for Cambridge v Oxford in 1829, introduced **round-arm bowling** to Australia on 26 Dec 1832. The style was unpopular among both spectators and opposition players.

William Still, playing for Eleven Natives v Eleven Officers and Immigrants in May 1834, became the first player in Australia to go out to bat wearing **pads and gloves**.

A cricketer referred to as 'Shiney' scored three consecutive ducks for Carlton, Tasmania, in 1835. This is the first mention of an **Aboriginal** playing cricket.

The first recorded reference to **'sledging'**— the 'low slang and insulting remarks so often resorted to by Australians', as the *Commercial Journal* so neatly put it—was reported on 7 Feb 1838. Sledging continues in Australian cricket at all grades to this day.

Cricket was first mentioned in **Western Australia** on 5 Apr 1835 in a Perth newspaper advertisement, in which a group of builders working on the new Government House challenged some builders working on the Commissariat building. The *Perth Gazette* of 13 Apr 1835 mentions the Perth Club, which it stated had 22 members, who met each Saturday afternoon at the Flats; this was the first mention of a club in Western Australia. The first match for which scores were kept and are still extant was played in May 1846 when the Perth Tradesmen (38 and 26) lost to the Perth Club (45 and 21–5) by five wickets.

Cricket was first mentioned in **South Australia** in an advertisement on 3 Nov 1838 in the *South Australian Register* and in the *South Australian Gazette*. It was directed at 'gentlemen cricket players' and announced that a meeting of patrons of the 'old English and manly game of cricket' would take place at the London Tavern, Adelaide, with the aim of forming a club. The first recorded match in South Australia was contested by Eleven Gentlemen of Royal Victoria Independent Club and Eleven Gentlemen of Adelaide at the Thebarton Cricket Ground, Adelaide, for 22 guineas a side on 28 Oct 1839. The Independent Club won by 11 runs.

Melbourne Cricket Club was formed on 20 Nov 1838, the first club in **Victoria**. Two days later it staged the first recorded match in Victoria against the Military; the result has not been traced. The *Sydney Morning Herald* of 18 Apr 1844 mentioned the formation, in South Brisbane, of the Albion Cricket Club—the first known mention of cricket (or a club) in **Queensland**. The first known match was reported in the *Moreton Bay Courier* of 27 June 1846, between an eleven of working men and an eleven of gentlemen for a stake of £5/10/- a side. The earliest Queensland match for which scores were recorded and preserved was won by the Squatters XI (40 and 48) v Drayton XI (24 and 21) after a race meeting at Drayton, Toowoomba, in May 1850.

The first **inter-colonial match** was between Van Diemen's Land (to become Tasmania in 1855) and the newly created colony of Victoria at Launceston in Van Diemen's Land in February 1851. The match score is appended.

The first **Australian cricket annual**, *The Australian Cricketer's Guide*, edited by H. Biers and William Fairfax, was published by Fairfax in Melbourne in 1857. Two further annual publications appeared under the sole editorship of Fairfax.

The earliest surviving **Australian cricket photograph** dates from November 1859. It shows a match at the Entally ground in Tasmania, between Entally and Westbury. Among the spectators visible on the photograph was Charles Du Cane, the Governor of Tasmania.

Six-ball overs were employed for the first time in any first-class cricket on 24–25 Feb 1871, Victoria v Tasmania at Melbourne. In 1880–81

The First Inter-Colonial Match in Australia

VICTORIANS

Time	Name	Score	How Out	Bowler	Total	Score	How Out	Bowler	Total	Time
		1st INNINGS—Time: 2 hours and 5 minutes					2nd INNINGS—Time: 1 hour and 20 minutes			
22 m.	Cooper	121	Bowled	McDowall	4		Bowled	Henty	0	
36 m.	W. Phillpott	123311213	Caught by Maddox	McDowall	17	111	R.O.S. by Marshall	Henty	3	15 m.
30 m.	Hamilton	41212	Bowled by Marshall	McDowall	10	312121412 21414213	Leg before wicket	McDowall	35	1 hr
33 m.	Lister	3111211	R.O.S. by Marshall	McDowall	10	12	Caught by Maddox	W. Field	3	5 m.
15 m.	Thomson	1	Bowled	McDowall	1		Bowled	Henty	0	
40 m.	R. Phillpott	311111121	Bowled	Henty	12	1	Caught by Westbrook	Henty	1	18 m.
3 m.	Antill	0	Stumped by Marshall	Henty	0		Not Out		0	
33 m.	Brodie	44111114	Caught by Henty	McDowall	17	1121	Caught by Tabart	Henty	5	10 m.
8 m.	Marsden	11	Bowled	Henty	2	2	Bowled	McDowall	2	5 m.
	Hall	2211	Not Out		6	114	Leg before wicket	McDowall	6	30 m.
	Harvey		Bowled	Henty	0	1	Caught by McDowall	Henty	1	3 m.
Byes 1	..	..	..	..	1		..	..	1	
Leg Byes 11	..	..	..	..	2		..	..	0	
Wides and No Balls	..	..	..	..	0		..	..	0	
				Total	82			Total	57	
									82	
									139	

Henty Bowled 13 overs—54 runs obtained
McDowall 13 overs—28 runs obtained
—
82

Henty Bowled 9 overs—27 runs
McDowall 5 overs—21 runs
Field 3 overs— 9 runs
—
57

TASMANIANS

Time	Name	Score	How Out	Bowler	Total	Score	How Out	Bowler	Total	Time
		1st INNINGS—Time: 2 hours and 40 minutes					2nd INNINGS—Time: 1 hour and 14 minutes			
1 h. 35 m.	G. Du Croz	1121413312 11411	Bowled	Antill	27	11211	Bowled	Antill	6	30 m.
1 h. 45 m.	Marshall	1111113121	Caught by Lister	Antill	13		Caught by Antill	Antill		
	W. Field		Bowled	Antill		1	Caught by Thompson	Brodie	1	5 m.
10 m.	Maddox	1	Bowled	Antill	1					
30 m.	G. Gibson	11213	Bowled	Hamilton	8	1	Bowled	Antill	1	3 m.
38 m.	Westbrook	514	Bowled	Antill	10	121	Caught by Cooper	Antill	4	20 m.
	C. Arthur	1	Bowled	Antill	1		Caught by Harvey	Antill	0	10 m.
10 m.	Tabart	2	Bowled	Hamilton	2	11234112	Not Out		15	
30 m.	Giblin	11131	Not Out		7	1	Bowled	Antill	1	5 m.
5 m.	Henty		Bowled	Antill						
20 m.	McDowall	13322	Caught by Antill	Hamilton	11	31	Not Out		4	
Byes—231122	..	..	..	..	..	11	3	..	..	3
Leg Byes—11111	..	..	..	..	..	5	2	..	..	2
Wide and no ball—8 (2 Antill, 6 Lister)			..				0			0
				Total		104			Total	37
									First Innings	104
									Grand Total	141

Lister bowled 12 overs—32 runs obtained
Hamilton 8 overs—30 runs obtained
Antill 12 overs—42 runs obtained
—
104

Antill bowled 6 overs—21 runs obtained
Brodie 7 overs—16 runs obtained
—
37

Tasmania winning by 2 runs and 3 wickets to go down

Opposite H. H. Stephenson, a doctor's son who became a professional, led the first England team to Australia in 1861–62 and spread cricket's gospel far and wide.

The picture looks 'artificial' and posed. A local entrepreneur hired out a ladder to enable spectators to secure vantage points in the trees surrounding the playing area.

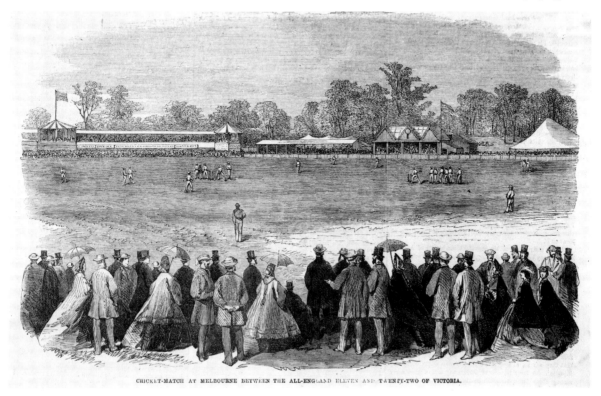

CRICKET-MATCH AT MELBOURNE BETWEEN THE ALL-ENGLAND ELEVEN AND TWENTY-TWO OF VICTORIA.

the D. Long Trophy was donated for competition between Victoria and New South Wales; the first **inter-colonial trophy** and precursor of the Sheffield Shield.

On 10 Oct 1887 William Vincent Duffy was appointed the first **professional coach** in Western Australia, being engaged by the Metropolitan Club of Perth for £100 a season.

TOURING TEAMS

The first **tourists** to Australia were an English team, under H. H. Stephenson, and sponsored by the Melbourne catering firm of Spiers and Pond, in 1861–62. Twelve matches were played, all against various odds, of which the tourists won six, lost two, with five drawn. Of matches on this tour there was the first mention of a **'Test match'**. (See Test match section.)

Two touring teams from England visited Australia in the same season for the first time in 1887–88. George Vernon's side, captained originally by the Hon. Martin Hawke, played 26 matches, winning eleven and losing one, while Lillywhite, Shaw and Shrewsbury's team under C. Aubrey Smith won 14 and lost two of its 25 matches. The two parties joined forces to play one Test, under Walter Read, which was won.

BATTING FIRSTS

John Rickards, of Sydney, scored 57 not out for Single v Married in Sydney in May 1833, the first **half century** recorded in Australia. The first **century** was by F. A. Powlett, for Melbourne Cricket Club v Melbourne Union Cricket Club on 17 Jan 1839, the first in Tasmania was 137 not out by E. Emmett for South Esk v Launceston at Launceston in 1840, the first in New South Wales was 112 not out by John Tunks for Currency Club v Victoria Club in January 1845, and the first in Queensland 118 by James Morrisey Bolger for Moreton Bay Club v North Australian Club at Brisbane on 29 July and 4 Aug 1859.

Probably the first bona fide century in South Australia was the 109 scored by John Collard Cocker in a single wicket challenge match against a player called Wilkins in Adelaide in 1855–56. Several years earlier, however, W. H. (later Judge) Bundy reckoned that he had scored a century with a home-made bat at Woodside, near Adelaide, while a boy. Perhaps the first century in a proper, even-handed match was by F. D. Harris, 101 out of 163 for St Peter's College, Adelaide, v the Young Cricketers' Club in Adelaide in 1870.

Richard Wardill, opening the batting for Victoria v New South Wales at Melbourne, 27–30 Dec 1867, scored 110, the first **century in a first-class match** in Australia. He added 113 for the fourth wicket with George Robertson, the first **century stand** in Australian first-class cricket.

The first **double century** in Australia was 256 scored by Billy Midwinter for Bendigo v Sandhurst at Bendigo, Victoria, in 1869–70. The first stand of over 200 was when Bransby Cooper and James Slight added 218 for the second wicket for South Melbourne v East Melbourne in 1874–75.

The first double century in a first-class match and also the first **triple century** in any grade of cricket in Australia, was the 321 made by Billy Murdoch for New South Wales v Victoria at Sydney, 10–15 Feb 1882. He hit 38 fours, 9 threes and 41 twos and added 245 for the fourth wicket with Samuel Jones, the first **stand of more than 200** in Australian first-class cricket. The New South Wales total of 775 was the first of **more than 700** in all first-class cricket. In the Victorian first innings of 315 Joe Palmer (76*) and William Cooper (29) added 100 runs together, the first **century stand for the last wicket** in Australian first-class cricket. In any grade of Australian cricket firsts were achieved by Alick Bannerman, who scored 111 and 104 for Carlton v Albert at Sydney in 1881–82, the first instance of a batsman scoring a **century in each innings** of a match, and by James Slight and John Rosser, the first **stand of over 300**, 395 for the first wicket for South Melbourne v St Kilda at Melbourne in 1882–83. The first of over **400** was 442 for the eighth wicket by Edward Noble and Syd Gregory

for Sydney v Warwick at Sydney in 1890–91. The first over **600** was 641 by T. Patton and N. Rippon for Buffalo v Whorouley at Gapsted, Victoria, in 1913–14.

The first **individual score over 500**, and still the highest ever by an Australian batsman, was the 566 compiled by Charles Eady in 7 hr 53 min, with 13 fives and 68 fours for Break-O'-Day (911) v Wellington at Hobart on 15 and 21 Mar and 2 Apr 1902. This remains a world record for club cricket.

BOWLING FIRSTS

George Gilbert, captain of New South Wales and a cousin of W. G. Grace, achieved the first **hat-trick** in a first-class match in Australia, taking the wickets of T. F. Wray, G. Elliott and G. Marshall with consecutive balls, on 12 Jan 1858, the first day of Victoria v New South Wales at the Richmond Paddock, Melbourne. However, Victoria won the match.

George Ulyett, for the England XI v New South Wales at the Sydney Association Ground, 7–10 February 1879, took the wickets of Edwin Evans, Edwin Tindall, Dave Gregory and Fred Spofforth, the first instance of a bowler taking **four wickets with successive balls** in Australian first-class cricket. In the first innings of this match Billy Murdoch scored 82 not out in the South Wales total of 177; the first time that an opener had **carried his bat** in an Australian first-class game.

Playing for a team at Bendigo in 1881–82 Fred Spofforth took **all 20 wickets** for 48 runs; the first such performance anywhere; all his victims were bowled.

OTHER FIRSTS IN NON-FIRST-CLASS CRICKET

Seven stumpings were made by E. J. Long for North Sydney v Burwood at Sydney in 1909–10. Les Andrews made **9 catches in an innings** for Bankstown-Canterbury v Sydney University on 27 Nov 1962.

Ken Mackay was the first cricketer to score a **triple century and take all ten wickets** in an innings in 1939–40.

TEAM FIRSTS

The first match between New South Wales and Victoria was played on Melbourne Cricket Ground on 26–27 Mar 1856; NSW (76 and 16–7) beat Victoria (63 and 28) by three wickets. Victoria's second innings score was the first **first-class score under 30**, John McKone took 5–11 and Victoria's top scorer was William Philpott with 11.

The first first-class score **under 20** was when Tasmania were out for 18 in the first innings of their match against Victoria at Melbourne, 12–13 Feb 1869. Sam Costick took 6–1 in 21.1 overs as the Tasmanian innings was completed on the first morning. Although Tasmania made 131 in their second innings, Victoria won by an innings and 265 runs.

The ultimate score, **all out for 0**, was first recorded in Australia in 1876–77, by Marlborough v Undaunted at Moore Park, Sydney. The first **tied match** in Australia was between 15 of New South Wales and Victoria (138 and 97) and an Australian XI (123 and 112) at Melbourne in 1877–78.

The first **total of 500 or more** was when Commercial Bank were dismissed for exactly that by the Joint Stock Bank on the Sydney Association Ground in 1877–78. More than **600 or 700** was first attained by East Melbourne, 742 v Tasmania at Melbourne, 1879–80. Tom Horan scored 250 not out and William Gaggin 100.

In a match on the East Melbourne ground on 17–19 and 21 Mar 1887, the Non-Smokers scored 803 v the Smokers, the first score of **over 800** in all first-class cricket. The teams comprised a mix of the English tourists and leading local players. The English captain Arthur Shrewsbury scored 236, his compatriot William Gunn 150 and Australian William Bruce 131. Shrewsbury and Gunn added 310 for the third wicket, the first **partnership of over 300** in Australian first-class cricket. The match was eventually drawn.

The first **innings total of over 1000** in any cricket match was the 1094 amassed by Melbourne University v Essendon at Melbourne on 5, 12, 19 and 23 Mar 1898. **Five centuries** were made for the first time: L. Miller 205, E. C.

Osborne 190, I. J. Quirk 179, E. Feilchenfield 176, H. Bullivant 139*.

In a first-class friendly match played at Melbourne on 2–3, 5 Feb 1923, a total of over 1000 runs was scored for the first time in first-class cricket. Victoria were all out for 1050 against Tasmania. Top scorer was Bill Ponsford, who with 429 in 477 minutes with 42 fours, scored the first **quadruple century** in Australian first-class cricket. The only other century maker was 'Hammy' Love (156).

GEORGE GIFFEN

George Giffen was the first bowler to take **all ten wickets in an innings** in Australian first-class cricket: 10–66 in 26 overs for the Australian Team v a Combined Eleven at the Sydney Association Ground. His side won the match, held on 15–18 Feb 1884, by nine wickets. He achieved a match analysis of 17–201 (9–91 and 8–110) in 116.2 overs for South Australia v Victoria at the Adelaide Oval, 13–17 Mar 1886, the first and only time that a bowler has taken **17 wickets** in an Australian first-class match. For South Australia v New South Wales at Adelaide on 19–23 Dec 1890, he became the first bowler to bowl more than **500 balls in an innings**, as his first innings analysis was 83.3 6-ball overs (501 balls), 35 maidens, 150 runs, 6 wickets. In 1891–92 he became the first player to achieve the double of **500 runs and 50 wickets in an Australian first-class season**; 509 runs av. 50.90 and 50 wickets av. 17.30 in six matches, including the first instance of a **double century and 16 wickets** in a first-class match: 271 and 9–96 and 7–70 for South Australia v Victoria at Adelaide, 7–11 Nov 1891. Giffen improved in 1894–95 to 902 runs av. 50.11 and 93 wickets av. 22.55 in eleven matches; figures unapproached since. In that season he had figures of 5–309 in 87 6-ball overs for South Australia v the English tourists at Adelaide, 28 Mar–2 Apr 1895 in a score of 609; the first instance of a bowler **conceding 300 or more runs** in an innings (only once subsequently exceeded).

In non-first-class cricket Giffen became the first to make **two centuries on one day against two different teams**. For Norwood in 1889 he

Charles Turner—first to take 250 wickets in a season in 1888; his calendar year's total of 365 is unbeaten and unbeatable.

Rick McCosker, perhaps underrated due to his 'Packer' days, holds the Sheffield Shield as captain of New South Wales.

scored 129 not out v Adelaide and 140 not out v South Adelaide.

SEASON'S FIRSTS

Charles Turner became the first, and only, bowler to take **100 wickets in first-class matches in an Australian season** in 1887–88, when in 12 matches he took 106 wickets for 1441 runs, av. 13.59, bowling 4267 balls in a mixture of 6- and 8-ball overs. His innings by innings figures, for New South Wales and Australian Test and representative teams: 4–22 & 6–23, 7–106 & 2–40, 7–117 & 0–21, 5–17 & 4–97, 8–39 & 8–40, 1–79 & 5–102, 1–80 & 3–19, 5–44 & 7–43, 5–128 & 1–34, 5–64, 4–71 & 7–48, 7–72 & 4–135.

The first batsman to score **1000 runs in an Australian season** was Clem Hill, who reached this figure during his 170 for South Australia v New South Wales at Sydney on 21 Feb 1898. In 1897–98 his total was 1196 runs av. 66.44 in eleven matches. Archie McLaren and K. S. Ranjitsinhji also completed 1000 in this season.

SHEFFIELD SHIELD

The major Australian domestic competition was named after the 3rd Earl of Sheffield, who in 1891–92 organised a tour to Australia and donated £150 for the advancement of cricket in Australia. The money was invested in a shield, competed for by the major colonies (now states).

The **first match** was at Adelaide Oval on 16–17, 19–21 Dec 1892, when South Australia (212 and 330), following on, beat New South Wales (337 and 148). The first ball was bowled by George Giffen to Sammy Jones (NSW). Giffen took the first wicket, that of Jones for 0 in the first over, and became the first man to take **five wickets in an innings** with 6–133 in 74.1 overs. He took a further six wickets in NSW's second innings but was beaten to the feat of first to take **ten wickets** in a match by Michael Pierce, 8–111 and 5–154 for NSW for a match total of 13–265 in 85.2 overs. For New South Wales Harry Donnan

(120) scored the first **century**, and put on 151 for the fourth wicket with Harry Moses (99), the first **century partnership**. A team did not win again after following on in the competition until 1965–66.

George Giffen of South Australia achieved several more Sheffield Shield firsts. He scored the first **double century**, 205 in 390 minutes v New South Wales at Adelaide, 15–16 and 18–19 Dec 1893, and in only his ninth match he reached a **career total of 1000 runs** during an innings of 94 not out against Victoria at Adelaide on 30 Nov, 1 and 3 Dec 1894; after this his total was 1088 runs av. 72.53. Against New South Wales at Adelaide on 5, 7–9 Jan 1895 he became the first to take **15 or more wickets in a match**, 8–77 in 42.2 overs and 8–109 in 48.1 overs, for a match total of 16–186 in 90.3 overs. In his 13th match, v Victoria at Adelaide on 9, 11–13 Nov 1895, he became the first to take **100 wickets**. His 100th victim was John Carlton (or Charlton), and although Giffen took eight wickets in the match, South Australia lost by 66 runs. At the end of the match Giffen's career figures were 25 innings (2 not out), 1263 runs av. 54.91; 101 wickets for 2258 runs, av. 22.35.

CAREER FIRSTS

The first batsman to reach **2000 runs** in the Shield was Frank Iredale, in an innings of 75 in his 30th match for New South Wales against South Australia at Sydney on 9–12 Jan 1900, having made his debut in 1892–93. Iredale's total at the end of the match was 2048 runs in 54 innings av. 40.15.

Clem Hill made his debut for South Australia in 1894–95. Against New South Wales on 17–20 Dec 1900 he scored the first Shield **triple century**, 365 not out in 515 minutes, with 35 fours and one hit for eight (after over-throws). He became the first batsman to pass **3000, 4000, 5000** and **6000 runs**, as follows:

Bradman with Maurice Leyland, reputedly taken in January 1930, when Bradman was in Australia.

Hill's final career total was 6274 runs av. 52.28. The first man to surpass this total was Don Bradman, who went on to become the first to the **7000** and **8000** targets. He reached the former in his 49th Shield game for South Australia v Queensland at Adelaide on 26 Dec 1938. At the completion of that match his record was 7139 runs in 78 innings (12 not out) for an average of 108.16. He passed **8000 runs** during 90 not out in the same fixture less than a year later, to total 8053 runs in 86 innings (15 not out) in 55 matches, av. 113.42. His final career record was 8926 runs av. 110.19. Bradman's total was eventually passed by John Inverarity, who exceeded **9000 runs** during an innings of 44 for South Australia v NSW at Adelaide on 17–20 Feb 1984 in his

Target	against	venue	date		Shield total
3000	NSW	Sydney	9–13 Jan	1903	3020 av. 52.06, 34 matches
4000	NSW	Adelaide	15–18 Dec	1906	4055 av. 50.68, 46 matches
5000	Victoria	Melbourne	1–6 Jan	1910	5066 av. 53.89, 54 matches
6000	NSW	Adelaide	9–12 Jan	1914	6004 av. 51.75, 66 matches

149th Sheffield Shield match. Inverarity's final career figures were 9341 runs, av. 38.44 in 159 matches.

Ernest Jones was the first to take **200 wickets** in Shield matches, reaching that figure for South Australia v NSW at Adelaide on 19–20, 22–23 Dec 1902. After the match his figures were 201 wickets av. 25.84 in 37 matches; he retired at the end of the season, having taken a further eight expensive wickets.

Clarrie Grimmett, a New Zealander, who did not make his Shield debut until he was aged 32, took his **300th wicket** in his 46th match, for South Australia v NSW at Adelaide on 15–16, 18 Dec 1833. Then his record was 303 wickets av. 26.75. He went on to be the first to take **400** and **500** wickets: for South Australia v NSW at Sydney on 19–20, 22–23 Feb 1937 and v Queensland at Brisbane on 6, 8–10 Jan 1940 in the last competition before the war in the Pacific stopped the action for seven years. His final Shield career figures were 513 wickets for 12976 runs av. 25.29 in 70 matches.

Although several other players emulated George Giffen's 1000 runs and 100 wickets, it was not until 66 years later that the first man reached **2000 runs/200 wickets**. Richie Benaud took his 200th wicket when playing for New South Wales v Victoria at Melbourne, 23–28 Dec 1961, and at the end of that game his figures for 57

matches were 2928 runs av. 37.53 and 201 wickets av. 27.72. Shortly afterwards his team-mate Alan Davidson also reached this target, as subsequently did another NSW all-rounder Johnny Martin.

Jim Kelly was the first **wicket-keeper to obtain 100 dismissals**, as five for New South Wales v Victoria at Melbourne on 24–28 Dec 1904 took his tally to 103 (67 catches, 36 stumpings) in 40 matches. He retired after one more match, when injury prevented him from adding to the total.

Don Tallon was the first to **200** when he obtained five dismissals for Queensland v South Australia at Brisbane, 30 Jan–3 Feb 1953. After one more match and one more stumping he retired the following season with 205 Shield dismissals, 144 catches and 61 stumpings.

John Maclean of Queensland dismissed South Australia's Paul Sleep at Brisbane, 19–22 Jan 1979, to become the first wicket-keeper to record **300 dismissals**. He had 277 catches and 23 stumpings in 82 matches; by the time he retired at the end of the season he had increased those to 289 and 24 in 86 matches, a total since exceeded only by Rod Marsh of Western Australia.

SEASON FIRSTS

The first man to score **1000 runs in a Shield season** was Bill Ponsford, 1091 in eight

Opposite John Inverarity beat Bradman's record total of Sheffield Shield runs. Less memorably for him, above, *he falls lbw to Underwood, enabling England to square the 1968 rubber. Interestingly, this Oval scene includes every England player. From left: R. Illingworth, T. Graveney, J. Edrich, E. Dexter, C. Cowdrey, D. Underwood, A. Knott, J. Snow, D. Brown, C. Milburn, B. D'Oliveira.*

Below Clarrie Grimmett, seen here bowling in England in 1934, started his career late, but was the first to 200 *Test wickets and remains the Sheffield Shield's most prolific wicket-taker.*

innings (av. 136.37) for Victoria in 1926–27: 214 & 54, 151, 352, 108 & 84, 12 & 116. He again scored 1000 runs the following season, 1217 av. 152.12, still the record, including the first **quadruple century** in the Sheffield Shield: 437 in 621 minutes against Queensland at Melbourne on 16–17, 19–20 Dec 1927. The first bowler to take **50 wickets in a season** was the left-arm spinner 'Chuck' Fleetwood-Smith in six matches for Victoria in 1934–35. His analyses: 5–57 & 4–81, 6–107 & 5–121, 2–74 & 4–96, 5–39 & 6–90, 7–113 & 8–113, 5–60 & 3–186 for a total of 60 wickets for 1137 runs, av. 18.95. This remains the season's record.

TEAM FIRSTS

New South Wales scored 807 v South Australia at Adelaide on 16, 18–20 Dec 1899, the first Shield **total in excess of 600**, and won by an innings and 392 runs. At Sydney in the next season, on 5–7, 9 Jan 1901, NSW scored 918, the first **total over 900**, and the first in all first-class cricket to include **five centuries**: Frank Iredale 118, Monty Noble 153, Syd Gregory 168, Reggie Duff 119 and Les Poidevin 140 not out. The innings took only 560 minutes and NSW then dismissed South Australia for 157 and 156 to win by an innings and 605 runs.

Finally Victoria scored 1107 v New South Wales at Melbourne on 24, 27–29 Dec 1926, the only score over **1000** ever to be obtained in a first-class competitive match anywhere (Victoria having scored 1050 in a friendly in 1923). Top scorers were Bill Ponsford 352 and Jack Ryder 295.

Victoria, needing 298 runs to avoid an innings defeat by New South Wales at Sydney, 25–28 Jan 1907, were all out for 31, the first Shield total **under 40**. The first and only total **under 30** was by South Australia (27) v NSW at Sydney on 18 Nov 1955. Phil Ridings was top scorer with 8 and Keith Miller took 7–12.

INDIVIDUAL FIRSTS

The first **double century partnership** was the 286 runs put on for the fifth wicket by Monty Noble (200) and Syd Gregory (176) for New South Wales who beat South Australia by an innings and 392 runs at Sydney, 16–20 Dec 1899. The same pair were the first to be together for a **stand of over 300**, 315 for the fourth wicket v Victoria at Sydney, 25–31 Jan 1908. Noble scored 176 and Gregory 201, but the NSW first innings total of 461 was insufficient to avoid a 211-run defeat. No stand of 400 has been achieved, the closest being 397 for the fifth wicket by Warren Bardsley (235) and Charles Kelleway (168) for NSW v South Australia at Sydney, 3–9 Dec 1920.

Warwick Armstrong (Victoria) took the first **hat-trick** when he dismissed NSW's Alick Mackenzie (21), Bert Hopkins (0) and Charles Gregory (0) at Melbourne, 26–29 Dec 1902. So far the only bowler to take **four wickets with successive balls** is Halford Hooker for NSW v Victoria at Sydney, 24–29 Jan 1929. His victims were Hans Ebeling, Herbert Gamble and Bert Ironmonger, to complete the Victorian first innings, and Ernest Austen with the first ball of their second innings.

Joe Travers was the first man to take **nine wickets in an innings**, 9–30 in 22.4 overs for South Australia v Victoria at Melbourne, 31 Dec 1900–3 Jan 1901. Victoria were all out for 76 but recovered to score 446 in the second innings and won the match. **All ten** was first achieved by Tim Wall, 10–36 in 12.4 8-ball overs for South Australia in New South Wales's first innings at Sydney, 3–6 Feb 1933. Again NSW rallied in their second innings and won the match.

Wally Grout became the first **wicket-keeper to take eight dismissals in an innings** in any first-class match, for Queensland v Western Australia at Brisbane on 15 Feb 1960.

AUSTRALIAN DOMESTIC LIMITED-OVERS COMPETITIONS

The great success of limited-overs competitions in England prompted Australia to start its own in 1969–70. The participants were the five Sheffield Shield teams plus Tasmania who played a preliminary round on a knock-out basis with the winners joined by New Zealand in the semi-finals. Sponsors for the first two seasons were the Vehicle and General Insurance Group; Coca-Cola took over in 1971–72, Gillette in 1973–74 and the present sponsors, McDonalds, from 1979–80. The over limit was originally 40 8-ball overs per innings, changed to 50 6-ball overs from 1979–80.

The **first match** was at Melbourne on 22 Nov 1969 when Tasmania scored 130–9 and Victoria needed only 21 overs to score 131–2 to win. Kevin Brown scored the first run in the first over,

bowled by Victorian fast bowler Alan Thomson. The first wicket to fall was that of Baden Sharman, caught at the wicket by Norman Carlyon off left-arm paceman Robert Rowan. For Victoria Ken Eastwood (69) scored the first **half-century** and with Ken Thomas put on the first **century partnership**, 115 for the first wicket.

In the third match at Sydney on 7 Dec 1970 Ian King, the first Torres Strait Islander to play for an Australian state, took 5–33 in 8 overs, the first **five wickets in an innings** analysis, for Queensland v New South Wales, the match winners.

New Zealand became the first **knock-out competition winners** when their captain Graham Dowling put Victoria in to bat on 1 Jan 1970. Victoria made 129 in 34.6 overs and New Zealand replied with 130–4 in 31.4 overs. The following season Western Australia defeated Queensland by 91 runs at Melbourne on 6 Feb 1971 to become the first Australian State to win the trophy.

The first **score over 200** was in the first match of the second season, 202–5 by South Australia, who had been set 200 to win by Victoria at Adelaide on 18 Oct 1970. On 4 Nov 1970 at Launceston, Tasmania, dismissed for 205 in 39 overs, were the first team to lose when scoring over 200, Western Australia having made 218.

The first **century** was made by Bill Lawry, 108 not out including 10 fours and a six in 165 minutes, as he skippered Victoria (192–2) to defeat South Australia by eight wickets in the final at Melbourne on 6 Feb 1972.

The first occasion on which a side was **set less than 100 to win** was when Queensland (94–1 in 25 overs) won by nine wickets, having dismissed New South Wales for 92 in 29.7 overs at Brisbane on 14 Jan 1973.

The first score **over 300** was at Sydney on 3 Dec 1981 when New South Wales made 310–4 v South Australia. Rick McCosker scored 164, the first **individual innings over 150**, and opening with John Dyson (100) he put on 253, the first **double century partnership**. The first batsman to score **1000 runs** in the competition was Julian Wiener for Victoria 1977–85, 1003 runs av. 55.72 in 20 matches.

INDIA

MILESTONES

Cricket is known to have been first mentioned in India in 1721 when some sailors employed by the East India Company played at Cambay, a Gujerati port. The first known **cricket club** in existence was the Calcutta Cricket Club in 1792.

The first known **cricket book** in India was a 119-page book of scores published by the Free School, Calcutta: *Calcutta Cricket Club Matches 1844-54*. The first known instructional book was reported to have been published at Agra, Uttah Pradesh, in 1867.

The first known **tied match** was between 5th Royal Lancers (114 and 95) v 102nd Fusiliers (119 and 90) at Lucknow in 1868.

BATTING FIRSTS

The first recorded **century**, anywhere overseas, was made by Robert Vansittart, who scored 102 for Old Etonians v The Rest of Calcutta at Calcutta in 1804. Private Sheiring scored 228, the first recorded **double century** in India, and added 186 for the tenth wicket with Colonel Coles, 54 not out, the first recorded **century stand**, at Shahjehanpur in 1872.

Score of over 600: Bolan Pass XI, 678 v Subordinates at Peshawar in 1880.

Stand over 200 and 300: Lt C. Mackenzie and Lt Taylor, 321 for first wicket, Simla v Queen's Royal West Surrey Regiment at Simla in 1884. The first **stand of over 200 for the tenth wicket** anywhere in the world was that of 215 unbroken by J. Henderson (128*) and H. R. Fagan (113*) for Calcutta v United Services at Calcutta, 1886-87.

Century in each innings: Edward Wynyard, 123 and 106, Visitors v Residents at Naini Tak in 1885.

Triple century: Gustavus Henry Spencer Fowke, 309 for the Gordon Highlanders v Queen's Regiment at Peshawar in 1905.

BOWLING FIRSTS

Playing for Deolati v Igatpuri in 1876, Quartermaster-Sergeant Miller was the first bowler to take **all ten wickets in an innings** and to take

18 wickets in a match. The first **hat-trick** was achieved by Mehallasha Edalji Pavri in 1885.

The first to take all ten wickets in a first-class innings in India was Frank Tarrant, with 10-90 in 35.4 overs, having already scored 182 not out in an innings total of 265 by the Maharaja of Cooch-Behar's XI v Lord Willingdon's XI at Poona Gymkhana, 12-13 Aug 1918. Tarrant added 173 for the ninth wicket with S. Aikut, who made just 5. Despite his efforts Cooch-Behar finished the match fighting to stave off defeat.

TOURS

The first **tour of an Indian side to England** was by the Parsees, captained by Dr D. H. Patel, coincident with the Colonial and Indian Exhibition in London in 1886. Of 28 matches played, the Parsees lost 19, drew 8 and won just 1, a one-day game against Normanhurst.

The first **team from the British Isles to tour India** was in 1889-90. Captained by George Vernon, it was composed entirely of amateurs, few of whom were regular first-class cricketers. The team played eleven even-handed games in India, of which eight were won, two drawn and one lost. The tour has never been regarded as first-class, and it is not feasible to upgrade the status now.

In 1892-93 Martin Bladen, the 7th Baron Hawke, took a team to India which the Association of Cricket Statisticians considers was the first to play **first-class cricket**. These four such games were:

22-24 Dec: Loss to Parsees by 109 runs at Bombay Gymkhana.

26-28 Dec: Win over Bombay Presidency XI by 8 wickets at Bombay Gymkhana.

29-31 Dec: Win over Parsees by 7 runs at Bombay Gymkhana.

26-28 Jan: Win over All-India XI by innings and 5 runs at Allahabad.

Arthur Hill, with 132 in the last match, made the first **first-class century** in India.

The first **All-India touring team** to England went in 1911 under the captaincy of His Highness the Maharaja of Patiala. They played 14 first-class matches, winning 2 and losing 10. No Test

Above *The Parsees of 1886—first side from India to tour England. Back: A. B. Patel, S. Bezonjee; Third row: C. Payne (umpire), N. P. Banerjee, C. P. Major, S. N. Bhedwar, D. D. Khambatta, A. C. Major, J. D. Pochkhana; Seated: A. P. Libuwalla, P. D. Daster, D. H. Patel (Capt), M. Framjee, B. P. Balla; On ground: J. M. Morenas, B. B. Baria, S. H. Harvar.*

Below *First Indian Tourists in 1911 at Hove.*

matches were played.

The first visit of an **MCC side to India** was in 1926–27 under Arthur Gilligan. Twenty-six matches were accepted as first-class, with 8 victories and 18 draws. A member of the tour party, Andrew Sandham, became the first batsman to **exceed 1000 runs in a season** of first-class matches in India, reaching this figure against Bombay Presidency at Bombay on 10, 12–13 December, with final figures of 1525 runs (av. 63.54). He also scored 15 in one innings in Burma, and 216 in three in Ceylon, for a tour first-class total of 1756 av. 62.71. In all first-class matches on the tour, including India, Burma and Ceylon, Maurice Tate became the first player to achieve the **double overseas**, with 1193 runs av. 36.15 and 116 wickets av. 13.78.

BOMBAY TOURNAMENT

Research by members of the Association of Cricket Statisticians and others suggests a convincing case for the first match of **first-class status** in India to be that between the Bombay Presidency and the Parsees at the Bombay Gymkhana ground on 26–27 Aug 1892. Presidency made 104 (M. D. Kanga 4–30), Parsees 54–4, but no play was possible on the second day due to rain.

This was the first match played in the **Bombay Tournament**, which lasted until 1947–48, when communal cricket was abandoned. The Hindus entered the tournament in 1905–06, and it became triangular in 1907–08, with the re-entry of the Parsees. It became quadrangular in 1912–13 with the entry of the Muslims, and pentangular in 1937–38 when 'The Rest' entered for the first time. The following firsts in arguably first-class cricket in India occurred in matches in this competition:

Bowler to take **ten wickets in a match:** Ernest Raikes, 10–79 in 44 overs, Bombay Presidency v Parsees, Poona, 19–21 Sep 1892.

Hat-trick: Harry Browne, Europeans v Parsees, Poona, 26–27 Sep 1895.

Total under 40: Europeans, 30 v Parsees, Poona, 26–27 Sep 1895. Robert Poore top scored

with 11, and B. M. Billimoria took 8–11 in 11.4 overs.

Total under 30: Muslims, 21 v Europeans, Poona, 9–11 Sep 1915. This remains the lowest on record in India. There were nine 'ducks', the best scorer being 'extras' with 9. Frank Tarrant had bowling figures of 5–6 in 7 overs, Harry Simms 4–2 in 3 overs.

The first man to score a **thousand runs in the Tournament** was John Greig. He went on to make the first **double century** in first-class cricket in India, 204 for Bombay Presidency XI v Oxford University Authentics at Bombay Gymkhana, 17–19 Nov 1902.

THE RANJI TROPHY

The competition for the Cricket Championship of India was inaugurated at a meeting of the Board of Control for Cricket in India at Simla in July 1934. The provincial cricket associations were to compete annually for a trophy presented by the then Maharaja of Patiala and named after the celebrated Indian batsman K. S. Ranjitsinhji ('Ranji'), who had died the previous year. In its first year, 15 teams competed in four zones— East: Central India, Central Provinces and Behar; North: Delhi, Northern India, Southern Punjab, The Army and United Provinces; South: Hyderabad, Madras and Mysore; West: Bombay, Gujerat, Maharashtra and Western India. The winner of each zone went into the semi-finals, the winners of which contested the final. In 1957–58 the zonal rounds were reorganised on a league basis, and in 1986 a record 27 teams entered what had become the world's largest first-class cricket competition.

The **first match** took place on 4 Nov 1934 between Madras and Mysore on turf at the Chepauk Ground, Madras. The damp conditions favoured the bowlers and Madras won in one day. The first ball was bowled for Madras by Morappakam Joysan Gopalan to N. Curtis, who scored the first run off Gopalan. The first wicket to fall was that of P. McCosh, who was dismissed by A. G. Ram Singh. The latter became the first to take **five wickets in an innings** and **ten**

The Ranji Trophy was presented for the National Championship of India in 1934, offering annual competition between the Provincial Cricket Associations of India and perpetuating the name of the great 'Ranji'.

† First in any Indian first-class match.

wickets in a match, with 6–19 and 5–16 for match figures of 11–35 in 27.5 overs (11 maidens).

The first **Ranji Trophy winners** were Bombay. Under the captaincy of Laxmidas Purshottamdas Jai they defeated Northern India by 208 runs at Bombay on 9–11 Mar 1935. Scores: Bombay 266 (P. J. Chury 58, L. P. Jai 41, Mubarak Ali 4–71) and 300 (V. M. Merchant 120, D. R. Puri 6–101); Northern India 219 (Agha Raza 50, G. E. B. Abell 43) and 139 (Agha Raza 62*, H. J. Vajifdar 8–40).

BATTING FIRSTS

Century: Syed Mohammed Hadi, 132 not out for Hyderabad v Madras, Hyderabad, 23–25 Nov 1934, his Ranji Trophy debut.

Double century: George Abell, 210 in 225 minutes with 28 fours for Northern India v The Army, Lahore, 4–6 Dec 1934. This was the first century by a wicket-keeper and the first by a European. With Agha Raza he added 304 runs for the second wicket, the first **double/triple century stands**.

Triple century† : Vijay Hazare, 316 not out in 387 minutes with 37 fours for Maharashtra v Baroda, Poona, 21–23 Jan 1940 in a total of 650–9.

Quadruple century† : Bhausahib Babashaheb Nimbalkar, 443 not out in 494 minutes with 49 fours, for Maharashtra v Kathiawar, Poona, 16–18 Dec 1948. The Kathiawar captain, His Highness Thakore Singh of Rajkot, conceded the match late on the third day when Nimbalkar was just 9 runs short of the highest score in first-class cricket. Nimbalkar added 455 with K. V. Bhandarkar, then a world record for the second wicket.

Century in each innings: S. M. Kadri, 105 and 114, Bombay v Western India, Poona, 20–22 Dec 1935.

400/500 stand: Vijay Harzare, 288, and Gul Mahomed, 319, 577 for the fourth wicket, Baroda v Holkar (the final) at Baroda, 7–11 Mar 1947. This stand, which took 533 minutes, remains the highest for any wicket in first-class cricket.

Completed match aggregate under 200: Bihar (49 and 46–2) beat Orissa (58 and 35) by 8 wickets. Orissa's 20 wickets total of 93 was also

'Ranji's' memorabilia cabinet at his palace in Jamnagar, India, containing passport and glass eyes (because he lost an eye during a shooting accident in England).

the first **under 100**.

Total over 400: Northern India, 459–7 dec v The Army, Lahore, 4–6 Dec 1934. They won by an innings and 52 runs.

Total over 500: Bengal, 515 from 120.2 6-ball overs when defeating Madras by an innings and 285 runs, Calcutta, 21–24 Jan 1939.

Total over 600: Maharashtra 650–9 dec (see triple century above) to qualify for the semi-finals on first innings lead in a drawn game.

Total over 700: Maharashtra 798 v Western India, Poona, 22–25 1941. This semi-final match was extended from three to four days to enable a first innings decision to be reached, Maharashtra qualifying for the final.

The peak score in the competition was reached with the first total over **800/900:** Holkar 912–8 dec v Mysore, Indore, 2–5 Mar 1946. For the first and only time in first-class cricket **six centuries were scored in one innings:** K. V. Bhandarkar 142, C. T. Sarwate 101, M. M. Jagdale 164, C. K.

Nayudu 101, B. B. Nimbalkar 172, R. Pratap Singh 100. At the end of the fourth day Mysore, 213 runs behind, with four second innings remaining, conceded the match.

Three firsts occured in the Ranji Trophy final at Bombay on 4–9 Mar 1945. The **match aggregate** of 2078 was the first to exceed **2000 runs** in first-class cricket, and remains the highest scored for the loss of all 40 wickets. The Holkar spin bowler Cottari Subbana Nayudu achieved firsts and world records for the most **balls bowled**, 917 in the match, and for **conceding** 428 runs, the first over **400**, with 6–153 in 64.5 6-ball overs (10 maidens) and 5–275 in 88 overs (15 maidens) in Bombay's scores of 462 and 764 (Vijay Merchant 278). Holkar scored 360 and 492 (Denis Compton 249*).

BOWLING FIRSTS

Eight wickets in an innings: P. Tata Rao (Hyderabad), 8–73 in 21.4 overs (3 maidens) in

Madras second innings 169, Hyderabad, 23–25 Nov 1934.

Nine wickets in an innings: R. R. Wadkar (Bombay), 9–38 in 23.3 overs in Western India first innings, Jamnagar, 2–4 Nov 1937.

All ten wickets in an innings: Premanshu Mohan Chatterjee (Bengal), 10–20 in 19 overs in Assam first innings, Jorhat, 26–29 Jan 1957. Assam totalled 54 and lost by an innings and 206 runs.

Hat-trick: Mohammed Baqa Jilani, bowling medium paced off breaks for Northern India v Southern Punjab at Amritsar, 5–7 Feb 1935. Southern Punjab were dismissed for 22 in just 97 balls having been set 114 runs for victory. This was the first **score under 30** and remains the lowest score in the competition. Mohamed Nissar top-scored with 6, Jilani took 5–7 in 25 balls, D. R. Puri 3–3 in 24 balls.

Hat-track on debut: J. S. Rao in 6–24 in 13 overs, Services v Jammu & Kashmir, the Army ground, New Delhi, 24–25 Nov 1963. In his second match, four days later, Rao became the first man to achieve **two hat-tricks in an innings** in his 7–30 in 11 overs for Services v Northern Punjab at the Gandhi ground, Amritsar. Shortly afterwards Rao became a paraplegic due to a parachuting accident.

SEASON'S FIRSTS

500 runs: S. M. Kadri, 515 av. 51.50 for Bombay in 1935–36: 40 & 4, 72 & 53, 105 & 114, 34 & 8, 83 & 2.

1000 runs: Rusi Modi, 1008 av. 201.60 for Bombay in 1944–45. His extraordinary, and still record, total was made up of the following innings: 160 v Sind at Karachi, 210 v Western India at Bombay, 245* and 31* v Baroda at Bombay, 113 v Northern India at Bombay, 98 and 151 v Holkar at Bombay.

50 wickets: R. B. Desai, 50 av. 11.10 for Bombay in 1958–59: 3–11 & 4–28, 6–63 & 1–58, 3–72 & 1–14, 5–10 & 6–28, 5–32 & 4–79, 2–35 & 3–30, 3–58 & 4–37.

CAREER FIRSTS

Vijay Merchant was the first to reach **1000 runs in the Ranji Trophy**, during an innings of 143

Vijay Merchant (left)—whose family name was Thackersey—scored prodigiously in the Ranji Trophy and when touring England, and averaged well in a short Test career. Yet his demeanour remained enviably modest. His partner Mushtaq Ali was a more explosive character with cricket inconsistency to match.

not out for Bombay v Baroda at Baroda, 18–20 Oct 1938. His career had started in 1934–35, and to this point he had 1006 runs av. 55.88 in eleven matches. He was also the first to reach **3000** during an innings of 278 v Holkar at Bombay in the final in March 1945, and after this his record was 40 innings (8 not out), 3003 runs av. 93.84.

Vijay Hazare was the first to reach **2000,** in the final between Baroda and Hyderabad, 26–29 Mar 1943, and he went on to be the first to **4000, 5000** and **6000** runs, in matches for Baroda on 18–24 Mar 1949, 16–19 Nov 1951 and 13–16 Mar 1958. His final career record according to *Indian Cricket* was 6312 runs av. 69.36 in 103 innings (12 not out). He was also the first to take **200 wickets,** passing this figure in the match for Baroda v Bombay at Baroda on 18–20 Nov 1949.

The first bowler to achieve **100 wickets** in Ranji Trophy matches was Amar Singh, right-arm fast medium, while playing for Nawanagar v Western India on 9–11 Nov 1939. A month later, v

The Duleep Trophy; India's Zonal equivalent of their National Championship, immortalising another cricket giant.

Baroda at Baroda, on 15–17 Dec 1939, he was the first to the **1000 runs/100 wickets** double. His first 31 wickets were taken in four matches for Western India 1934–36, the remaining 69 for Nawanagar.

The leg break bowler Vaman Kumar was the first to take **300** and **400** wickets, while playing for Tamil Nadu v Kerala at Tellicherry, 14–15 Nov 1970 and v Andhra at Salem, 4–6 Jan 1975 respectively. Rajendra Goel was the first to **500** and **600** wickets. The left-arm spinner achieved the first target when playing for Haryana v Delhi at Delhi, 12–14 Nov 1981 and the second for Haryana v Jammu & Kashmir at Rohtak, 29 Nov–1 Dec 1984, when he had match figures of 14–74 in 55.2 overs. Goel, who also played for Patiala and Delhi, and never appeared in an official Test, took a total of 636 Ranji Trophy wickets for 10950 runs, av. 17.21, in 122 matches to the end of the 1984–85 season.

THE DULEEP TROPHY

This competition, contested by five zones: Central, East, North, South and West, was named after the great batsman Kumar Shri Duleepsinhji, and began in 1961–62.

The **first match** was between South Zone and North Zone at Nehru Stadium, Madras on 30 Sep, 1–2 Oct 1961, the winners to play the winners of a three-team knock-out competition between the other three zones. The first ball was bowled by the medium pacer Surendra Nath for the North Zone to M. L. Jaisimha, who in the same over scored the first run of the competition, and who was also the first out, lbw to Surendra for 5. In this match A. G. Milkha Singh scored the first **century**, 151 for South Zone in 362 minutes, exactly half his side's first innings total. He was the son of A. G. Ram Singh, who had taken the first wicket in the Ranji Trophy, and his brother A. G. Kripal Singh captained the South Zone to victory.

The first **Duleep Trophy winners** were the West Zone, captained by Nariman Contractor, who beat South Zone by ten wickets at the Brabourne Stadium, Bombay, 20–23 Oct 1961: South Zone 175 (A. G. Kripal Singh 73, P. R. Umrigar 6–52) and 139 (Prabakhar Rao 48*, R. B. Desai 4–51); West Zone 234–9 dec (C. G. Borde 82*, Kripal Singh 4–66) and 82–0 (N. J. Contractor 44*).

BATTING FIRSTS

Double century: Hanumant Singh, 210 in 384 minutes for Central v South, Hyderabad, 14–16 Nov 1964.

Triple century: Raman Lamba, 320 for North v West, Bhilai, 21–26 Oct 1987.

Century on debut: Mansur Ali Khan, Nawab of Pataudi, 141 for North v South at Feroz Shah Kotla, Delhi, 23–25 Dec 1963.

Century stand: Suryaveer Singh and Salim

Durani, 138 for second wicket, Central v East at Brabourne Stadium, Bombay, 8–10 Oct 1961.

Double century stand: Salim Durani and Vijay Manjrekar, 205 for third wicket, Central v West, Baroda, 13–15 Oct 1961.

Triple century stand: Ajit Wadekar and Dilip Sardesai, 320 for third wicket, West v Central at Brabourne Stadium, Bombay, 24–27 Nov 1972.

Total over 500: West Zone, 555, in the final against Central Zone, Brabourne Stadium, Bombay, 13–15 Feb 1965, which they won by an innings and 89 runs.

Total over 600: South Zone, 623, batting second against Central, Jamodoba, 6–9 Jan 1984. Mohammed Azharuddin scored 226.

Total over 700: South Zone, 740, replying to West Zone's 516 in the final at Wankhede Stadium, Bombay, 31 Oct, 1–2, 4–5 Nov 1986. Their three century scorers were B. Arun 149, K. Srikkanth 112 and C. Saldanha 102. The aggregate total in this match, 1728 runs for 23 wickets was the first **over 1500** in the series.

Total over 800: North Zone, 868 v West at Bhilai, 21–26 Oct 1987 to ensure a victory in the final or first innings. Raman Lamba scored a competition record 320.

BOWLING FIRSTS

Five wickets in an innings: Ramakant Bhikaji Desai, 5–70 in 20 8-ball overs for West v Central, Baroda, 13–15 Oct 1961.

Ten wickets in match: 'Baloo' Gupte, 9–55 in 16.6 8-ball overs and 3–72 in 24 overs for 12–127, West v South, Calcutta, 24–26 Jan 1963.

CAREER FIRSTS

1000 runs: M. L. Jaisimha, in his 16th match, for South v West at Hyderabad in the final on 28 Feb, 1–3 Mar 1969.

2000 runs: Anshuman Gaekwad, in his 26th match, for the losing side West in the final v North at Bhilai, 21–26 Oct 1987.

50 wickets: Bhagwat Chandrasekhar, in his eleventh match, for South v North at the Chepauk Stadium, Madras, 13–15 Sep 1969. He eventually took 99 wickets, av. 24.26, the highest so far, in the Duleep Trophy.

500 runs and 50 wickets: Madan Lal in his 18th match, North v East at Delhi, 21–24 Dec 1980.

THE DEODHAR TROPHY

This was the first limited-overs competition in India. It was started in 1973 as an inter-zonal tournament to give leading Indian players experience in this type of cricket. India's success in recent limited-overs events is surely justification of the foresight of the Indian Cricket Board.

The **first match**, a quarter-final, was played at Madras on 21 Nov 1973, between South and East Zones at 60 overs a side, each bowler being restricted to 12 overs. East Zone's P. K. Hazarika faced the first ball from Test all-rounder Abid Ali, who had him caught at the wicket by Syed Kirmani for 11 when the score was 17, the first wicket to fall. East Zone scored 156–9, with Gopal Bose (52) making the first half century of the competition, but lost the match.

In the semi-final at Poona on 29 November, Kit Ghavri, with the first **five wicket** haul of 6–24 in 12 overs, helped West Zone dismiss North in 39 overs for 98, the first **total under 100**, and win the match by eight wickets. On 12 December at Bombay, the South scored 185 in 52.1 overs and then dismissed West for 101 in 38 overs to become the first **holders of the trophy**.

Due to rain the quarter-final between East and West at Poona on 2 Oct 1974 became the first to be decided by the **spin of a coin**, as just three overs play had been possible, during which East scored one run without loss. West were the lucky team.

In the semi-final between South and North at Madras, 23 Oct 1974, South's Abdul Hai, a left-hander, made 101 in 256 minutes to become the first **century** scorer. With Mansur Ali Pataudi, who joined him at 27–3, he added 103 for the fourth wicket, the first **century partnership**. Despite four run outs in their innings of 248–9, South beat North by 99 runs.

The first bowler to **concede more than 60 runs** was Dhiraj Parsana, left-arm medium, 1–56 in 12 overs, West v South at Hyderabad on 4–5 Nov 1974. With 73 not out he was one of three

Ravi Shastri is a guileful left-armed spinner and the most adaptable of batsmen.

THE WILLS TROPHY

This limited-overs competition, sponsored by the India Tobacco Co. Ltd., was started in 1978, when the first matches were played on 5 March. Karnataka met Uttar Pradesh at Bangalore, Bengal and the Wills XI played at Madras, and Sunil Gavaskar, for the Board President's XI v Gujerat at Hyderabad, scored the first **50** and **100** in the competition. With Venkat Sivaramakrishnan (92) he shared in the first **century stand**, 184 for the first wicket (which remains the record), and eventually reached 103.

Rajasthan were skittled for 73 in 41 overs by Bombay at Delhi, 1 Oct 1980, the first **completed innings total under 100**, and Bombay won by seven wickets.

Ravi Shastri, left-arm spinner, with 5–35 in 9.3 overs for Bombay v Wills XI at Indore on 1 Oct 1981, was the first bowler to take **five wickets in a match**. In this game with 102 not out for Bombay Sunil Gavaskar, in his tenth game, became the first **batsman to score 500 runs** in Wills Trophy matches.

The first instance of a bowler **exceeding his quota of overs** was when Azim Khan, for Maharashtra v Andhra at Gwalior on 1 Apr 1987 bowled 11 overs, one over the maximum. On realising their error the umpires deleted the runs scored from his last over. Maharashtra won by six wickets.

men to make 50s (also Yajurvindrasingh 67, Eknath Solkar 65) in the first **score of over 300:** West's 320–9 in 60 overs v North at Bombay on 24 Dec 1975. During this innings Rakesh Shukla had figures of 2–91 in 12 overs, the first instance of a **bowler conceding 90 runs** in a match.

Dilip Vengsarkar (85 not out) and Ashok Mankad (80 not out) added 154 for the West third wicket v East at Ahmedabad, 10–12 Oct 1976. This, the first **stand over 150**, was terminated only because West attained their winning target. The first **double century stand** came in the final at Sholapur on 15 Feb 1984, when Anshuman Gaekwad (94) and Ghulam Parkar (113) started the West innings of 309 in 48.4 overs with 211 together. West beat North by 43 runs.

The first side to win **without the loss of a wicket** was at Pune (formerly Poona) on 16 Apr 1987 when North Zone scored 177–0 in 38.5 overs after taking 53 overs to dismiss West for 174.

The first player to reach **500 runs in this competition** was Brijesh Patel during his 25 for South v West on 14 Sep 1980 at Madras; his 14th innings and match. Madan Lal became the first to capture **25 wickets**, when bowling for North v West at Delhi on 4 Jan 1987.

> *The first cricketer to play in* **six decades** *was C. K. Nayudu, who made his first-class debut for the Hindus in 1916–17, became India's first Test captain, against England in 1932, and played his last first-class match for the Maharashtra Governor's XI v Chief Ministers XI, on the last day of which, 4 Nov 1963 he was aged 68 years 4 days.*

NEW ZEALAND

MILESTONES

In his diary entry for 23 Dec 1835 Charles Darwin stated, of the voyage of HMS *Beagle*, that when his party arrived at Waiwata he saw young Maori farm workers playing cricket on a farm run by British missionaries. This is the first actual record of the game in New Zealand, but the implication must be that cricket had been played there for a number of years.

New Zealand became a British crown colony on 6 Feb 1840 and cricket was played in the Bay of Islands in 1841, although no further details are to hand.

The first mention of a **club**—the Wellington Cricket Club—was on 28 Dec 1842, when their 'blues' defeated the 'reds' by 126 notches to 124, after which they adjourned to partake of roast beef and plum pudding. This is the first recorded **match**.

The first **inter-provincial match** was played at Wellington (Mount Cook's Parade Ground) on 16 Mar 1860. Wellington 71 and 39 (G. K. Turton five wickets) lost to Auckland 43 and 69–6 by four wickets. Wellington were dismissed for 13 by Nelson at Nelson in 1862–63, the first **total under 20** in New Zealand. G. Phillips (8 not out) **carried his bat** through the Wellington innings, the first recorded instance in New Zealand. A score of 13 was equalled by Auckland v Canterbury on 31 Dec 1877, but never lowered.

On 27–29 Jan 1864 Otago, 78 (R. Taylor 6–21) and 74, beat Canterbury, 34 and 42 (F. Macdonald 6–17), by 76 runs after being put into bat at the South Dunedin Recreation Ground. This was the first inter-provincial match of more than one day, and is regarded as the first **first-class match** in New Zealand. A few days later George Parr's English team came from Australia—the first **touring team in New Zealand**. Their first match was against 22 of Otago on 2–4 February at Dunedin. England, 99 and 58–1, beat Otago, 71 and 83, by nine wickets. The tourists won three matches and drew one, all against teams of 22.

The first **tour by a New Zealand team** was by Canterbury to Victoria and Tasmania in January 1879.

The first known **century** in New Zealand was scored by J. W. Marchant, 117 for Up-Country XI v Invercargill at Invercargill in 1864–65. The first in first-class cricket was 175, including 17 fours, by G. Watson, who opened the innings for Canterbury v Otago at Hagley Park, Christchurch, 24–26 Jan 1881. In the same season Watson, 225 for Christchurch v Otago, scored the first known **double century** in New Zealand.

In what was almost certainly a first-class match at Hagley Park on 7 Feb 1867, Canterbury were all out for 25 and 32, beaten by an innings by Otago, 94. This was the first **match aggregate less than 160** in NZ first-class cricket and remains the lowest ever aggregate outside England. W. F. Downes had innings analyses of 6–8 and 4–14—the first bowler to take **ten wickets in a match** in NZ first-class cricket. At the same venue, on 28–30 Jan 1875, A. M. Ollivier (52) and C. C. Corfe (80) put on 119 for the second wicket for Canterbury v Otago—the first **century stand** in NZ first-class cricket.

The first **tied match** outside Britain was on 17–18 Mar 1874 between Wellington, 63 and 118, and Nelson, 111 and 70, at Basin Reserve, Wellington.

The first bowler to take **all ten wickets in an innings** in New Zealand was R. Halley for an undisclosed number of runs for Addington v United Club at Addington in 1884–85. A. E. Moss had figures of 21.3 overs, 10 maidens, 10 wickets for 28 runs for Canterbury v Wellington at Hagley Park, Wellington on 27 Dec 1889. This was the first and only instance of all ten wickets in an innings in a NZ first-class match, and is unique for a bowler making his first-class debut.

In first-class matches the first **hat-trick** was taken by Charles Frith, a right-arm medium paced bowler, for Otago v Canterbury at Carisbrook, Dunedin on 20–21, 23–24 Feb 1885, as in the first innings he dismissed J. Wheatley (c & b 4), H. Page (b 0), E. P. Barnes (lbw 0) in consecutive balls and Otago eventually won by two wickets. Alexander Downes, for Otago v Auckland at Dunedin on 1 Jan 1894, became the first, and so far only, bowler to take **four wickets with successive balls** when he dismissed R. L.

Sir Pelham Warner—international player, author and administrator. Involved in cricket at all levels in all guises. Universally known, usually respected, not invariably liked. He was the MCC manager on the 'bodyline' tour.

Holle, W. I. Stemson, J. R. Lundon and H. W. Lawson as Auckland's second innings score crashed from 145–5 to 145–9. Auckland still won the match, by 13 runs.

In 1885–86 W. G. Dixon, playing for Carisbrook v Excelsior at Dunedin, was reported to have scored a **double century** (219) and then taken **all ten wickets in an innings**—the first such feat anywhere.

The first **double century partnership** was 202 added by Sammy Jones (159) and Joe Palmer (76) for the first wicket for the Australians v 22 of Wellington at Wellington in 1886–87. The first **triple century stand** in NZ first-class cricket was 306 for the first wicket by Leonard Cuff and James Lawrence for Canterbury v Auckland at Lancaster Park, Christchurch on 5–6 Jan 1894. The first such stand in lower grade cricket was the 360 added for the sixth wicket by H. C. Wilson (200) and G. Marshall (252 not out), during the first **score of more than 600** in New Zealand, 609 by Napier United 'A' v Napier United 'B' at Napier in 1898–99. The first score **over 500** had been 510 by Midland v Rivals at Wellington in 1895–96.

The first **stand of over 500** in New Zealand was made by A. Young, 275, and L. McMahon, 226 not out, for the second wicket for Wanderers v Taraheru at Gisborne in 1910–11.

Arnold Williams scored 114 and 105 not out for Midland v Wellington at Wellington in 1897–98, the first instance on record of a **hundred in each innings of a match** in New Zealand. The first in a first-class game was by Charles Dacre, 127 not out and 101 not out for Auckland v Victoria at Eden Park, Auckland on 13–14, 16 Mar 1925. This remains the only instance of two not out centuries.

The first **double century** in NZ first-class cricket was scored by Pelham Warner, a member of Lord Hawke's English touring team, with 211, including 27 fours, v Otago at Dunedin on 13–14 Feb 1903. The first **triple century** in any grade of cricket was 335 by Warwick Armstrong for the touring Melbourne Cricket Club v Southland at Invercargill in 1905–06.

The first **innings total of over 600** in NZ first-class cricket was 658 by Sir Arthur Sims'

Australians v Auckland at Auckland on 6–7, 9 Feb 1914 in the opening match of their tour. Vernon Ransford scored 159, Edgar Waddy 130 and Warwick Armstrong 128. In the Australians' match v Canterbury at Christchurch on 27–28 Feb, 2 March, Victor Trumper and Arthur Sims completed the first **stand of more than 400** in NZ first-class cricket, with 433 for the eighth wicket. The stand lasted 3 hours, and in that time Trumper's 293 included 3 sixes and 44 fours. In minor matches on the tour Jack Crawford made the first **score of over 350** in New Zealand, 354 v 15 of South Canterbury, and the Australians made the first score of **over 700** in New Zealand, 709 v Southland at Invercargill.

Minor match firsts were achieved by Havelock, **all out for 0** v Whareti at Auckland in 1909–10, W. Blackie taking nine wickets; and by A. Rimmer, a 14-year-old schoolboy, who took **all 20 wickets in the match** (10–4, 10–12) for Linwood 7th Grade v Cathedral Grammar School at Christchurch in 1925–26, the only instance in New Zealand.

The first **cricket book** published in New Zealand was *Auckland Cricketers' Trip to the South 1873–74*. The first cricket annual covered the 1889–90 season: *A Record of the Past Season* was compiled by F. E. Brittain. It contained 54 pages, including a frontispiece and statistics. It appeared in the following three seasons as the *Wellington Cricketers' Association Cricket Annual* before ceasing publication.

In a match between Hawke's Bay and the touring New South Wales team on 24–25 Jan 1894, play on the first day was at the Recreation Ground, Napier and on the second at Farndon Park, Napier. This is a unique instance of a **first-class match arranged at two venues**.

New South Wales scored 752–8 dec in their only innings against Otago at Dunedin on 15–16, 18 Feb 1924. This was the first, and remains the only, **score of more than 700**, and the only occasion on which more than **600 runs have been scored in a day** (649–7), in NZ first-class cricket. It was in fact a record for all first-class cricket at the time and remains the best outside England.

Don Taylor (99 and 143) and Bert Sutcliffe (141 and 135), opening the batting for Auckland v Canterbury at Eden Park, Auckland on 7–8, 10–11 Jan 1949, scored 220 together in the first innings and 286 in the second, the first and only case of **two double century opening stands in a match**. Despite their efforts the match was drawn, Auckland losing on first innings.

The New Zealand captain John Reid became, in 1961–62, the first player to score **2000 runs in an overseas season**. He set a record in South Africa with 1915 runs in 17 matches (30 innings) for the New Zealand touring team; on the way there he had scored 62 and 4 v Western Australia, and on the way home 13 and 49 v South Australia and 0 and 40 v New South Wales. Finally back in New Zealand he made 105 in four innings against a Commonwealth team, for a grand total of 2188 runs av. 57.57 in 22 matches, 40 innings (two not out). His total was not exceeded until Mohinder Amarnath scored 2234 during 1982–83 in India, Pakistan and the West Indies.

Glenn Turner of Otago became the first batsman to score **1000 runs in a NZ first-class season**, with 1244 runs av. 77.75 in eleven matches, 20 innings, including four not outs. This total was surpassed by Martin Crowe with 1676 runs av. 93.11 in 1986–87.

THE PLUNKET SHIELD

Cricket, A Weekly Record of the Game reported on 26 Mar 1908 of the Plunket Shield, donated by the Governor-General Lord Plunket, that it 'was to be awarded at the end of the 1906–07 season to the Association which was considered by the Council to hold the best record of the year. Thereafter the Shield could only be wrested from the holders by another Association challenging and defeating them on their home ground. A vote of the Council awarded the Shield to Canterbury, and in December last Auckland, assisted by Relf, went to Christchurch in an endeavour to wrest the honour from them'.

Thus the first **Plunket Shield match** was played between Canterbury, the first holders, and Auckland at Christchurch on 14, 16–17 Dec 1908. Auckland wrested the shield as they won comfortably by an innings and 135 runs: Canterbury 190 (H. B. Lusk 66, A. E. Relf 6–64) and 214 (S. A. Orchard 51, A. Haddon 5–65), Auckland 539 (L. G. Hemus 148, Relf 157, J. H. Bennett 5–169).

Albert Relf, of Sussex and England, who was coaching in Auckland, bowled the first ball to Harold Lusk, a future New Zealand representative batsman, and took 6–64 in 27 overs, the first instance of a bowler taking **five wickets in an innings**. The first wicket to fall was that of William Patrick, lbw to Relf for 26 with the score on 93. For Auckland Lance Hemus scored the first **century** (148 with 12 fours in 258 minutes out of 347) and put on 100 for the first wicket with William Brook-Smith, the first **century stand**.

Auckland's first **score over 500** was improved by them to 579 v Otago at Auckland, 11–15 Feb 1910, when for the first time **three batsmen scored centuries**: Hemus 109, Relf 118 and Edmund Sale 121. Hemus achieved another first, a **double century stand**, when he added 216 for the third wicket with Sidney Smith for Auckland v Canterbury at Christchurch, 2–5 Jan 1920. Auckland's total of 643 was the first **over 600**, while Smith's 256 in 330 minutes was the first **double century** of the competition.

The first bowler to take **ten wickets in a match** was Alister MacDonald Howden, a Scottish-born leg-spinner, who achieved match figures of 12–148 (7–87 and 5–61) for Auckland v Otago at Auckland, 28–30 Dec 1908 in a match his side had to fight hard to save.

Thirteen wickets were first captured by leg-spinner Caleb Olliff for Auckland v Wellington at Auckland, 1–3 Jan 1913, in a total of 45 overs 6–62 and 7–42 including a spell over the two innings of 9–3 (3–0 and 6–3). At the end of the second day he was carried shoulder-high from the pitch, and Auckland won by nine wickets. The first instance of **15 wickets in a match** and **nine in an innings** was when Daniel McBeath, for Canterbury v Auckland at Auckland, 21–22, 24 Feb 1919 took 9–56 in 24 overs and 6–112 in 29 overs. His match figures of 15–168 remain the Shield record.

The left-arm bowler D. A. Orchard (Canterbury) took the first hat-trick in the Shield when he dismissed E. V. Sale, A. Haddon and W. Brook-Smith of Auckland at Auckland, 7–10 Jan 1910. However, he took no more wickets and Canterbury lost by seven wickets.

When Andrew (139) and Cyril (119) Snedden scored centuries for Auckland v Hawke's Bay at Auckland on 25, 27 Dec 1920, they were the first **brothers to score a century in the same innings**. Cyril's was the only century of his first-class career, and was made on his debut; none of their runs was scored together.

The first **match aggregate over 1500** in NZ first-class cricket was at Basin Reserve, Wellington, 23–27 Dec 1922, when Wellington (435 and 396) beat Auckland (386 and 337) by 108 runs. The first instance of one **team scoring more than 1000 runs** in a NZ first-class match was at Carisbrook, Wellington on 18–19, 21–23 Jan 1924 by Wellington (560 and 465) as they defeated Otago by 145 runs; the Otago openers, James Shepherd (76 and 92) and Rupert Worker (106 and 94) had first wicket stands of 154 in the first innings and 155 in the second, the first such instance in NZ first-class cricket.

The first **win by a margin of over 500 runs** was when Wellington (447 and 374) beat Auckland (191 and 118) by 512 runs at Wellington, 19–23 Feb 1926. Bert Kortlang scored 214 not out in the first innings and John Hiddleston 204 in the second, the first time **two double centuries** had been scored for one side.

After rain had caused severe disruption on all three days of the match between Otago and Wellington at Dunedin on 17, 19–20 Feb 1923, the idea of a fourth day being played was countermanded by the New Zealand Cricket Council, the first instance of a match being **abandoned** in such circumstances in world cricket. Wellington were to play Canterbury on 23 February.

Set to score 473 for victory by Auckland at Christchurch, 25–29 Dec 1930, Canterbury obtained the runs in 6 hr 15 min, with 4 minutes remaining, for the loss of six wickets. This was the first time in the Shield that a **team had won after being set to score more than 400**.

The first **triple century** in NZ first-class cricket was scored by Roger Blunt, 338 not out in Otago's second innings v Canterbury at

Bob Blair was a stalwart New Zealand pace bowler with most Plunket Shield bowling records. He had a moderate Test record and is best remembered for a heroic innings against South Africa in 1953, only hours after hearing of his fiancée's death in New Zealand.

Christchurch, 25–29 Dec 1931. Coming in at 49–1, Blunt batted throughout the rest of the innings of 589. He added 127 for the second wicket with Fred Badcock and 184 for the last wicket with W. Hawksworth (21), which remains a New Zealand record. Yet, set to score 279 for victory, Canterbury achieved the target with seven wickets down.

Charles Jackman was the first wicket-keeper to take **eight dismissals in a match,** five in the first innings (1ct 4st) and three (all stumped) in the second, for Canterbury v Wellington at Wellington, 24–27 Dec 1935. His **seven stumpings** remains a NZ record. The first **fielder to take five catches in an innings** was John Lamason for Wellington v Otago at Dunedin, 4–8 Feb 1938. Paul Whitelaw was the first batsman to make **centuries in each innings** of a Plunket Shield match, 115 and 155 for Auckland v Wellington at Auckland on 18–21 Jan 1935; these were his maiden first-class hundreds. When Whitelaw (195) and William Carson (290 in his second first-class innings) added 445 in 268 minutes for the third wicket, Auckland v Otago at Dunedin, 31 Dec 1936, 1–4 Jan 1937; it was the first **stand over 400** in the Shield. Whitelaw (108) was one of **four batsmen to score centuries in an innings** in Auckland's 590 v Canterbury at Auckland, 7–10 Jan 1938. The others were A. J. Postles 105, Verdun Scott 122 and Alexander Matheson 112. This remains a unique feat in New Zealand.

Wellington, after a first innings lead over Otago of 85 at Wellington, 24–27 Dec 1945, were all out for 42, leaving Otago the easy task of 128 runs for victory. This was the first **sub-50 innings** in the Shield.

CAREER FIRSTS

Lance Hemus (Auckland) was the first to **500 and 1000 runs**. He passed both figures in matches v Canterbury at Auckland: 142 on 24–27 Dec 1910 for a total at that time of 583 runs av. 53.00 in 12 innings, and 140 in his 14th match, 2–5 Jan 1920 to bring his total to 1045 runs av. 45.43 in 24 innings. His Plunket Shield career total was 1263 av. 37.14 in 21 matches to 1922.

The first to **2000 runs** was J. S. Hiddlestone, whose 114 for Wellington v Canterbury, 1–3 Jan 1927 took his total to 2108 runs av. 54.05 in 23 matches. He retired after one more match with 2137 av. 52.12. Bert Sutcliffe was the first to pass targets from **3000 to 6000 runs**. At the end of his epic innings of 385 (a NZ record) for Otago v Canterbury at Christchurch, 25–29 Dec 1952, his Shield career total was 3015 runs av. 87.17. The **4000** was passed in his 104 not out v Northern Districts at Dunedin, 26–28 Dec 1957, taking him to 4003 av. 72.78 in 34 matches, and **5000** during his 264 in 364 minutes v Central Districts at Dunedin, 5–8 Feb 1960, when his total was 5024 av. 64.41 in 48 matches, 84 innings. His **6000th** run came during his 57 for Northern Districts v Wellington at Wellington, 14–16 Jan 1963 (6029 av. 58.53 in 62 matches, 110 innings). Sutcliffe's Shield career finished in 1966, with 6800 runs av.

53.96 in 139 innings in 78 matches. The only other batsman even to reach 5000 runs was John Reid.

The first to take **50 wickets** was Donald Sandman, a right-arm leg break bowler, during 3–58 for Canterbury v Otago at Christchurch, 24–27 Dec 1921, his 14th match. His first 50 wickets cost 1078 runs av. 21.56. Alfred Brice passed **100** in the second innings for Wellington v Canterbury at Wellington, 31 Dec 1927, 1–2 Jan 1928. This was his 23rd match, and his 100 cost 21.66 runs each. His career finished that season, for a total of 108 wickets av. 22.00 in 25 matches.

Bob Blair was the first to take **200** Shield wickets, reaching 202 av. 15.11 in the Wellington v Central Districts match at Wanganui, 25–28 Dec 1959. He was also the first to **300**, taking that for Wellington v Otago at Dunedin, 18–21 Jan 1963, his 49th match, at which stage his career was 305 wickets for 4351 runs, av. 14.26. His final Plunket Shield career record was 58 matches, 352 wickets for 5146 runs, av. 14.61.

THE SHELL SERIES

In March 1975 it was announced that a Shell sponsored competition would commence the following season to take over as the main first-class competition in New Zealand. The Plunket Shield was reassigned for matches between North and South Islands. Initially the Shell Cup went to the winners of a first round of matches, the Shell Trophy to the winners of a second competition. After numerous changes over the years the Shell Trophy is now awarded to the winners of the single first-class inter-Provincial competition, the Shell Cup to the winners of a knock-out competition.

The first **Shell Cup matches** took place on 19–21 Dec 1975: Auckland v Northern Districts at Auckland, Central Districts v Wellington at Masterton and Otago v Canterbury at Dunedin. Jock Edwards of Central Districts, who hit the first six (off Ewen Chatfield) was the first batsman to be dismissed, caught by Jeremy Coney off Michael Coles for 31 out of 37. In this match Alistair Jordan, Central Districts' pace bowler, was the first to take **five wickets in an innings** (5–80 in 25 overs in the first innings), and Wellington's Jeremy Coney, 106 in 250 minutes with 1 six and 14 fours, hit the first century. For Auckland, Mark Burgess and James Riley hit the first **century stand**, 111 for the fourth wicket in 98 minutes in their first innings.

The first bowler to take **ten wickets in a Shell Cup match** was Hedley Howarth, who had figures of 4–58 and 7–75 for Auckland, who beat Otago by 10 runs at Dunedin, 30–31 Dec 1975, 1 Jan 1976. On those dates wicket-keeper Leslie Downes took **six dismissals** for Central Districts v Canterbury at Nelson.

Peter Petherick was the first bowler to take **nine wickets in an innings**, 9–93 in 35 overs in the first innings of the match, Otago v Northern Districts at Dunedin, 8–10 Jan 1976.

The first **double century** was 222 by Ian Rutherford for Otago v Central Districts at New Plymouth, 9–12 Mar 1979. He batted in all for 625 minutes, reaching his 200 in 555 minutes, and hit 2 sixes and 29 fours. Otago's total of 543–8 dec was the first **over 500**. Bad weather caused the match to be left drawn.

The first **innings score of less than 100** was when Central Districts were dismissed for 96 by Northern Districts at Hamilton on 26–28 Dec 1975, but they later forced a draw after rain.

CAREER FIRSTS

Glenn Turner (Otago) was the first batsman to reach **500 runs**, during an innings of 57 at Wanganui v Central Districts, his fourth match, at which time his record was 538 runs av. 76.85 in eight innings, and the first to **1000**, in his first match for Northern Districts, v Auckland at Pukekohe, 17–19 Dec 1976 during a second innings 93. That took his Shell record to 1009 runs av. 77.61, 16 innings (3 not out), eight matches.

Ian Rutherford reached **2000 runs** during his 222 for Otago in 1979 (see above) to take his total to 2050 runs av. 37.96 in 31 matches, 57 innings. John Wright had scored exactly **3000** after the Northern Districts v Auckland, Rotorua, 10–12 Jan 1984, 39 matches, 75 innings, average 41.66.

Bruce Edgar was the first to reach **4000 runs**, batting for Wellington v Otago at Wellington, 1–3 Feb 1987, making his record in 58 matches, 107

Opposite *Ewan Chatfield was nearly killed while batting before becoming a highly consistend New Zealand bowler.*

innings (9 not out), 4034 runs av. 41.16.

Ewen Chatfield (Wellington) became the first bowler to take **50 wickets**, v Canterbury at Christchurch on 7 Jan 1977; ending the match with 53 wickets for 1261 runs av. 23.79 in 12 matches. He reached **100** wickets on 16 Dec 1978, as did David O'Sullivan (Central Districts), but both were beaten to that first by one day by Stephen Boock, for Otago v Wellington at Invercargill. O'Sullivan went on to reach **200** first, v Auckland at Napier on 12 Jan 1981, but Boock was the first to **300**, for Otago v Wellington at Lower Hutt, 12–14 Jan 1984, and the first to **400**, in his 82nd match, in the first innings for Otago v Wellington at Centennial Park, Omaru, 2–4 Feb 1988. His 400th victim was Bruce Edgar, the first batsman to score 4000 Shell Trophy runs 12 months, to the day, previously.

LIMITED-OVERS COMPETITION

The first limited-overs inter-provincial competition in New Zealand was started in 1971–72, under the sponsorship of the New Zealand Motor Corporation. Gillette took over in 1977–78, there was no sponsor in 1979–80, and since then it has been contested for the Shell Cup. In the first two seasons matches were played at 40 8-ball overs per innings, this was then reduced to 35 8-ball overs, and further to 30 overs in 1977–78, before reverting to 35 in 1978–79. From 1979–80 50 6-ball overs has been standard.

The **first matches** were played on 5 Dec 1971, when first Auckland (139–3) beat Northern Districts (135) and then Wellington (243–7) beat Central Districts (196–5). In the former match Dennis Lloyd of Northern Districts was the first batsman to lose his wicket, caught by Roger Harris off John Williams, while in the latter Bruce Taylor scored the first 50 with an unbeaten 59 in 49 minutes, including 5 sixes, for Wellington.

The first **completed innings under 100** was 92 by Auckland in 32.3 8-ball overs v Wellington at Wellington on 12 Dec 1971.

The first **winners** were Canterbury, who beat Wellington 129–3 to 127 at Lancaster Park, Christchurch on 19 Dec 1971. Northern Districts scored 220–9 in their 40 8-ball overs at Seddon Park, Hamilton in reply to Auckland's 223 on 3 Dec 1972, the first losing total of 200 or more.

The first **century partnership** was 104 for the fifth wicket by Austin Parsons and Ross Morgan for Auckland v Wellington at Wellington on 16 Dec 1973, but they were on the losing side. The first **stand of over 150** was the 171 added in just 87 minutes by the Auckland captain Graham Vivian and John F. Reid (47 not out) for the fifth wicket v Wellington at Auckland on 12 Nov 1977. Vivian scored the first **century** in the competition, 126 in 103 minutes with 6 sixes and 9 fours.

Richard Collinge was the first bowler to take **five wickets in a match**, 5–23 in seven 8-ball overs for Wellington v Otago at Wellington on 8 Dec 1974. The first to take more was Willie Watson with 7–23 in 7 overs for Auckland v Otago at Auckland on 12 Jan 1985, including the first **hat-trick**, his victims being John Cushen, Stephen Boock and Vaughan Johnson.

Ross Dykes became the first wicket-keeper to take **five dismissals** (all caught), for Auckland v Wellington in the final at Wellington, 16 Dec 1973, and the first to take **six** was Ervin McSweeney for Wellington v Auckland at Wellington, 24 Jan 1983. At Palmerston North on 23 Nov 1975 Central Districts scored 223–9 in their 35 overs but Northern Districts had only reached 39–2 in 10 overs, when rain prevented further play. Central Districts were awarded the match, the first to be determined by the **spin of a coin**.

Ian Rutherford was the first, and so far only, player in this series to be dismissed **'obstructing the field'**, for 4 when opening for Otago v Canterbury at Dunedin, 6 Mar 1977.

Brian Dunning of Northern Districts was awarded the match v Wellington at Whangarei on 13 Mar 1977, which also celebrated the 50th anniversary of the Northlands Cricket Association, as a **benefit**. He did not bat as his team scored 180–1 to win by nine wickets, but he took 2–34 in 7 overs.

The first **tie** in the series was at Logan Park, Dunedin on 9 Dec 1979. Otago, 223–5, however went through to the final on the basis of losing

fewer wickets than Wellington, 223–9. Wellington's Stewart Cater was run out from the last ball of the match.

Three medium paced bowlers were the first to **concede more than 70**, **80** and **90 runs**. Graeme Thomson, left-arm, 1–76 in 10 overs, Otago v Wellington at Alexandria, 30 Dec 1980; then two right-armers on 16 Jan 1983: Bruce Blair, 3–80 in 10 overs, Otago v Central Districts at Omaru and later for Northern Districts v Auckland at Gisborne, Craig Presland had figures of 2–93 in 10 overs. The first century is eagerly awaited.

The first **total of over 300** was by Northern Districts, 306–2 (Barry Cooper 97*, John Parker 96*) in 50 overs at Gisborne on 16 Jan 1983, but Auckland replied with 309–8 (Tom Hellaby 80, John Bracewell 66) in 49.2 overs to win.

The career milestone of **1000 runs** in these limited-overs matches was first passed by John F. Reid on 15 Jan 1984 for Auckland v Central Districts, when an innings of 40 not out took his total to 1031 in 26 innings, av. 57.27. Bruce Edgar reached his 1000 later that season. First to **50 wickets** was Stephen Boock for Otago v Northern Districts at Gisborne on 29 Dec 1986.

PAKISTAN

MILESTONES

Pakistan was created as an independent dominion within the British Commonwealth on 15 Aug 1947, on the partition of former British India. First-class matches had, of course, been played previously in this territory, but the first **first-class match** in Pakistan was played at the Bagh-e-Jinnah Ground, Lahore on 6–8 Feb 1948: Governor's XI 277 (Fazal Mahmood 78) and 203–7 dec (Fazal Mahmood 77) drew with Punjab University 372 (Maqsood Ahmed 116, Mohammad Amin 5–117) and 68–2. Maqsood's 116 was the first **first-class century** in Pakistan, and the first **century stand** was 116 added for the sixth wicket by Fazal Mahmood and K. A. Saeed (68) in the first innings.

The first **touring team to Pakistan** was that of the West Indies led by John Goddard in 1948–49. Pakistan's first **international** match was a drawn game against that team at Bagh-e-Jinnah Ground, Lahore on 26–29 Nov 1948. In their second innings the Pakistan captain, Mohammad Mian Saeed (101) added 205 for the second wicket with Imtiaz Ahmed (131), the first **double century stand**, and the first **centuries** in Pakistan internationals.

Waqar Hassan (201 not out) made the first **double century** in Pakistan for Air Marshall Cannon's XI v Hassan Mahmood's XI at Karachi 2–4 Oct 1953 and, scoring 189, with Imtiaz Ahmed (209) put on 308 for the seventh wicket for Pakistan v New Zealand at Lahore, 26–31 Oct 1956; the first **stand of 300 or more** in Pakistan.

Aftab Ahmed, for Punjab v North-West Frontier Province at Peshawar on 19–21 Nov 1954, took 6–27 and 5–52, the first bowler to take **ten wickets or more in a match**. The first instance of **nine wickets in an innings** or **15 wickets in a match** was by Fazal Mahmood, 6–33 and 9–43, for Punjab v Services at Lahore, 7–12 Feb 1957.

The Karachi Whites were dismissed for 762 by Karachi Blues, Karachi 1–6 Feb 1957, the first **total of over 600/700** in Pakistan; while **800/900** was exceeded for the first time by Railways, who declared at 910–6 in their only innings v Dera Ismail Khan at Lahore, 2–4 Dec 1964. This remains the record total in Pakistan. The innings lasted until lunchtime on the third day, and Railways then demonstrated the amazing imbalance between the teams by dismissing their opponents for 32 and 27 during the remainder of the day to win by an innings and 851 runs, the most **overwhelming result** in first-class cricket anywhere.

In 1961–62 Hanif Mohammad became the first player to score **1000 runs** in first-class matches **in a Pakistan season**. He reached this total on 10 Mar 1962 during an innings of 77 for the East Pakistan Governor's XI v an International XI at Dacca. Twelve days later Imtiaz Ahmed also reached 1000 runs, soon followed by Mushtaq Mohammad and Alimuddin. Hanif's season's total was 1250 runs av. 59.52 in 13 matches, 21 innings.

The first bowler to take **100 wickets in a season** was Abdul Qadir of Habib Bank, 102 av. 22.98 in 1982–83.

The first **tie** in a Pakistan first-class match was at Bahawalpur on 30 Nov, 1–2 Dec 1961: Lahore B 127 and 278, Bahawalpur 123 and 282. It remained the only tie until 1983–84.

Shahid Mahmood, for Karachi Whites v Khairpur at Karachi in 1969–70 took all ten second innings wickets for 58 runs in 25 overs; the first instance of **all ten** in Pakistan first-class cricket. It remains a unique feat.

A **stand of over 400** was first achieved in Pakistan first-class cricket by Khalid Irtiza (290) and Aslam Ali (236), 456 for the third wicket, United Bank v Multan in 1975–76 at the National Stadium, Karachi. On the same ground **500** was first surpassed by Waheed Mirza (324) and Mansoor Akhtar (224*), 561 for the first wicket for Karachi Whites v Quetta on 7–9 Feb 1977. This is a record for the first wicket anywhere in the world.

QAID-I-AZAM TROPHY

This, Pakistan's first first-class tournament, means 'The Great Leader', after Mohammad Ali Jinnah, the nation's founder. It was inaugurated with eight teams: Bahawalpur, Karachi, Lahore,

The team group of the 1962 Pakistan tourists includes several who loom large in their country's cricket history.
They are (back row) left to right: *Saeed Ahmed, Mohammad Farooq, Imtiaz Ahmed, Javed Burki* (Capt), *Alimuddin, Ijaz Butt, Hanif Mohammed* (Vice Capt) *and Nasimul Ghani.*
Front row (left to right): *Intikhab Alam, Wallis Mathias, Mushtaq Mohammad, Asif Ahmed and Munir Malik.*

North-West Frontier Province, Punjab, Railways, Services and Sind, after two teams had dropped out, in 1953–54. Until then most of the Pakistani first-class cricket consisted of matches against overseas touring teams, so the need for strong domestic competition was identified as a sure way of enabling a steady supply of talented players for the national team. It has remained the premier first-class competition.

The **first matches** were played on 20–22 Nov 1953: Bahawalpur v Sind at the Dring Stadium, Baghdad-ul-Jadeed, and NW Frontier v Railways at Peshawar. In the former match the Sind captain, The Pir of Pagaro, won the toss and elected to bat. B. G. Irani faced the first ball from home skipper Khan Mohammad, while over at Peshawar the Railways skipper Masood Salahuddin inserted the opposition and himself opened the bowling to future Test stalwart Alimuddin. NW Frontier were dismissed for 90, the first **score under 100**, but the major statistical milestone was passed by Bahawalpur's Hanif

Mohammad, who opened the batting, scored the first **century** and became the first to **carry his bat**, with his 147 not out in his side's total of 252.

The next game was played at the Agha Khan Gymkhana Ground, Karachi on 4–6 Dec 1953, Combined Services v Karachi. The Services batted first after winning the toss, and they made the first **total over 400** in the competition, 407. Flt. Lt. M. E. Z. Ghazali (160) became the first batsman to make over **150** and with A/C Qamar Yusuf (76) added 203 for the sixth wicket, the first **century** and **double century stand**. In the second innings Ghazali opened with Capt. S. A. Rehman, and together they put on 109, the first first wicket century stand. Bahawalpur became the first **winners of the trophy**, beating Punjab by eight wickets in the final, staged at Karachi on 23–25 Jan 1954. The match was scheduled to be played to a finish, but it was all over in less than three days.

Hanif Mohammad went on to set many batting firsts and records. Opening for Karachi v Sind at

Opposite Javed Miandad is likely to hold all his country's Test batting records before his retirement. Pictured during his epic 260 for Pakistan v England at The Oval, 1987—his fourth Test double century.

the KPI Ground, Karachi, 19–21 Nov 1954, he scored the first **double century**, with 230 not out in a total of 452–3 dec, having scored 168 of these while batting throughout the first day. With his brother Raees Mohammad (118 not out) he added 255 (unbroken) for the fourth wicket, the first **stand of over 250**, while, with another brother Wazir Mohammad also playing, this was the first case of three brothers playing for the same side. In the next final, for Karachi v Services at the Karachi National Stadium, 21–24 Apr 1955, Wazir 118, Hanif 109 and Raees 110 all scored centuries, the first time **three brothers** had done this in Pakistan. During the Services innings Abdul Wahab achieved the first **hat-trick** in Pakistan first-class cricket. He dismissed M. E. Z. Ghazali (55), Anwar Saeed and Miran Baksh with successive deliveries to end the innings.

For Karachi v Bahawalpur at Karachi, 8–9, 11–12 Jan 1959 Hanif scored 499, the first **score over 300** and the first individual innings to last more than two full days in Pakistan; it remains the highest ever first-class score anywhere in the world, but he failed to make the 500 mark as he was run out trying to turn a single into two. This was the fifth of six successive centuries that he made in the competition; and he was the first to score **three or more consecutively**. They were: 228 Karachi Whites v Karachi Blues in 1956–57; 123 Karachi A v Sind B and 146* Karachi A v Sind A in 1957–58; 129 Karachi v Hyderabad, the 499, then 130 Karachi v Services in 1958–59. All these were at Karachi, except the fourth at Hyderabad. Hanif became the first batsman to score a **century in each innings**, 133 out of 223 and 148 in 275–6 dec for Karachi Whites v Karachi Greens, 10–12 Nov 1961 and was the first player to reach **1000, 2000** and **3000 runs** in the competition, achieving these figures in his 9th (in 1956–57), 13th (1958–59) and 21st (1961–62) match respectively.

The first to reach **4000, 5000, 6000 and 7000 runs** was Shafiq Ahmed in his 50th (1982–83), 59th (1983–84), 77th (1985–86) and 88th (1986–87) matches.

In the first match in 1956–57 Fazal Mahmood, for Punjab v Peshawar at Peshawar, 25–26 Dec 1956, took 8–21 in 19 overs in Peshawar's first innings 64. This was the first case of **eight wickets in an innings** and was followed a few days later by the first case of **ten wickets in a match** in the competition, when Mahmoud Hussain had figures of 2–39 in 15 overs and 8–95 in 34.5 overs for Karachi Whites v Karachi Greens at the KPI Ground, 28–30 December.

Fazal improved both records in the semi-final against Services at Punjab University Ground, Lahore, 7–12 Feb 1957, with 6–33 in 39 overs and 9–43 in 30.1 overs, for the first **nine wickets in an innings** and **15 wickets in a match** (15–76), as he led Punjab to an innings victory. In the other semi-final, which had been played at the Karachi Gymkhana Ground on 1–6 Feb 1957, a **match aggregate of over 1000** was comfortably exceeded for the first time when, after Karachi Blues, who had won the toss, made 314, Karachi Whites amassed 762, the first score ever **over 500**. The match aggregate was 1392 for 29 wickets.

At Hyderabad Municipal Gardens, 4–5 Jan 1957, Sind were dismissed for 44 in their first innings by Karachi Whites—the first **total under 50**.

Fazal Mahmood was the first to take **50 wickets** in the competition, reaching this in his 8th match in 1956–57. Shujauddin in his 20th match, was the first to **100** in 1961–62 (and, two matches later, the first to the **double of 1000 runs and 100 wickets**), and the first to **200** and **300** wickets was Mohammad Nazir in his 42nd (1981–82) and 60th (1984–85) matches respectively.

Batting for Karachi B v Quetta at BVS Parsi School Ground, Karachi, 11–12 Oct 1957, Karachi's Ghaffar A. Khan scored 102 in his only innings, 17 **more than the combined total** of Quetta's two innings. In a match seven days later at the KPI Ground even greater domination was shown as Karachi A scored 277–0 dec (Hanif Mohammad 146 not out, Alimuddin 131 not out) and then dismissed Sind for 92 and 108 to become the first side to **win a match without losing a wicket**.

When Sind A met Sind B at Hyderabad Municipal Gardens, 25–27 Oct 1957, the **match was abandoned** before lunch on the second day due

to a disagreement over interpretation of some cricket laws—the first such occurrence.

Qasim Omar was the first batsman to score **1000 runs in a Qaid-I-Azam season**: 1078 in 1982–83.

THE WILLS CUP

The first **limited-overs tournament** between first-class teams in Pakistan was the Wills Cup, started in 1980–81. This was arranged in two leagues of five teams each, with the top two progressing to knock-out semi-finals and final.

The **first matches** were played in Hyderabad on 12 Mar 1981. At the Iqbal Stadium the House Building Finance Corporation lost to United Bank by eight wickets, and at the Niaz Stadium the Industrial Development Bank beat Karachi by two wickets. Mansoor Akhtar scored 50 not out for United Bank and Shaukat Mirza 52 for IDB.

The first **century** was made by Mansoor Akhtar the next day, with 113 for United Bank at Faisalabad as his team (250–7) beat Lahore (164–5) by 86 runs. He eventually became the first batsman to complete **1000 runs in the Wills Cup**, reaching this against Pakistan International Airlines (PIA) at Shahi Bagh Stadium, Peshawar on 6 Oct 1986. Imran Khan was the first bowler to take **five wickets in an innings**, 5–20 in 8.3 overs for PIA v Habib Bank at Qaddafi Stadium, Gulberg, Lahore in the semi-finals on 25 March, enabling PIA to win by one wicket. In the first **final** at the Qaddafi Stadium on 27 March PIA, captained by Zaheer Abbas, scored 230 and became the first **champions**, as United Bank made 225 in 44.1 overs despite Mudassar Nazar carrying his bat for 109 not out.

The first **century partnership** was 126 added for the fourth wicket by Qasim Omar (80) and Ijaz Faqih (66) for Muslim Commercial Bank v PIA at the Niaz Stadium, Hyderabad on 21 Mar 1981; nonetheless PIA won by six wickets. The first **double century partnership** was an unbroken 241 for the first wicket by Agha Zahid (101 not out) and Arshad Pervez (102 not out) for Habib Bank v Railways at the Niaz Stadium on

Saleem Jaffar bowling for Pakistan in the B&H final at Perth, January 1987.

16 Feb 1982. This was also the first time that **two individual centuries** had been made for one team, but Railways replied with 244–7 to win.

The first **total over 300** was made by PIA, 302–4 in 45 overs v Lahore at the Qaddafi Stadium on 10 Feb 1982. Zaheer Abbas contributed 158 not out, the first **individual innings over 150**, and PIA won by 147 runs.

Bowling for Pakistan Railways v Karachi City CA at the National Stadium, Karachi on 9 Sep 1985, Saleem Jaffar achieved figures of 7–32 in his 9 overs—the first and only time that a bowler has taken **six wickets or more in one match**.

SOUTH AFRICA

MILESTONES

Tradition has it that cricket was played during the British occupation of the Cape in 1795–7, but it has not been possible to confirm this. It seems that the first definite reference occurred in the winter of 1807–08, when there was certainly at least one game recorded at Cape Town—between the Artillery Mess and Cape Colony Officers at a ground on Green Point Common, which is still used for cricket. The first known **club** was that of Port Elizabeth, founded on 15 Jan 1843, and the first South African Cricket Guide was a 24-page **booklet** published in 1871–72.

The first **match** for which full scorecard details are preserved is Pietermaritzburg v Durban at Maritzburg, 2 May 1860. Durban won by three wickets.

The first known **century** in South Africa was 110 not out by B. Taylor for Civilians v Military at Wynberg, Cape Town in the 1841–42 season.

The leading competition in South Africa, until the Currie Cup replaced it, was for the **Champion Bat**. A silver shield was presented for competition amongst the towns of the Cape Colony by the municipality of Port Elizabeth. The first **winners** were Kingwilliamstown, who won all three matches in the first tournament, played on a league basis in 1875–76. Some of the later matches in this competition were arguably first-class, and it was last contested in 1890.

The first mention anywhere of **coconut matting wickets** was in a tournament at Bloemfontein in 1880.

During the 1882–83 season the first **total of 500** or more was obtained: 505–5 (D. C. Davey 177 not out) by Winberg v Brandfoot in Orange Free State; and the first **century stand**: 187 for the third wicket by J. Spens, 125 and C. Fowler, 89, 85th Regt. v Victoria County, Natal.

The first **bowlers to take 16 and 17 wickets** in an 11-a-side match were I. R. Grimmer, 16–83 (8–45 and 8–38) for Stray Klips v Western Province at Wynberg, Cape Town in 1886–87, and H. L. Allen, 17–26 for Kroonstadt v Heilbron at Kroonstadt, Orange Free State in 1887–88. These figures were matched in a South African

first-class match for the first time when Bill Howell took 17–54 (8–31 and 9–23) for the Australians v Western Province at Newlands, Cape Town on 5–6 Nov 1902. The first bowler to take all **ten wickets in an innings** was S. W. Long, 10–6 for Potchefstroom v Moss Valley, Transvaal in 1887–88.

The first **English team to tour South Africa** was captained by C. Aubrey Smith and played 19 matches in 1888–89, winning 13 and losing four. The first match was lost to Western Province at Cape Town on 21–23 Dec 1888. The first match now recognised as **first-class** in South Africa was that between the tourists and South Africa at St George's Park, Port Elizabeth, 12–13 Mar 1889. This was subsequently generally recognised as the first **South African Test match**, although it was certainly not considered such at the time, and it is interesting to note that seven of the twelve England players in the two 'Tests' on this tour did not play any other Test matches. Bobby Abel, with 120 in the second first-class (and Test) match, at Newlands, Cape Town, scored the first **first-class century** in South Africa.

On 22–23 Mar 1892 W. W. Read's English tourists played a match against a Malay 18, which they won by ten wickets. This was the first, and remains the only, time an **English touring team has played against a non-white side** in South Africa.

The first **South African team to tour England** was captained by Herbert Castens and played 24 matches (none first-class), of which 12 were won, 5 lost and 7 drawn, on their tour in 1894.

The first **score under 40** in a first-class match in South Africa was the 30 for which South Africa were dismissed by England in the second innings of their Test on 13–14 Feb 1896. It remained the lowest Test score until New Zealand's 26 in March 1955.

James Sinclair became the first player to **score a century and take all ten wickets in an innings**, with 157 not out and 10–103, Johannesburg v Stray Klips at Johannesburg in 1895–96, and the following season he became the first man to score a **triple century** in South Africa, with

301 not out for G. Beves' XI v Roodeport at Johannesburg.

For the MCC tourists in 1909–10 Jack Hobbs scored 1194 runs (av. 62.84) in first-class matches, the first such **season's total over 1000**, and David Denton scored 139 and 138 v Transvaal at Old Wanderers, Johannesburg on 18–19, 21 Feb 1910, the first instance in SA first-class cricket of a **century in each innings**. On the next MCC tour in 1913–14 Sydney Barnes became the first bowler to take **100 wickets in a season** of SA first-class matches: 104 av. 10.74.

First-class batting firsts in 1919–21 were the first South African to score a **century on his debut**: Charles Frank with 108 for Transvaal v the Australian Imperial Forces at Old Wanderers, Johannesburg, 25, 27–28 Oct 1919; the first **triple century**: Dave Nourse's 304 not out for Natal v Transvaal at Old Wanderers, Johannesburg, 2–3, 5 Apr 1920; and the first **century before lunch**: John Zulch, as he went on to 185, opening for Transvaal v Orange Free State at Bloemfontein on 8–9 Apr 1921.

The first bowler to take a **hat-trick in his first over in first-class cricket** was R. R. Phillips for Border v Eastern Province, 1939–40.

FIRSTS IN NON-FIRST CLASS CRICKET

In any grade of cricket several South African firsts were set in the 1889–90 season. E. Breech scored 117 not out and 132 for Pirates v Kimberley at Kimberley, the first instance of a **century in each innings**. Kimberley became, in a home match v Arabs, the first side to **total over 600** with 682, of which Charles Mills scored 297, including 7 fives, 19 fours and 25 threes, the first **double century**; with J. H. Chapman he added 202 for the fifth wicket, the first **double century stand**. A total of **500** was not passed in a first-class match until the English tourists scored 537–6 dec v Transvaal at Johannesburg on 4, 6–7 1899.

The first authenticated **partnership of more than 300** was 303 for the first wicket by Captain R. Mainwaring (193) and L. Lowndes (117)

for Royal Dublin Fusiliers v Civilians at Pietermaritzburg 1897–98. The first **stand over 400** was when Charles Fichardt (229) and Lionel Richardson (113) added 401 for the second wicket, Ramblers v Town at Bloemfontein 1904–05.

Paul Hugo, for Smithfield v Aliwal North at Smithfield, Orange Free State in February 1931, was the first bowler anywhere to take **nine wickets with successive balls**.

THE CURRIE CUP

The Currie Cup was presented by the shipowner Sir Donald Currie in 1888–89 to Kimberley, the team to have performed best against the English tourists. The following year it became the national first-class competition of South Africa, and thrives to this day, under the name of the 'Castle Currie Cup'.

Kimberley were challenged by Transvaal for the first inter-provincial match of the series which was held at Kimberley (Eclectics Ground) on 5, 7–8 Apr 1890. The first ball was bowled by Charles Vintcent of Transvaal to Bernard Tancred, who scored the first run and whose second innings 106 was the first **century**. Vintcent took the first wicket, that of Robert Sneddon for 13. George Glover, a slow spin bowler, achieved the first ever **five wicket** analysis, 5–60. Transvaal won by six wickets: Kimberley 98 (A. B. Tancred 42, B. Wimble 4–8, C. A. Smith 4–36) and 235 (A. B. Tancred 106, C. E. Rutherford 55, C. H. Vintcent 5–70); Transvaal 117 (M. P. Bowden 63, G. K. Glover 6–50) and 224–4 (M. P. Bowden 126*, C. H. Vintcent 60*).

Transvaal played Kimberley at Johannesburg on the seven days 4, 6–11 Apr 1891; the first **cricket match** anywhere in the world to **last more than five days**. The match aggregate was 1402 runs for 40 wickets, the first to **exceed 1000** in South Africa, and a South African record until 1925–26. For Transvaal John Piton, 13–204, became the first bowler to take **ten wickets in a match** in the Currie Cup.

Progressive low scoring firsts have been: **Under 40:** Griqualand West 34 (James Sinclair

Political considerations destroyed the Test career of brilliant South African left hander Graeme Pollock, seen here in 1970. His Currie Cup record, far superior to any other, confirms his awesome quality, and unfulfilled Test potential.

† First in South African first-class cricket.

6–12, Johannes Kotze 3–19) in their second innings v Transvaal, Port Elizabeth on 6–7 Apr 1903; after 66 in the first innings to lose by an innings and 216 runs. **Under 30:** Border all out for 23 (Claude Carter 6–11, Joe Cox 4–9) before lunch on 12 Mar 1921 at East London against Natal, who replied with 209 (Harvey 5–70), before Border made 123 to lose by an innings and 63 runs. W. H. T. Harvey was their top scorer in both innings, 6 and 28. The same teams were involved at East London on 19, 21–22 Dec 1959 for the first **score under 20**: after Natal had scored 90, Border made just 16 in 23 overs. Top scorer was N. During with 9, Trevor Goddard took 6–3 and John Cole 4–13. Left to get 369 for victory Border again collapsed to a second innings total of 18, with Peter Tainton top scorer on 7; Geoff Griffin took 7–11 and Cole 3–4, and Natal wicket-keeper Malcolm Smith established a South African record of **seven dismissals in an innings**, having top-scored with 33. Border's **match aggregate** of 34 for 20 wickets is the first and only **under 40 in first-class cricket**.

George Glover, with a match analysis of 15–68 for Griqualand West v Eastern Province at Cape Town, 20–21 Mar 1894, was the first to take **15 wickets in a match**. The first to **16** in a match was Albert Vogler, 6–12 and 10–26 for Eastern Province v Griqualand West at Johannesburg (Wanderers) on 26–28 Dec 1906. His second innings feat was the first instance of **all ten** wickets in an innings. He bowled 12 6-ball overs, 2 maidens and only once required 'outside help', with 6 bowled, 2 caught and bowled, 1 lbw, and the last one caught by H. T. Hibbert. All ten wickets in an innings were also taken by Steve Jefferies, 10–59 for Western Province v Orange Free State at Newlands, Cape Town, 26–28 Dec 1987.

OTHER CURRIE CUP FIRSTS

Hat-trick: Johannes Kotze, Transvaal v Griqualand West, Port Elizabeth, 6–7 Apr 1903.

Four wickets in four balls†: Albert Borland, Natal v Griqualand West, Kimberley, 3–4 Jan 1927.

Century in each innings: Ronald Draper,

129 and 177, Griqualand West v Border, Kimberley, 12–13, 15 Dec 1952.

Double century†: Albert Paine, 220, Western Province v Griqualand West, Old Wanderers, Johannesburg, 16–17 Mar 1897.

Double century stand: Paine and T. E. Etlinger, 225 for fourth wicket in above match in Western Province's 483, which enabled them to win the match by an innings and 338 runs.

Triple century stand: Stanley Coen and Mick Commaille, 305 for second wicket, Orange Free State v Natal, Bloemfontein, 30–31 Dec 1926, 1 Jan 1927.

Quadruple century stand: Jack Siedle and John Nicolson (252*), 424 for first wicket in above match for Natal, enabling them to save the game.

Score over 600: Western Province 601 v Border, Cape Town, 26–28 Dec 1929. S. S. L. Steyn scored 261 not out and WP won by an innings and 163 runs.

Alan Hill, opening for Orange Free State v Griqualand West, scored 103 in 414 minutes on 11–12 Mar 1977. This was the first **century to be entirely devoid of a boundary** to be scored in first-class cricket under modern conditions.

Eddie Barlow's performances for The Rest of the World confirmed his reputation as an all-rounder. He showed natural qualities of leadership in the Currie Cup and for Derbyshire.

Vintcent van der Bijl brought his devastating Currie Cup bowling to England for one memorable season with Middlesex in 1980.

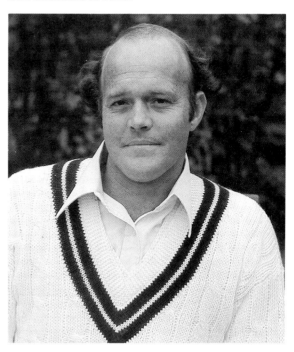

CAREER MILESTONES

Graeme Pollock, for Eastern Province and Transvaal, became the first player to pass each **1000 run milestone in a Currie Cup career from 7000** in 1977–78 **to 12 000** in 1985–86. On his retirement in 1987 he had scored 12 409 runs in 157 matches, with 261 innings for an average of 54.66. This total is 4528 ahead of the second highest by Eddie Barlow. Previous run milestones had been achieved as follows:

1000 Louis Tancred, Transvaal v Griqualand West, 20–21 Mar 1911
2000 Dave Nourse, Natal v Orange Free State, 22, 24 Dec 1923, his 27th match
3000 Dave Nourse, Western Province v Natal, 31 Dec 1929, 1 Jan 1930, his 38th match
4000 Dudley Nourse, Natal v Eastern Province, 4–6 Jan 1951, his 46th match

5000 Ali Bacher, Transvaal v Rhodesia, 15, 17–18 Dec 1973
6000 Barry Richards, Natal v Rhodesia, 8–10 Nov 1975

Dave Nourse had Currie Cup career figures of 3482 runs av. 51.97 and his son Dudley 4478 runs av. 65.85. Bacher's figures were 5460 runs av. 42.32 and Richards 7551 runs av. 60.40. Dave Nourse was the first to score **500 runs in a season**, 589 av. 98.16 for Natal in 1906–07: 25 & 33, 212, 80, 123, 4 & 112*. Barry Richards was the first to score **1000 in a season**: 1089 av. 77.78 for Natal in 1971–72: 63 & 104, 169, 34 & 134, 219, 24*, 12 & 73, 35 & 1, 76 & 27, 94 & 24.

The first bowler to take **100 wickets** in Currie Cup competition was James Sinclair, a medium paced bowler who had gained early batting fame as a hitter. He reached 100 wickets with the 11th of 13 he took for Transvaal v Eastern Province at Port Elizabeth on 8–9 Apr 1903. On retirement his career figures, which remain unchallenged, were 164 wickets av. 13.45 in 27 matches.

John Waddington was the first to **200 wickets**, in the match for Griqualand West v Transvaal at Kimberley on 10, 12–13 Jan 1953, and to **300** wickets, v North Eastern Transvaal at Pretoria on 30–31 Jan, 2 Feb 1959. His total was 317 wickets av. 21.75 in 59 matches.

Vintcent van der Bijl, who played for Natal and Transvaal, retired with figures of 572 wickets av. 16.42 in 109 matches. He was the first to **400** wickets in 1979–80, and to **500**, for Natal v Eastern Province at Durban on 30–31 Jan, 1 Feb 1982; his 500th victim was Robert Armitage.

The first bowler to take **50 wickets in a season** was Alfred Hall, 52 av. 12.50 in six matches for Transvaal in 1926–27. His figures: 6–42 & 5–56, 3–47 & 2–92, 6–35 & 8–80, 4–14 & 5–48, 3–71 & 3–35, 2–69 & 5–61.

SOUTH AFRICAN INTER-PROVINCIAL LIMITED-OVERS COMPETITION

The competition was started, under the sponsorship of Gillette, for the 1969–70 season. Based on the English Gillette Cup, the matches were of 60 overs per side, with no bowler being allowed more than 12 overs until 1981–82, thereafter 55/11.

The opening games were played on 30 Mar 1970: Natal v Orange Free State at Durban, Transvaal v North Eastern Transvaal at Johannesburg, Eastern Province v Border at Port Elizabeth, Western Province v Griqualand West at Cape Town.

In these games were the following firsts:

Score over 300: Western Province 333–6, Eastern Province 319–9.

Century: Brian Bath (Transvaal) 100.

Century stand: Graeme Pollock (102) and Colin Bland (69), 155 for fifth wicket for Eastern Province.

Five wickets in innings: Peter Heger (Border) 5–103 in 11 overs; he is still the only bowler to **concede more than 100 runs** in a match.

The first **winners of the Cup** were Western Province, who beat Natal by two runs at the Wanderers ground, Johannesburg on 6 Apr 1970. Western Province batted first and scored 132 in 36.1 overs; Natal replied with 130 in 42.1 overs.

The first **double century stand** was by Eddie Barlow (148) and Hylton Ackerman (127), 241 for first wicket for Western Province (360–4) who beat Border by 245 runs at East London on 21 Nov 1970. In Border's innings Grahame Chevalier, 6–32 in 7.2 overs, was the first to take **six wickets in an innings**. The first to take **seven** was Peter Henwood, 7–21 in 12 overs, Natal v Border at East London, 21 Oct 1972.

The first **hat-trick** was by Denys Hobson, Western Province v Northern Transvaal at Pretoria, 19 Oct 1974. On the same day Graeme Pollock scored the first **double century in any limited-overs competition**, 222 not out for Eastern Province v Border at the Jan Smuts ground, East London. In 164 minutes he faced 165 balls and hit 26 fours and 6 sixes. Eastern Province scored 372–4 in 60 overs and won by 206 runs. Pollock became the first to reach **1000 runs in a career** on 8 Feb 1975, batting for Eastern Province v Western Province at Port Elizabeth, at which stage his record was 1031 runs av. 79.30 in 14 innings, and the first to reach **2000**, for Transvaal v Griqualand West at Kimberley on 21 Nov 1981, for 2052 runs av. 68.40 in 35 innings. He retired in 1987 with career figures of 2936 runs av. 62.46, over 1000 runs more than the next best, Jimmy Cook.

The first, and only, **declaration in top-class limited-overs cricket** anywhere came when Natal reached 361–2 in the 54th over v South African XI at Kingsmead, Durban, 25 Oct 1975. Alan Barrow (202*) and Henry Fotheringham (128*) added 303 unbeaten for the third wicket, the first **triple century stand**. Their opponents replied with 78 in 39 overs.

Vintcent van der Bijl became the first bowler to take **50 wickets in a career** during the Natal v Transvaal A match at Durban on 10 Nov 1979. He retired with figures of 62 wickets av. 17.32.

SRI LANKA

MILESTONES

The first cricket **club** in Ceylon (Sri Lanka from 1972) was the Colombo CC, formed on 8 Sep 1832. Its first **match** was a nine wicket defeat by the 97th Regiment of the British Garrison at the Galle Face ground on 3 Nov 1832. The club's first **overseas success** came with victories by all-English teams in India in 1885, against Bombay and the Parsees.

The first known **century** in Ceylon was 105 by C. H. A. Ross for Dikoya v Dimbula at Radella, and the first **double century partnership** 250 for the first wicket by G. S. Saxton (152) and G. van der Spaar (117) in a Colombo Club match, both in 1878–79. The first **double century** was when T. Y. Wright was reported to have scored 202 not out in an unidentified match in 1895–96. J. C. O. Ernst passed **250** with his 252 for YMCA v Royal College at Colombo 1916–17 and M. Wanduragala (306) scored the first **triple century**, for Mackwoods v Volkart at Colombo 1956–57.

The first **stand of over 400** was the 462 added, unbeaten, for the second wicket by Bandula Warnapura (294), Sri Lanka's first Test captain, and Annura Tennekoon (221) for Ceylon President's XI v a Malaysian Cricket Association team at Colombo in 1971–72.

First **totals over:**

400—447 Kandapolla v Dikoya at Dikoya, 1887–1888

500—518 Dimbula v ABCD at Dimbula, 1895–96

600—619 Railways and Public Works Dept. v Government Services at Colombo, 1917–18

700—925 Colombo Municipality v Irrigation Department at the Vihara Mahadevi Park, Colombo on the afternoons of 5–6, 20–22 July 1959.

The first instance of **ten wickets in an innings**, but in a 12-a-side match, was 10–43 by A. J. Denison for Nuwara Elya v a Colts' team in 1887–88. The first in an 11-a-side game was by A. J. Grant-Cook, 10–34 for Colombo CC v Kalutara in 1909–10. Tommy Kelaart took the first **hat-trick** in a club game in Colombo in 1891–92.

Welihinda Bennett became the first **wicket-keeper** anywhere to **take ten dismissals in an innings**, with four caught and six stumped for Mahinda College v Galle CC at the Galle Esplanade on 1 Mar 1953.

TOURING TEAMS AND REPRESENTATIVE MATCHES

The first **touring team to play in Ceylon** was the Hon. Ivo Bligh's team, who beat 18 of Colombo on first innings (Colombo 92 and 16–7, England 155) in a match played on 13–14 Oct 1882 on their way to Australia. Similarly the Australians (75) beat 18 of Ceylon (49) at Galle Face on their way to England in 1884. The first extended tour of the island was made by George Vernon's English team in November and December 1889, and the first Australians to do so were the Rev. E. F. Waddy's New South Wales team in 1914. Against them Ceylon recorded their first **victory**, in the second match.

The Ceylon Cricket Association was formed in 1922, and Ceylon's first **official tour** was to India in 1932–33, under the captaincy of Dr Churchill Hector Gunasekera. Of ten matches played, two were won, one lost and seven drawn, including Ceylon's first match against All-India, played at Delhi. In this match Sargo Jayawickrema scored the first **century for Ceylon**, 130 in a total of 305, in reply to India's 383, in which Edward Kelaart took 5–95. India made 188–7 in their second innings.

Ceylon played **unofficial 'Tests'** against various touring teams, and recorded their first **win** against Pakistan 'A' in 1964, followed by a win over India at Ahmedabad in India on 2–5 Jan 1965, the third of a three-match series. On both occasions Michael Tissera was the successful captain. Following their win in the ICC Trophy in 1979, Sri Lanka were granted Test status, and their first **Test** was against England at Saravanamuttu Stadium, Colombo on 17–18, 20–21 Feb 1982. England 223 and 171–3 beat Sri Lanka (218 and 175) by seven wickets.

Opposite *Sidath Wettimuny opened the Sri Lankan batting in their first Test in 1982 and became their major batsman.*

Sri Lankan party on their first Test tour of England 1984. Most readily recognisable to English eyes is scorer Geoffrey Saulez (far right), formerly of England.

FIRST-CLASS CRICKET IN SRI LANKA

It is far from easy to ascertain what has been **'first-class'** in Ceylon, as in other non-Test playing nations. The first such match, as suggested by the Association of Cricket Statisticians, was played at Colombo on 12–13 Feb 1926 when Dr John Rockwood's XI recovered from a first innings deficit to defeat W. E. Lucas's Bombay XI by seven wickets. Walter Greswell bowled the first ball, but the first wicket to fall was that of Bombay's B. E. Kapadia, run out for 30. The first Ceylon bowler to take a wicket was R. M. M. de Silva, and their captain Francis Brooke (56) scored the first half century.

The next first-class matches and the first played by a bona fide touring side were those by the MCC in January and February 1927. For the MCC, in their second match Maurice Tate (121) made the first **first-class century** on the island, soon followed by Bob Wyatt (124).

The first bowler to take **ten wickets in a match** of possible first-class status was C. Horan for Dr Rockwood's XI v Bombay at the Nondescripts Ground, Colombo in December 1929.

The first bowler to take **nine wickets in an innings** was Ron Oxenham for Australians v All-Ceylon at the Sinhalese Sports Club, Colombo in 1935–36. His 9–18 remain unmatched, and he had 11–31 in the match, won by the Australians by an innings and 127 runs.

The first **total over 500** was the 513 by the West Indians v Ceylon 1949. In their previous match, at Colombo Oval on 19–22 February, the West Indians had made the first **partnerships over 200 and 250**: Allan Rae (116) and George Carew (77) 200 for the first wicket, Everton Weekes (133*) and Clyde Walcott (125*) for an unbroken third wicket stand of 258.

For the Commonwealth XI v Ceylon at Colombo Oval on 16–18 Feb 1951 Frank Worrell (285) scored the first **double century** and with Billy Sutcliffe (95) added 310 for the fifth wicket, the first **triple century stand**.

Derek Underwood uniquely obtained **15 wickets in a first-class match** in Ceylon: 8–10 and 7–33 for International XI v Ceylon President's XI at Colombo, 5–7 Mar 1968.

The first instance of **two centuries in a match** was by Ashok Mankad, 105 and 100 not out for an Indian XI v President's XI at St Anthony's College, Kandy on 1–3 Feb 1974.

WEST INDIES

MILESTONES

Although cricket had almost certainly been played in the West Indies many years earlier, the first definite mention of cricket there came on 12 May 1806 in a newspaper report of a meeting of St Anne's Cricket Club in Barbados. By 1840 cricket was being played in British Guiana and Antigua; the first **club** to be mentioned in Jamaica was the Kingston Cricket Club, formed in 1843–4, and in British Guiana the still surviving Georgetown Cricket Club in 1857.

The first **inter-colonial match** was contested by Barbados and Demerera (now part of Guyana, formerly British Guiana) at Garrison Savannah, Bridgetown on 15–16 Feb 1865. Ranked as **first-class** by the Association of Cricket Statisticians, Barbados 74 and 124 beat Demerera 22 and 33 by 143 runs; the Barbados captain F. B. Smith took six wickets in the first innings and four in the second to become the first bowler to take **ten wickets in any match in the West Indies**. A return fixture, on 11–12 Sep 1866 at Georgetown was the first **first-class match played on the South American continent**. The first first-class match in Trinidad was played at Port-of-Spain on 14–15 Jan 1869, when Trinidad beat Demerera by five wickets.

The first **first-class inter-colonial tournament** was contested by Barbados, Demerera and Trinidad from 1–10 Sep 1891 on the Wanderers Ground, Bay Pasture, Barbados. Barbados were champions, winning all their three matches. This competition continued, largely on a biennial basis until 1938–39.

The first recorded **century** in the West Indies was made by E. M. Sealy, c. 1860, while at Codrington College, Barbados. The first score of **150** or more was exactly that by C. W. Sherrard for Kingston v Spanish Town at Kingston, 1875–76.

The first known **score of over 300** in the West Indies came in 1872–73 when Kingston scored 342 v Spanish Town, who were then dismissed for 7, the first known West Indian score of **under 10**. The first **century partnership** was 110 for the fifth wicket by E. Agostini and G. Wehekind

for Trinidad v Demerera on the Parade Ground, Georgetown, 1876–77. In the Demerera second innings E. G. Penalosa of Trinidad achieved figures of 8–33 in 20.2 5-ball overs, the first instance of a bowler taking **eight wickets in an innings** in the West Indies. In the corresponding match in 1882–83, E. F. Wright made the first **first-class century** in the West Indies, 123 out of 168 for Demerara, who beat Trinidad (72 and 90) by an innings and 6 runs.

The first **tour by a West Indian team** was under L. R. Fyfe to Canada and the USA in August and September 1886. They played 13 matches (none first-class), of which six were won and five lost. This tour was described in the first known cricket book in the West Indies, by C. G. A. Wyatt and L. R. Fyfe, published by Argosy in Demerera. Its 92 pages contained scores, pictures and statistics of the tour.

The first **visit of an English touring team** to the West Indies was one captained by Robert Slade Lucas in 1894–95. Of eight first-class matches played, four were won and three lost. In the opening match at Bourda, Hugh Bromley-Davenport achieved the first **hat-trick** in West Indian first-class cricket, as he dismissed Demerera's A. B. Clarke, W. E. Goodman and W. P. Weber in their second innings of 46. In the second match of the tour, at Bridgetown, 5–9 Feb 1893, Barbados won the toss and taking first innings, scored 517, the first **total over 500** in any cricket in the West Indies. The **match aggregate** of 1373 runs for 40 wickets was the first **over 1000**. Bromley-Davenport became the first bowler to exceed **50 wickets in a West Indian first-class season**, reaching that target in the final match when he dismissed All-Jamaica's H. D. B. Castle for 8, and he ended with 56 wickets for 561 runs av. 10.01 in eight matches; later in this match his team-mate Fred Bush also took his 50th wicket.

Playing for Harrisonians v Codrington College at Bridgetown, Barbados in 1892–93, H. C. Clarke took 10–30, the first known instance of a bowler taking **all ten wickets in an innings** in the West Indies. The first ten wickets in an innings in a first-class match was F. Hinds, 10–36 for A. B. St Hill's team v All-Trinidad at Queen's

The first of the modern day West Indies teams to tour the UK in 1923.

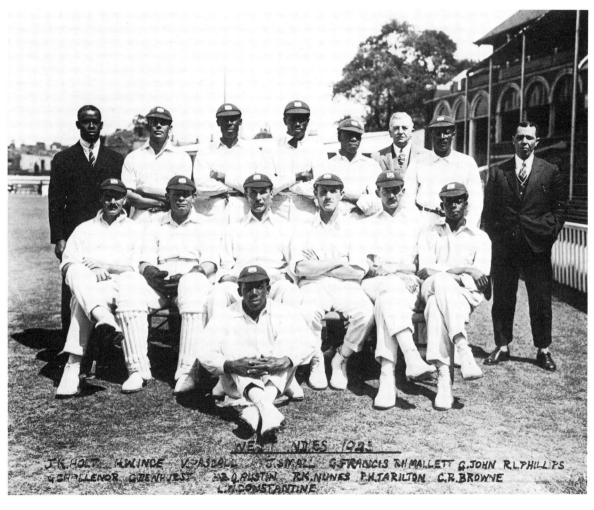

J.K.HOLT H.W.INCE V.PASCALL J.SMALL G.FRANCIS R.H.MALLETT G.JOHN R.L.PHILLIPS
G.CHALLENOR G.DEWHURST H.B.G.AUSTIN R.K.NUNES P.H.TARILTON C.R.BROWNE
L.N.CONSTANTINE

Park, Port-of-Spain 10–11 Jan 1901, but this was in a 12-a-side game. The first first-class 'all-ten' did not come until Eddie Hemmings, the England and Nottinghamshire off spinner, playing for an International XI against a West Indian XI at Kingston, 25–28 Sep 1982, took 10–175 in 49.3 overs in a score of 419. This remains the most expensive 'all-ten' ever.

For Barbados v Trinidad at Bridgetown, Barbados, 7–10 Sep 1897, G. B. Y. Cox and Harold Austin added 263 for the second wicket, the first **stand of over 200** in West Indian first-class cricket. Cox scored 161 and Austin 129, and Barbados won by an innings and 235 runs. The first two **partnerships of over 300** in any West

Indian cricket were scored in the 1922–23 season: C. M. Morales (111) and K. D. Andrews (212), 335 for the first wicket, Kingston v St Catherines at Kingston; and K. I. R. Fitzpatrick (185) and J. E. Chabroll (156), 320 for the third wicket, British Guiana v Georgetown at Bourda. The first of over 300 in first-class matches was 330 for the fifth wicket by Percy Holmes (244) and Ewart Astill (156) for MCC v Jamaica, 18–20 Mar 1926.

Playing for R. A. Bennett's English touring team v All-Jamaica at Sabina Park, Kingston, 8, 10 Feb 1902, leg-spinner Edward Dowson achieved figures of 8–21 in 9 overs and 8–37 in 27 overs, for match figures of 16–58, the first bowler to take **16 wickets in a first-class match** in the

West Indies. These figures remain the best ever.

The first recorded **double century** in the West Indies was 207 not out by L. D. Samuel for Kingston v Melbourne at Kingston in 1902–03: the first in a first-class match was also the first **triple century**, as Percy Tarilton scored 304 not out in a total of 623–6 dec (the first innings total over 600) for Barbados v Trinidad at Bridgetown, 11–14 Feb 1920. Tarilton, who batted for 6 hr 50 min, hit 1 six, 1 five and 31 fours.

The first instance of a batsman scoring **two separate centuries in a match** was in 1903–04 when A. H. Brebner made 140 and 104 not out for Georgetown II v British Guiana II at Georgetown.

The match between Jamaica and MCC at Kingston, 2–5 Apr 1911 ended in a **tie**—the first

in first-class cricket in the West Indies. MCC scored 269 and 131, Jamaica replied with 173 and 227.

In minor matches, an **innings total of over 600** was first exceeded in 1912–13 at Kensington, Barbados when Wanderers scored 673 v Pickwick. George Challenor scored 195 and Harry Ince 109. These two also starred in 1920–21 in the first **match in which more than 1500 runs were scored**. Challenor scored 206 and 133, Ince 106 and 150 for Wanderers (590 and 489) as they beat Pickwick (436 and 284) at Bridgetown, when the aggregate was 1799 runs for 39 wickets.

The first **score over 700** in West Indian first-class cricket was made by Barbados, 715–9 dec v

Opposite *A typical shot of George Headley, the first indisputably great West Indian batsman, known as 'The Black Bradman'.*

Members of the 1928 West Indian team to England. Players in foreground are J. A. Small, C. V. Wight, R. K. Nunes, L. N. Constantine (feeling the cold!), and W. St. Hill. In the background is M. P. Fernandes.

British Guiana at Bridgetown, 17–21 Jan 1927. In their next match, at the same venue on 26 Jan–2 February, Barbados scored 726–7 dec v Trinidad, with the match aggregate of 1677 runs for 37 wickets, the first over 1500 in first-class matches.

The first series of 'official' Test matches in the West Indies was in 1929–30. In the first innings of the fourth Test, at Kingston, 3–5, 7–12 Apr 1930, England scored 849, the first, and still the only, **score of over 800** in West Indian first-class cricket. Then the longest ever Test, rain prevented play on the last two days, and the match was left drawn with West Indies 408–5 in their second innings, still 427 runs short of England's total. 'Patsy' Hendren scored 1765 runs (av. 135.76) on the tour, having become the first batsman to score **1000 runs in a West Indian season** during the second Test match at Port-of-Spain, 1, 3–6 February. His 205 not out in the second innings was the first double century in matches between the two countries.

George Headley (344*) and Clarence Passailaigue (261*) put on an unbeaten 487 together in just 245 minutes for the sixth wicket, Jamaica v Lord Tennyson's XI at Kingston, 20, 22–24 Feb 1932, the first **stand over 400** in the West Indies, and it remains a world record for the sixth wicket. The first **stand over 500** came when Frank Worrell (308*) and John Goddard (218*) added 502 unbeaten for the fourth wicket, Barbados v Trinidad at Bridgetown, 12, 14–16 Feb 1944.

Trinidad were dismissed for 16 by Barbados at Bridgetown on 20 July 1942; the first and only **total under 20** in West Indian first-class cricket. Derek Sealy took 8–8.

SHELL SHIELD

Inter-colonial cricket had dated from 1865, and the inter-colonial matches had been extended to four colonies for the first time in 1956 when Jamaica joined Barbados, British Guiana and Trinidad, and to five in 1961 with the introduction of a combined team from the Leeward and Windward Islands. However, the major annual competition was initiated in 1966, under the sponsorship of the Shell Oil Company.

The **first match** was staged at St John's, Antigua between Combined Islands and Jamaica on 27–29, 31 Jan 1966. The first ball was bowled by A. Freeland for the Islands to Teddy Griffith of Jamaica. The first wicket to fall was that of Easton McMorris, bowled by E. Gilbert for 24 with the score at 52. Griffith went on to score a splendid 150, third man out at 248; the first **century** in the Shell Shield. Freeland took his wicket and became the first bowler to take **five wickets** or more, with 6–49 in 22.2 overs in this innings. With Maurice Foster (41), Griffith added 125 for the third wicket, the first **century partnership**. In Jamaica's second innings Griffith scored 44 and put on 108 for the first wicket with McMorris, who went on to score 134. McMorris scored 553 runs av. 92.16 in the 1966 season, a total not surpassed until 1984.

The first **innings total over 500** was made in the fifth match of this first season; Barbados, in reply to a British Guiana score of 227 made 559–9 dec from 189 6-ball overs, which enabled them to win the match by an innings and 15 runs. Gary Sobers scored 204, the first **double century** of the competition, and shared the first **double century stand**, 214 for the fifth wicket with Rawle Brancker (132).

The first **total over 600** was 641–5 dec by Guyana v Barbados at Georgetown on 28 Feb, 1–3 Mar 1967. There were three century makers: Roy Fredericks (127), Rohan Kanhai (144 retired hurt) and Basil Butcher (183*).

The first **triple century stand** was made by Richard Austin (131) and Maurice Foster (234) who added 308 together for the second wicket for Jamaica v Trinidad at Montego Bay, 13–16 Jan 1977. They came together with the score 75–1 when Jeffrey Dujon retired hurt; the three batsmen actually added 339 runs for the wicket. After Austin's dismissal Dujon resumed to add 56 for the third wicket with Foster.

The first **innings score below 100** came when, needing 117 to win against Combined Islands at Castries, St Lucia on 11–12, 14 Mar 1966, Trinidad collapsed to 85 all out.

The first bowler to take **ten wickets in a match** was Kaleb Laurent, who had figures of 11–170 (6–76 and 5–94) in 58 overs for the Windward Islands v Guyana at St George's, Grenada on 15–18 Mar 1967. **Ten wickets and a century in a match** was first achieved by Arthur Barrett (102* and 28, 5–39 and 5–43) for Jamaica v Combined Islands at Castries, St Lucia, 14–17 Mar 1970.

Seven wickets in an innings was first achieved by Geoff Greenidge, 7–124 in 29.2 overs for Barbados v Jamaica at Bridgetown, 22–23, 25, 27 Mar 1967; **eight** by Richard Austin, 8–71 in 35 overs for Jamaica v Trinidad at Queen's Park Oval, Port-of-Spain, 9–12 Feb 1978, and **nine** by Deryck Parry, 9–76 in 39.5 overs in the second innings for Combined Islands v Jamaica at Sabina Park, Kingston, 21–24 Mar 1980. Parry had taken 6–25 in 21 overs in the first innings to have match figures of 15–101, a record for the competition. His team won by six wickets. The first to take **12 or more wickets in a match** had been the Trinidad slow bowler Inshan Ali against Jamaica at Queen's Park Oval, Port-of-Spain, 28 Feb, 1–3 Mar 1974. With 6–78 and 7–20 he had match figures of 13–98 as Trinidad won by five wickets.

Willie Rodriguez performed the first **hat-trick**, for Trinidad v the Windwards at Port-of-Spain, 17–18, 20–21 Jan 1969. His victims were A. Gregoire, R. Brandford and D. Cambridge.

The first bowler to exceed **30 wickets in a Shield season** was Ranjie Nanan, 32 wickets for 677 runs av. 21.15 in 1982 for Trinidad.

CAREER MILESTONES

First batsman to score:

	Name	Match	No. matches
1000 runs	Peter Lashley	Barbados v Jamaica, Bridgetown, 7–11 Feb 1969	11
2000 runs	Peter Lashley	Barbados v Combined Islands, Roscau, 4–7 Feb 1972	22
3000 runs	Maurice Foster	Jamaica v Guyana, Georgetown, 29 Mar–1 Apr 1975	34
100 wickets	Arthur Barrett	Jamaica v Trinidad, Port-of-Spain, 6–9 Feb 1976	28
1000 runs/ 100 wickets	David Holford	Barbados v Guyana, Bridgetown, 21–24 Jan 1977	30

WEST INDIAN LIMITED-OVERS COMPETITION

The first **inter-Territorial limited-overs** competition commenced in 1976, under the sponsorship of Gillette. The six teams were split into two groups of three: 'North'—Barbados, Jamaica and the Leewards, and 'South'—Guyana, Trinidad and the Windwards, played on a league basis, with the winners meeting in the final. Geddes Grant/Harrison Line took over the sponsorship two years later, and throughout the matches have been over 50 overs per innings.

The **first matches** were due to be played on 18 or 19 Feb 1976, but were marred by rain. Leewards v Jamaica at Besseterre was washed out, but some play was possible on the 19th at Castries, where Guyana scored 78-4 off 16.1 overs v Windwards. The first result came on 21 February when Barbados made 187-9, thanks largely to 79 from Gordon Greenidge, the first half-century, and beat the Leewards (156-9), for whom Lipton Griffin had taken 5-35 in his 10 overs, the first **five wickets in an innings**. Although rain had spoilt the competition, the two strongest teams reached the final at Bridgetown on 28 February, when Barbados, 191 in 49.3 overs, beat Trinidad, 148 in 39.5. The first final **'man-of-the-match'** was Barbados all-rounder Stephen Farmer, who top-scored with 63 and took 2-38, a performance all the more notable for the fact that his father, the former Barbados player Wilfred Farmer, had died only days before.

Emerson Trotman of Barbados scored the first individual **century**, reaching exactly 100 not out from the last ball of the innings v Guyana at Georgetown on 26 Jan 1977. With his captain David Holford, he added 113 for the sixth wicket, the first **century stand**. Barbados won by 19 runs, and their score of 239-6 was the **first of over 200**. Barbados also won the second final, when they dismissed Trinidad, who batted first, for 95 in 33.3 overs, the first **completed innings total under 100**.

At Bridgetown on 26 Apr 1979 Neil Phillips, the Barbados pace bowler knocked off the bails before delivering the ball with Clive Lloyd, captain of Guyana, out of his ground. Phillips had denied Lloyd (41) the normal courtesy of a warning, and this was the first instance in this competition of a **run out while backing up**. In this match Guyana pace bowler Syd Matthews was hit for 63 runs in 7 overs for 0 wickets, the first time a bowler had conceded 60 runs.

In the final at St John's on 3 May 1980, Guyana scored the first **total over 300**, 327-7 v the Leewards, for whom James Harris had figures of 0-73 in his ten overs, the first bowler to **concede 70 runs**. There were **two separate century stands** for Guyana: Roy Fredericks (119) added 114 for the first wicket with Tyrone Etwaroo and 103 for the third with Randy Gomes (57).

The first **stand of over 150** was at Guaracara Park, Trinidad for the Trinidad second wicket by Richard Gabriel (108 not out) and Larry Gomes against Jamaica on 17 Mar 1982. Gomes became the first player to complete a **career total of 500 runs** in the competition during this innings.

Playing for Barbados v Guyana at Bridgetown on 30 Jan 1985, Terry Hunte scored 114, with 3 sixes and 8 fours, the first **century on debut** in the competition. Hunte still ended on the losing side. On 14 Feb 1985 for the Leewards v Barbados at Bridgetown, Enoch Lewis (55 not out) joined his brother Edward (on his debut) (145 not out, the record score) with the score at 177-3, and together they took the score to 289-3. This was the first **century stand between brothers** in this event.

Left-arm pace bowler Desmond Collymore became the first bowler to **concede 80 runs**, with 1-82 for the Windward Islands v Barbados at Bridgetown on 15 Jan 1986. Barbados 276-3 won the match by 171 runs. Captaining Trinidad against Barbados at Bridgetown on 9 Apr 1987, the off-spinner Ranjie Nanan, in his 25th match, became the first bowler to take **35 wickets** in the competition.

TEST CRICKET

Frederick Robert Spofforth ('The Demon'). The Australian fast bowler of saturnine countenance and Yorkshire ancestry enforced respect for Australian cricket.

MILESTONES

The first mention of a **'Test match'** was of matches played by the first tourists to Australia, the English team, under H. H. Stephenson, in 1861–62. W. J. Hammersley's *Victorian Cricketers' Guide* stated that 'Of the thirteen matches, five only can be termed "test matches", the three played at Melbourne and the two played at Sydney'. These were the two matches against Victoria, the one with New South Wales and the two against combined teams from these colonies.

The first **Test match played on level terms** was between England and Australia at Melbourne on 15–17, 19 Mar 1877. Only many years later was it dubbed a 'Test match' but it was recognised as a full international match by the contemporary sporting press, so there can be very little argument that it has been given its rightful place.

The first ball in Test cricket was bowled by Alfred Shaw, of England and Nottinghamshire, a slow round-arm bowler of legendary steadiness and accuracy, to the Australian opening batsman Charles Bannerman, whose antecedents were most interesting. He was an adopted Australian, born in Kent of a well-known Dundee family. He could almost be regarded as the first Scot to play Test cricket. Bannerman became the first Test **century** maker; his 165, retired hurt out of 245 in the first innings of this first match took him 285 minutes and included 16 fours. He had scored the first run, off Shaw, and the first batsman to be dismissed was his opening partner Nathaniel Thompson, another adopted Australian, originally from Birmingham. The taker of this first wicket was England's Yorkshire pace bowler Allen Hill, who bowled Thompson for a single with the score on 2. In England's reply of 196 Billy Midwinter, another English-born (Gloucestershire) Australian, took 5–78 in 54 4-ball overs (23 maidens), the first instance of **five wickets in an innings** in Tests.

Australia became the **winners** of the first Test match, by 45 runs, and the first winning **captain** was Dave Gregory of New South Wales. During the England first innings of the third Test match,

at Melbourne, 2–4 Jan 1879, Fred Spofforth took the wickets of Vernon Royle, Francis MacKinnon and Tom Emmett in successive balls, to complete the first **hat-trick** in Test cricket. With 6–48 in this innings and 7–62 in the second, he became the first bowler to take **ten wickets or more in a Test match**, as Australia won by ten wickets, dismissing England for 113 and 160. In Australia's 256, Tom Emmett had beaten Spofforth to be the first to take **seven wickets in an innings** with 7–68.

Billy Midwinter, who had played for Australia in the first two Tests in 1877, played for England v Australia at Melbourne on 2–4 Jan 1882, and was thus the first man to play **Test cricket for two countries**. In this match the run aggregate of 1049 for 33 wickets was the first **over 1000**. Midwinter returned to Australia's ranks in 1883.

Australia's 63 in the first innings v England at The Oval on 28–29 Aug 1882 was the first **completed innings score of under 100**, but Australia (122 in their second innings) still won a low scoring match by 7 runs as they dismissed England for 101 and 77. It was as a result of this victory that the Ashes came into being, with the famous notice in *The Sporting Times* that the body of English cricket would be cremated and the ashes taken to Australia. Spofforth improved his previous figures with the first case of **14 wickets in a Test**: 7–46 and 7–44.

The first **innings victory** in Tests was at Melbourne on 19–20, 22 Jan 1883, when England 294 beat Australia 114 and 153 by an innings and 27 runs. Billy Bates starred for England with 55, 7–28, including a hat-trick and 7–74.

In the 1884 series in England, in the first Test at Old Trafford, 10–12 July, George Bonnor (Aus) became the first batsman to be given out **hit wicket** in Test cricket, for 6 to Yorkshire slow left-armer Edmund Peate. In the second Test, the first ever played at Lord's, William Murdoch became the first **substitute fielder to take a catch** when holding Henry Scott, one of his own players, off Allan Steel. Murdoch, Australia's captain scored 211 in his side's only innings of the third match of the series, at The Oval, 11–13 August, the first Test **double century**. With Scott (102) he put on 207 runs for the third wicket, the first Test **double century stand**, and Australia's 551 was the first **over 500** in Tests. In this innings **every member of the side bowled** for England, the first such happening in Test cricket, with wicket-keeper Hon. Alfred Lyttelton taking 4–19 in 12 overs.

England were the first team to field an **unchanged side throughout a five match Test series**, beating Australia 3–2 in 1884–85. In contrast, in the second Test, Australia fielded a totally different team from that of the first Test, with nine men making their debuts; this was due to the fact that the previous set of players had demanded half the gate money for this match.

In the first Test of the 1886–87 series at Melbourne, Australian captain Percy McDonnell **won the toss and put the opposition in to bat**, the first time this happened in Tests, and England were dismissed for 45, the first **completed Test innings under 50**; however, Australia lost by 13 runs. In the second Test, at Sydney, George Lohmann, the English medium-paced bowler,

became the first to take **eight wickets in a Test innings**, 8–35 in 25 4-ball overs in the first innings, an analysis which remains a record for England in Australia.

In their second Test, at Newlands, Cape Town on 25–26 Mar 1889, South Africa became the first team to be **twice dismissed for under 50**: 47 and 43, with Bernard Tancred the first Test batsman to **carry his bat through an innings**, for 26 not out in the first innings. For England Johnnie Briggs had a match analysis of 15–28 (7–17 and 8–11); the first bowler to take **15 wickets in a Test**, and he took them all on one day (26 March).

The first **Test played over six days** was at Sydney on 14–15, 17–20 Dec 1894. The **match aggregate** of 1514 runs was the first in **excess of 1500** in any cricket match; England (325 and 437) beat Australia (586 and 166) by 10 runs. In the second Test, at Melbourne, Arthur Coningham of Australia became the first bowler to take a **wicket with his first ball in Test cricket**, on 29 Dec 1894. In the five Tests George Giffen took 34 wickets for 820 runs for Australia, the first time a bowler had taken **30 wickets in a series**. He also scored 475 runs for an unsurpassed all-round achievement. For England Tom Richardson followed him by taking 32 wickets.

In the 1895–96 series in South Africa, George Lohmann of England followed first Test figures of 7–38 and 8–7 with 9–28 in 14.2 5-ball overs in the first innings of the second Test at the Old Wanderers ground, Johannesburg, 2–4 Mar 1896. This was the first time that a bowler had taken **nine wickets in a Test innings**, and only Jim Laker (1956) has returned a better analysis. Lohmann took 35 wickets av. 5.80, the first over 30 in a three-Test series. In the second Test in 1896, at Old Trafford, England included Sussex batsman K. S. Ranjitsinhji, the first **Indian to play in a Test match**. On the third morning, 18 July, during his second innings of 154 not out, he added 113 to his overnight score as the first **pre-lunch century in Test cricket**. In this match George Giffen became the first player to complete the double of **1000 runs and 100 wickets in Tests**. In the third and final Test George Lohmann and William Gunn refused to play for

England, demanding better terms; this was the first **'strike'** in Test history.

During the first Test of the 1897–98 series, at Sydney on 13–17 December, Australia's Joe Darling scored 101 in the second innings v England, becoming the first **left-handed Test century maker**. During the England first innings of 551 wicket-keeper Jim Kelly **did not concede a single bye**, the first such instance **in a score of over 500**. Darling scored 537 runs in seven innings in the series, the first run **aggregate over 500**, and in the third Test, at Adelaide, he completed his century with the first hit for six in Test cricket.

With 106 and 6–26 for South Africa v England at Cape Town on 1–4 Apr 1899 James Sinclair was the first to **score a century and take five wickets in an innings** in Tests.

When making his final Test appearance for England v Australia at Trent Bridge W. G. Grace was 50 years 320 days old on the final day, 3 June 1899, thus becoming the first **50-year-old Test player**. In the fourth Test, at Old Trafford, of the 1902 series Victor Trumper of Australia scored 103 not out, a **century before lunch on the first day**, 24 July, the first such occurrence in Tests. Having batted in all for 115 minutes and added just one more run, he was out five balls later. Australia won the match by just three runs.

For England v Australia at Sydney in the first Test on 11–17 Dec 1903, Reg 'Tip' Foster scored 287, the first **double century on a Test debut**. His 209 runs in one day was the first over 200, and he was also the first batsman to share three century partnerships in the same Test innings.

In 1905 for England v Australia Hon. Stanley Jackson became the first **Test captain to win the toss in each match of a five-Test series**; England won twice, with three drawn.

Australia's Warren Bardsley became the first batsman to score a **century in each innings** of a Test, with 136 and 130, each of 225 minutes, against England at The Oval, 9–11 Aug 1909.

For England v South Africa at Lord's, Durban, 21–26 Jan 1910, Neville Tufnell became the first **substitute to make a stumping** after he replaced Herbert Strudwick for England.

In the fourth Test of the 1911–12 series against Australia, at Melbourne on 9–13 February, Jack Hobbs (178) and Wilfred Rhodes (197) added 323 for the first wicket, the first Test **triple century partnership**. It was Hobbs's third century of the series, another first.

In the first match of the first, and only, triangular Test series, the Australian bowler Jack Matthews took a **hat-trick in each innings** v South Africa at Old Trafford, 27–28 May 1912, a unique feat. The tournament was won by England, who won four and drew two of their six matches.

At Johannesburg, 26–30 Dec 1913 for England

Old Trafford 1956, and Jim Laker has just taken nine Australian wickets for 37. He shakes hands with A. A. Mailey of Australia, the only other nine wicket Test bowler at the time. It all became academic when in the second innings Laker took all ten, for a unique 19 wicket match haul.

in their second test of the series v South Africa, Syd Barnes had a match analysis of 17–159, the first time **16 wickets** had been taken in a Test. Although playing in only the first four Tests Barnes became the first bowler to take **40 wickets in a series**. His final figures of 49 wickets av. 10.93 was made up of: 5–57 & 5–48, 8–56 & 9–103, 3–26 & 5–102, 7–56 & 7–88. England's Herbert Strudwick dismissed 21 batsmen, the first **wicket-keeper to take more than 20 in a series**.

Arthur Mailey had match figures of 10–302 (5–160 and 5–142) in the third Test v England at Adelaide, 14–20 Jan 1921, the first time a bowler had **conceded 300 runs or more in a match**. Mailey repeated the feat four years later, and remains the only Australian to do so. In this series Australia won all five Tests, the first 'whitewash' in a five-Test rubber.

On the second day of the second Test between England and South Africa at Lord's, 29 June 1924, England scored 503 runs for the loss of two wickets, a unique feat of one **Test team scoring more than 500 runs in a day**. Jack Hobbs (211) and Herbert Sutcliffe (122) put on 268 together and Frank Woolley was undefeated on 134 with Patsy Hendren 50 when England declared at 531–2 the following day.

Eight-ball overs were bowled for the first time in Tests in the Australia–England series in 1924–25, when Herbert Sutcliffe became the first to score **four centuries in a series**. In the second Test at Melbourne, 1–8 Jan 1925, after Australia had scored 600, the first **Test innings of 600 or more**, Hobbs and Sutcliffe batted together throughout the third day, adding 283 runs—the first time that **no wicket had fallen in a full day's play in a Test**. The stand was

Bottom of page *Herbert Sutcliffe; one of a line of unflappable Yorkshire openers, but with the demeanour and accent of the Southern stockbroker belt.*

Below *The young Bradman returning to the Leeds pavilion in 1930 having scored 334—then the highest Test score.*

broken immediately the following day; they scored 154 and 176 respectively. In the fourth Test at Melbourne, Australia's Bert Oldfield became the first wicket-keeper to take **five dismissals in a Test innings**, including a record for stumpings.

The first **fielder to take five catches in an innings** was Vic Richardson for Australia v South Africa at Durban on 3 Mar 1936.

For England v Australia in 1928–29 Walter Hammond became the first man to score **over 900 runs in a series** or to score **double centuries in successive Tests**. His scores: 44 & 28, 251, 200 & 32, 119* & 177, 38 & 16 for an aggregate of 905 av. 113.12. This total was bettered only by Don Bradman, 974 av. 139.14 for Australia v England in 1930, in the third Test of which, at Headingley on 11–15 July, he became the first **Test batsman to score 300 runs in a**

Australian skipper Bill Woodfull ducking under a Larwood flier at Brisbane 1933. Like many Australians, Woodfull showed his distaste and disdain for the 'bodyline' tactics which nearly caused a break in Anglo-Australian cricket relations, and were a successful counter to the Bradman menace.

Opposite *Len Hutton's record score resplendent on The Oval scoreboard. For 50 years it has remained the England record.*

day, an unbeaten 309. He went on to 334 the next day, and was the first to score **three double centuries in a series**, with 254 in the second and 232 in the fifth Tests.

In the fourth and final Test of their series against West Indies, played at Kingston, 3–10 Apr 1930, England totalled 849 and 272–9 dec, a match aggregate of 1121 for 19 wickets, the first time a side had **surpassed 1000 in a Test match** or **700 in an innings**. O. C. 'Tommy' Scott achieved first innings figures of 5–266, the first time a Test bowler had **conceded 200 runs in an innings**. Andrew Sandham's 325 for England was the first Test **triple century**.

The first Test crowd of **over 50 000** attended the second day of the third Test of the 'bodyline' series, at Adelaide on 14 Jan 1933. In his 336 not out for England v New Zealand at Eden Park, Auckland, 31 Mar–3 Apr 1933, Walter Hammond became the first to hit **ten sixes in a Test innings**.

In the fifth Test, at The Oval, 18–22 Aug 1934, Bill Ponsford (266) and Don Bradman (244)

added 451 in 316 minutes for the second wicket in the first innings for Australia v England. This was the first **stand of over 400**, and remains a Test record, although equalled in 1983. The first for the first wicket was 413 by Vinoo Mankad (231) and Pankaj Roy (173) for India v New Zealand at Madras, 6–11 Jan 1956.

When England made 903–7 dec v Australia in the fifth Test at The Oval on 20, 22–24 Aug 1938, several Test records were set. The total remains a record as is England's victory margin of an innings and 579 runs. It was the first **total over 900**, and Len Hutton's 364 was a record until Gary Sobers made 365 not out for West Indies v Pakistan in 1958. The Australian bowlers toiled hard for a total of 335.2 overs (2012 balls)—this was the first **innings in which more than 300 overs were bowled** in any first-class match. 'Chuck' Fleetwood-Smith bowled 87 overs (1–298), Bill O'Reilly 85 (3–178), Mervyn Waite 72 (1–150), Stan McCabe and Sid Barnes 38 each, Lindsay Hassett 13, and captain Don Bradman 2.2.

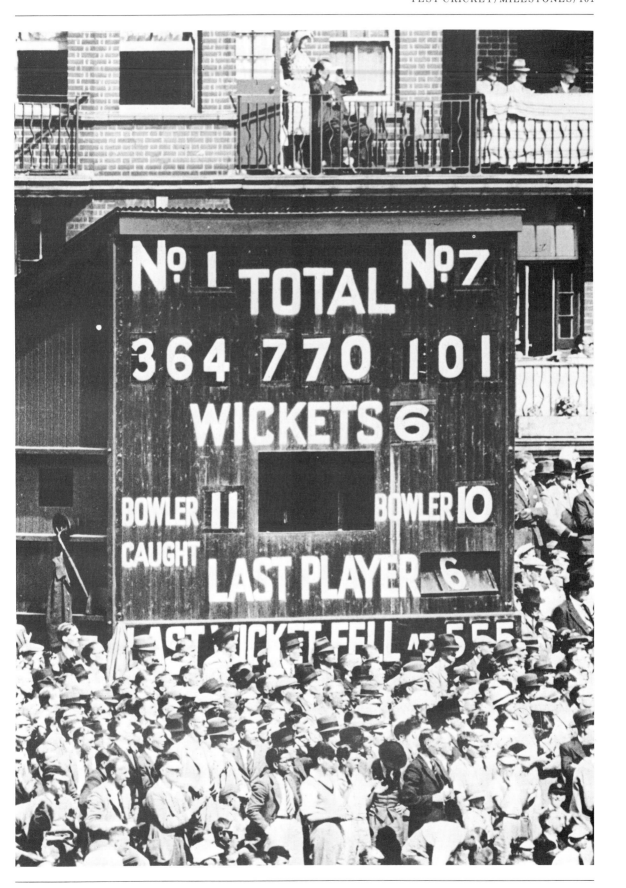

In the final Test of the South Africa–England series in 1938–39 at Kingsmead, Durban **play was spread over ten days** for the first time. England, set 696 to win, reached 654–5 before having to leave to catch the boat home. This was the first time a **team had exceeded 600 runs in the fourth innings**, and remains unique. The match produced a Test record aggregate of 1981 runs.

The Australian opener Bill Brown was **run out** by Indian left-arm spinner Vinoo Mankad **when backing up too far**—the first instance in Tests—at Sydney, 12–17 Dec 1947. The first to be dismissed **'obstructing the field'** was Len Hutton, for England v South Africa at The Oval on 18 Aug 1951, after deliberately obstructing wicket-keeper Russell Endean taking a catch. Endean himself achieved a Test first v England at Cape Town on 5 Jan 1957 when he was dismissed **'handled the ball'**.

Everton Weekes became the first batsman to score **centuries in five successive Test innings** when he made 162 and 101 for West Indies v India at Calcutta, 31 Dec 1948–4 Jan 1949. His previous innings had been 141 v England at Kingston, 128 v India at Delhi, 194 v India at Bombay. In the next Test he was run out for 90.

For the series against India in 1952 the England selectors appointed Len Hutton as the first **professional captain to lead England in a home rubber**. England won the first three Tests clearly with the fourth drawn.

Playing for Pakistan v India at Lucknow, 23–26 Oct 1952, Nazar Mohammad became the first player to be **on the field for every ball of a Test match**, including carrying his bat for 124 out of 331 in 515 minutes.

For West Indies v Australia in 1955 Clyde Walcott became the first batsman to hit **five centuries in a Test series**. His scores in the five Tests: 108 & 39, 126 & 110, 8 & 73, 15 & 83, 155 & 110. For Australia at Kingston in the fourth Test, 11–17 June, for the first time **five batsmen scored centuries in one Test innings**: Colin McDonald 127, Neil Harvey 204, Keith Miller 109, Ron Archer 128 and Richie Benaud 121 and, also a first, **five bowlers conceded over 100 runs**: Tom Dewdney, Frank King, Denis

Atkinson, Collie Smith and Frank Worrell, with Gary Sobers conceding 99, in Australia's 758–8 dec.

The fourth Test of the 1956 series against Australia at Old Trafford on 26–28, 30–31 July featured England's off-spinner Jim Laker, who had a match analysis of 19–90 in 68 overs. Bowling from the Stretford Road end he took 9–37 in 16.4 overs in the first innings and 10–53 in 51.2 overs in the second. **Ten wickets in an innings** is unique in Test cricket and **19 wickets in a match** in any first-class match. England won by an innings and 170 runs, having made 459 in 491 minutes, including 307–3 on the first day before the pitch began to break up. Australia lost eleven wickets on the second day, one on the third when rain permitted only 45 minutes play, none in the hour possible on the fourth, before Laker finished the job with the eight remaining by 5.27 p.m. on the final day.

On the first day of the first Test between Pakistan and Australia at Karachi, 11 Oct 1956, only 95 runs were scored for the loss of 12 wickets, the first and only time that **fewer than 100 runs have been obtained in a full Test day's play**. Australia were out for 80 (Fazal Mahmood 6–34, Khan Mohammad 4–43), Pakistan 15–2.

Batting for India v Australia at Calcutta, 23–28 Jan 1960, M. L. Jaisimha became the first player to **bat on all five days of a Test**. Coming in at number nine for a few minutes on the first day, he continued to 20 not out on the second. He reappeared as night-watchman (no. 4) for 0 not out in the second innings on the third day, batted throughout the fourth for 59 not out and was dismissed for 74 on the fifth morning.

Australia and West Indies achieved the first **tie** in Test history at Brisbane, 9–14 Dec 1960, the first match of that series. Having been set 223 to win in 310 minutes Australia lost their last wicket from the penultimate ball of the match, when Joe Solomon ran out Ian Meckiff. A further 26 years passed before the next tie.

Playing for India v England in 1963–64 Budhi Kunderan became the first **wicket-keeper to exceed 500 runs in a Test series**, with 525 in five Tests.

The first case of **two sides scoring over 600**

in an innings in the same Test was at Old Trafford, 23–28 July 1964, when Australia made 658–8 dec and England replied with 611.

Ken Barrington's 148 not out for England v South Africa at Durban, 4–8 Dec 1964 made him the first **batsman to score a century in Tests in all seven Test playing countries** (as then known). His other firsts were: 128 in West Indies 1960, 151* in India 1961, 139 in Pakistan 1962, 132* in Australia 1963, 256 in England 1964, 126 in New Zealand 1963. Barrington was also the first man to score **Test centuries at all six Test grounds** in England.

In the fifth Test v West Indies at The Oval, 18–22 Aug 1966, Ken Higgs (63) and John Snow (59*) added 128 for England's last wicket to become the first **numbers 10 and 11 to score fifties in the same Test innings**.

While playing for England v Australia at Edgbaston, 11–16 July 1968, Colin Cowdrey became the first **player to appear in 100 official Test matches**. He celebrated the event by scoring his 21st century and completing a career total of 7000 runs.

Batting for Australia v West Indies at Sydney, 14–16, 18–20 Feb 1969, Doug Walters scored 242

and 103—the first instance in Test cricket of a batsman making **a century and a double century in the same match**. Australia won by 382 runs. Lawrence Rowe was the first player to score a **hundred in each innings of his first Test**, with 214 and 100 not out for West Indies v New Zealand at Kingston, 16–21 Feb 1972.

The Australian pace bowler Bob Massie became the first player to take **eight wickets in each innings and 16 in a match on his Test debut**, v England at Lord's 22–26 June 1972; 8–84 in 32.5 overs and 8–53 in 27.2 overs. He played only five more Tests, taking a further 15 wickets.

When India scored 524–9 dec v New Zealand at Kanpur, 18–23 Nov 1976, it was the first occasion on which a **Test side had exceeded 500 without an individual century**; Mohinder Amarnath top scored with 70.

With his 14th Test century, 191 in 629 minutes for England v Australia at Headingley, 11–15 Aug 1977, Geoff Boycott became the first player to **reach 100 first-class centuries in a Test match**.

A batting helmet is now standard equipment; the first to bat in one in a Test was Graeme

Mohammed Azharuddin sowed the seeds of greatness in his unparallele entry to the Test arena—centuries in his first three Tests: 110, 48 & 105, 122 & 54* against England in India in Jan–Feb 1985.

Yallop for Australia v West Indies at Bridgetown, 17–19 Mar 1978.

Bob Taylor was the first **wicket-keeper to take ten dismissals in a Test match** with seven in the first and three in the second innings, all caught, for England v India in the Golden Jubilee Test at Bombay, 15–19 Feb 1980.

Record Test run-scorer Sunil Gavaskar of India (see table) scored his **30th Test century** with 236 not out against West Indies at Madras, 24–29 Dec 1983. At this venue v Australia on 18–22 Sep 1986 he became the first man to appear in **100 consecutive Tests** played by his country. His run started with the fifth Test v West Indies, 23–29 Jan 1975 and he eventually reached 106 in succession before standing down as he did not wish to play at Calcutta, the venue for the second Test v Pakistan, 11–16 Feb 1987.

FIRST TEST AND FIRST VICTORY BY EACH COUNTRY

AUSTRALIA

1st Test	v Eng, Melbourne, 15–19 Mar 1887	
1st Win	as above	1st match

ENGLAND

1st Test	v Aus, Melbourne, 15–19 Mar 1877	
1st Win	v Aus, Melbourne, 31 Mar–4 Apr 1877	2nd match

SOUTH AFRICA

1st Test	v Eng, Port Elizabeth, 12–13 Mar 1889	
1st Win	v Eng, Old Wanderers, Johannesburg, 2–4 Jan 1906	12th match

WEST INDIES

1st Test	v Eng, Lord's, 23–26 June 1928	
1st Win	v Eng, Georgetown, 21–26 Feb 1930	6th match

NEW ZEALAND

1st Test	v Eng, Christchurch, 10–13 Jan 1930	
1st Win	v WI, Auckland, 9–13 March 1956	45th match

INDIA

1st Test	v Eng, Lord's, 25–28 June 1932	
1st Win	v Eng, Madras, 6–10 Feb, 1952	25th match

PAKISTAN

1st Test	v Ind, Delhi, 16–18 Oct 1952	
1st Win	v Ind, Lucknow, 23–26 Oct 1952	2nd match

SRI LANKA

1st Test	v Eng, Colombo, 17–21 Feb 1982	
1st Win	v Ind, Colombo, 6–11 Sep 1985	14th match

MILESTONES IN TEST CRICKET FOR EACH COUNTRY—BATTING

First to 1000 runs

Team	Player	Match	No. games needed
Eng	Arthur Shrewsbury	E v A, Lord's, 17–19 July 1893	21
Aus	Charles Bannerman	A v E, The Oval, 14–16 Aug 1893	27
SA	Aubrey Faulkner	SA v A, Melbourne, 31 Dec 1910–4 Jan 1911	15
WI	George Headley	WI v A, Sydney, 2–4 Mar 1931	9
Ind	Vijay Hazare	I v WI, Bombay, 4–8 Feb 1949	13
NZ	Bert Sutcliffe	NZ v SA, Johannesburg, 24–29 Dec 1953	13
Pak	Hanif Mohammad	P v WI, Bridgetown, 17–23 Jan 1958	19
SL	Arjuna Ranatunga	SL v P, Colombo, 14–18 Mar 1986	17

First to 2000 runs

Aus	Clem Hill	A v E, Adelaide, 13–20 Jan 1904	27
Eng	Jack Hobbs	E v A, The Oval, 19–22 Aug 1912	23
SA	Dave Nourse	SA v E, Johannesburg, 9–13 Feb 1923	39
WI	George Headley	WI v E, Lord's, 24–27 June 1939	17
Ind	Vijay Hazare	I v WI, Port-of-Spain, 21–28 Jan 1953	26
NZ	Bert Sutcliffe	NZ v I, Madras, 6–11 Jan 1956	26
Pak	Hanif Mohammad	P v I, Bombay, 2–7 Dec 1960	28

First to 3000 runs

Aus	Clem Hill	A v E, Adelaide, 7–13 Jan 1911	42
Eng	Jack Hobbs	E v SA, Edgbaston, 14–17 June 1924	34
SA	Bruce Mitchell	SA v E, Durban, 16–20 Dec 1948	38
WI	Everton Weekes	WI v A, Port-of-Spain, 11–16 Apr 1955	31
Ind	Polly Umrigar	I v E, Kanpur, 1–6 Dec 1961	51
NZ	John Reid	NZ v P, Lahore, 2–7 Apr 1965	54
Pak	Hanif Mohammad	P v A, Melbourne, 4–8 Dec 1964	42

First to 4000 runs

Eng	Jack Hobbs	E v A, Lord's, 26–29 June 1926	45
Aus	Don Bradman	A v E, Melbourne, 1–2 Jan 1937	31
WI	Everton Weekes	WI v E, Headingley, 25–27 July 1957	42
Ind	Sunil Gavaskar	I v WI, Calcutta, 29 Dec 1978–3 Jan 1979	43
Pak	Zaheer Abbas	P v I, Hyderabad, 14–19 Jan 1983	56

First to 5000 runs

Eng	Jack Hobbs	E v A, Melbourne, 8–16 Mar 1929	55
Aus	Don Bradman	A v E, Headingley, 22–25 Jul 1938	38
WI	Gary Sobers	WI v E, Headingley, 4–8 Aug 1966	56
Ind	Sunil Gavaskar	I v A, Bangalore, 19–24 Sep 1979	52
Pak	Zaheer Abbas	P v NZ, Lahore, 16–20 Nov 1984	72

First to 6000 runs

Eng	Walter Hammond	E v SA, Johannesburg, 24–28 Dec 1938	70
Aus	Don Bradman	A v I, Melbourne, 1–5 Jan 1948	45

Opposite *Miraculous catching has been a feature of Ian Botham but even he has human frailties. Here he puts down Rick McCosker off Derek Underwood— Sydney 1979–80.*

BATTING MILESTONES (*cont.*)

WI	Gary Sobers	WI v E, Georgetown, 28–30 Mar 1–3 Apr 1968	65
Ind	Sunil Gavaskar	I v A, Adelaide, 23–27 Jan 1981	65
Pak	Javed Miandad	P v E, The Oval, 6–11 Aug 1987	86

First to 7000 runs

Eng	Walter Hammond	E v I, The Oval, 17–20 Aug 1946	85
WI	Gary Sobers	WI v I, Georgetown, 19–24 Mar 1971	79
Aus	Greg Chappell	A v P, Sydney, 2–6 Jan 1984	87
Ind	Sunil Gavaskar	I v P, Lahore, 10–15 Dec 1982	80

First to 8000 runs

WI	Gary Sobers	WI v E, Kingston, 16–21 Feb 1974	91
Eng	Geoff Boycott	E v I, Delhi, 23–28 Dec 1981	107
Ind	Sunil Gavaskar	I v WI, Delhi, 29 Oct–3 Nov 1983	95

First to 9000 runs

Ind	Sunil Gavaskar	I v A, Adelaide, 13–17 Dec 1985	110

First to 10 000 runs

Ind	Sunil Gavaskar	I v P, Ahmedabad, 4–9 Mar 1987	124

BOWLING MILESTONES

First to 100 wickets

Eng	Johnny Briggs	E v A, Sydney, 1–4 Feb 1895 (Day 1)	25
Aus	Charles Turner	A v E, Sydney, 1–4 Feb 1895 (Day 3)	17
Ind	Vinoo Mankad	I v P, Bombay, 13–16 Nov 1952	23
WI	Alfred Valentine	WI v E, Georgetown, 24 Feb–2 Mar 1954	20
SA	Hugh Tayfield	SA v E, The Oval, 13–17 Aug 1955	22
NZ	Dick Motz	NZ v E, The Oval, 21–26 Aug 1969	32
Pak	Fazal Mahmood	P v WI, Karachi, 20–25 Feb 1959	22

First to 200 wickets

Aus	Clarrie Grimmett	A v SA, Johannesburg, 15–17 Feb 1936	36
Eng	Alec Bedser	E v A, Lord's, 25–30 June 1953	44
WI	Lance Gibbs	WI v NZ, Wellington, 7–11 Mar 1969	46
Ind	Bishen Bedi	I v E, Madras, 14–19 Jan 1977	51
Pak	Imran Khan	P v I, Karachi, 23–28 Dec 1982	45
NZ	Richard Hadlee	NZ v E, Trent Bridge, 25–29 Aug 1983	44

First to 300 wickets

Eng	Fred Trueman	E v A, The Oval, 13–17 Aug 1964	65
WI	Lance Gibbs	WI v A, Perth, 12–16 Dec 1975	75
Aus	Dennis Lillee	A v P, Brisbane, 27 Nov–1 Dec 1981	56
NZ	Richard Hadlee	NZ v A, Wellington, 21–24 Feb 1986	61
Ind	Kapil Dev	I v SL, Cuttack, 4–7 Jan 1987	83
Pak	Imran Khan	P v E, Headingley, 2–6 July 1987	68

WICKET-KEEPING MILESTONES

First to take 50 dismissals:

Aus	Jack Blackham	A v E, Sydney, 29 Jan–1 Feb 1892	30
Eng	Dick Lilley	E v A, Sydney, 11–17 Dec 1903	18
SA	Jock Cameron	SA v E, The Oval, 17–20 Aug 1935	26
WI	Clyde Walcott	WI v A, Kingston, 26–31 Mar 1955	29
	(including matches playing as a fielder)		
NZ	Arthur Dick	NZ v E, Lord's, 17–22 June 1965	17
Ind	Narendra Tamhane	I v P, Kanpur, 16–21 Dec 1960	20
Pak	Imtiaz Ahmed	P v WI, Port-of-Spain, 26–31 Mar 1958	23

First to 100 dismissals:

Aus	Bert Oldfield	A v E, Lord's, 22–25 June 1934	41
Eng	Godfrey Evans	E v I, Lord's, 19–24 June 1952	42
SA	John Waite	SA v E, The Oval, 18–23 Aug 1960	36
WI	Deryck Murray	WI v A, Sydney, 3–7 Jan 1976	33
Pak	Wasim Bari	P v WI, Kingston, 15–20 Apr 1977	45
Ind	Syed Kirmani	I v E, Bombay, 15–19 Feb 1980	42
NZ	Ian Smith	NZ v WI, Wellington, 20–24 Feb 1987	33

First to 200 dismissals:

Eng	Godfrey Evans	E v WI, Headingley, 25–27 July 1957	80
Aus	Rodney Marsh	A v WI, Brisbane, 1–5 Dec 1979	53
Pak	Wasim Bari	P v I, Karachi, 30 Jan–4 Feb 1983	73

First to 300 dismissals:

Aus	Rodney Marsh	A v NZ, Christchurch, 19–22 Mar 1982	83

First fielders to take 100 catches:

Eng	Walter Hammond	E v WI, Old Trafford, 22–25 July 1959	76
WI	Gary Sobers	WI v I, Port-of-Spain, 13–19 Apr 1971	81
Aus	Bobby Simpson	A v I, Perth, 16–21 Dec 1977	54
Ind	Sunil Gavaskar	I v E, Edgbaston, 3–8 July 1986	115

Imran Khan in 1980; for Pakistan & Sussex, he was the leading all-rounder of the following decade.

TEST CRICKET EXTRAS

On 16 June 1880 James Southerton, who played for England in the first two Test matches, died at his home, The Cricketers Inn, Mitcham, Surrey, from pleurisy and lung congestion. Aged 52, born in Sussex on 16 Nov 1827, he was the first **Test cricketer to die**. The scheduled third Test between England and Australia at Old Trafford on 25–27 August 1890 was the first Test match to be **abandoned without a ball being bowled**. Old Trafford has also been the venue on the occasion of the first **complete day being abandoned due to rain**, the first day of the first Test England v Australia 10 July 1884.

The first and only instance of **a country simultaneously playing two Test series** was when England sent teams to New Zealand (won one Test, three drawn) and to West Indies (1–1 with two drawn) in January–February 1930. Even so, several of the best England Test players stayed at home.

The first **fielding captain to appeal against the light** in a Test match was Herbert Wade at Johannesburg v Australia on 28 Dec 1935. A heavy storm ended the match with Australia needing 125 runs for victory with eight wickets in hand.

For the first time in Test cricket an **extra day** was added to the Test between New Zealand and England at Christchurch in 1947. Originally scheduled for 21–22 and 24 March, as the third day's play was washed out, it was determined to play also on 25 March, but rain again prevented play, and the game was left drawn.

The first Test match to be **played on Christmas Day** was at Adelaide, Australia v West Indies third Test, 25 Dec 1951. West Indies won their present, winning by six wickets, half-way through this the last day of the match.

Indian captain Bishen Bedi declared his first innings closed at 306–6 in **protest against intimidatory bowling** by West Indies in the fourth Test at Sabina Park, Kingston, Jamaica on 21–25 Apr 1976. After West Indies had scored 391, the Indians made just 97 in their second innings, with five men absent hurt. Three had been injured in the first innings: Anshuman Gaekwad, Gundappa Viswanath and Brijesh Patel, and they were joined as absentees by Bedi and Bhagwat Chandrasekhar, injured while fielding.

The first **scheduled Test to be cancelled due to political factors** was that due to be played at Georgetown, Guyana on 28 Feb–5 Mar 1981, the second Test between West Indies and England. The Guyana government refused to allow one of the English team, Robin Jackman, permission to stay in the country due to his South African connections. England therefore refused to take part in the Test.

The first **teenager** to play Test cricket was Tom Garrett, Australian medium-fast bowler, who was 18 years 232 days old when the first ever Test match started on 15 Mar 1877.

Although there must be doubts about the exact ages of some cricketers, according to their official birthdays the first **17-year-old** was

Derek Sealy, 17 years 122 days for West Indies v England at Bridgetown, Barbados, 11 Jan 1930; the first **16-year-old** was Khalid Hassan, 16 years 352 days for Pakistan v England at Trent Bridge, 1 July 1954, and the first **15-year-old** was Mushtaq Mohammad, 15 years 124 days for Pakistan v West Indies at Lahore, 26 Mar 1959.

The first **teenager to score a Test century** was Archie Jackson, at 19 years 152 days, 164 on his Test debut for Australia v England at Adelaide, 1–8 Feb 1929. The first **17-year-old** was Mushtaq Mohammed at 17 years 82 days, 101 v India at Delhi, 8–13 Feb 1961. The first **teenager to score a double century** was Javed Miandad at 19 years 141 days for Pakistan v New Zealand at Karachi, 30 Oct–4 Nov 1976. In this match Imran Khan of Pakistan, after bowling three bouncers at Richard Hadlee, was the first person to be **banned from bowling in a Test match for intimidatory bowling**; the umpire was former Pakistani cricketer Shuja-ud-din.

The first **black Test cricketer** was Samuel Morris who opened the batting for Australia v England at Melbourne, 1–5 Jan 1885. His parents came from Barbados to Tasmania in the 1850s, and Morris, who was born in Hobart, played for Victoria from 1881 to 1892.

The first **Malaysian Test cricketer** was the Sikh, Lall Singh, who, having made a century for the Federated Malay States, where he lived in Kuala Lumpur, went to India for the trials for the 1932 tour to England. He gained selection and played in the Lord's Test.

The first **one-eyed Test cricketer** was John Sharpe, who had lost an eye while young, who played three times for England v Australia, 1890–2. One-eyed also was fast-medium right-arm bowler 'Buster' Nupen (also the first-born of Norwegian parents), who played 17 Tests for South Africa, 1921–36, taking 50 wickets.

A unique experience of **playing his one first-class match in a Test** was that of Joe McMaster, an Irishman who toured South Africa with Major Wharton's team in 1888–89. He played in the second 'Test' at Cape Town on 25–26 Mar 1889, got a 'duck' and did not bowl.

The first officially appointed **Test selectors** were Lord Hawke, Dr W. G. Grace and H. W. Bainbridge, appointed as England selectors by the Board of Control in 1899.

The first full-time **England cricket manager** was Micky Stewart, appointed on 1 Apr 1987. The former Surrey captain had played in eight Tests, 1962–4.

The pay for an England cricketer per Test first reached **£100** in 1957 and **£1000** in 1978.

FAMILIES

The first **brothers** and first **father–son Test cricketers** were the Gregorys of Australia. In the first ever Test match Dave was captain and E. J. 'Ned' Gregory also played. Ned had the misfortune to make the first **Test duck**; his son Syd played in 58 Tests from his first, against England at Lord's on 21–23 July 1890, to 1912 on his eighth tour of England. The fourth member of the family to play Test cricket was Jack Gregory, the son of Charles, brother of Dave and Ned. All the family played for New South Wales.

The first instance of **three brothers in a match** were the Graces, W.G., E.M. and G.F. in the first Test in England, at The Oval, 6–8 Sep 1880. E.M. and W.G. put on 91 together in the first innings of the match, E.M. scoring 36 and W.G. going on to 152, **England's first Test century**. W.G. put on 120 for the second wicket with A. P. Lucas, the first **century partnership** in Test cricket. Fred, however, bagged a **'pair'**, the first in Test history.

Brothers on opposing Test teams were the Hearnes at Newlands, Cape Town on 19–22 Mar 1892. Frank, who had played twice for England against South Africa in 1889, made his debut for South Africa, while on the opposing England team were his brothers Alec and George.

Ian and Greg Chappell became the first **brothers each to score a hundred in the same Test innings**, 118 and 113 respectively for Australia v England at The Oval, 10–16 Aug 1972, and the first to score hundreds in both innings of a Test match: Ian 145 and 121, Greg 247* and 133, v New Zealand at Wellington, 1–6 Mar 1974.

The first instance of **four brothers playing Test cricket** were the Mohammads of Pakistan:

Hanif, Wazir, Sadiq and Mushtaq, although they never all played together. A fifth brother Raees Mohammad was once 12th man for Pakistan.

The first **father and son Test captains** were the Manns of Middlesex, who both took England teams to South Africa, Frank T. Mann in 1922–23 and F. George Mann in 1948–49. On both occasions England won the five-Test series. George played in two further Tests against New Zealand in 1949, but Frank had no other Tests.

The first **fourth generation Test cricketer** was Paul Sheahan, who made his debut for Australia v India at Adelaide on 23, 25–28 Dec 1967. His great-grandfather William Cooper played twice for Australia, 1881–4.

TEST UMPIRES

George Coulthard was probably the youngest ever Test umpire at 22 years 154 days when he stood at Melbourne in the Australia–England match, 2–4 Jan 1879. His next Test appearance was when he became the first **umpire to play Test cricket**, for Australia v England at Sydney, 17–21 Feb 1882, when he batted at no. 11 for 6 not out and did not bowl. Then he umpired again in the fourth Test of this series. He died of tuberculosis in 1883—the first **Australian Test cricketer to die**.

In February 1879 at Sydney Coulthard gave Billy Murdoch run out in the New South Wales v England match, and the crowd rioted, causing play to be abandoned for the day. Umpiring at the other end was Edmund Barton, later the first **first-class umpire to go on to become a prime minister**, as he was Australia's first, 1901–3.

The first man to **umpire in different countries**, and the first to stand in **20 or more Tests** was the Australian Jim Phillips, who had been a useful all-rounder for Victoria and for Middlesex, travelling regularly between Australia and England in the 1890s. He first umpired in a Test at Melbourne, 21–25 Mar 1885, and first umpired in a Test in England at Lord's, 17–19 July 1893. While still playing first-class cricket he accompanied the Australian team to England

Jim Phillips, an Australian of uncertain age, played Sheffield Shield for Victoria, County Championship for Middlesex, and became the first internationally recognised umpire.

in 1896. His 20th Test match was at Sheffield, 3–5 July 1902, and he ended his umpiring career (29 Tests) when he completed a unique triple by umpiring all five Tests in the South Africa–England series in 1905–06.

The first umpire to stand in **30 or 40 or more tests** was Frank Chester in England. A promising all-rounder for Worcestershire, he lost an arm in World War I and his first Test as an umpire was at the age of 29 in 1924. His 30th Test was England–India at The Oval, 17–20 Aug 1946, his 40th England–South Africa at Trent Bridge, 7–12 June 1951 and his last, his 48th, England–South Africa at Headingley, 21–26 July 1955.

The first **brothers to umpire a Test match** were Stanley and Dalkeith Collins, South Africa v New Zealand at Cape Town, 1–5 Jan 1954.

The first occasion on which **four umpires stood in a Test match** was at Edgbaston, the fifth Test England v Australia on 10–12, 14 July 1975. The original pair were Dicky Bird and Arthur Fagg. Bird withdrew with an injured back; Alan Oakman took over after tea on the third day and Tom Spencer on the fourth day.

The first Test to be conducted with a **stand-by umpire** was when Ray Julian fulfilled that role in the England–Australia match at Lord's, 13–18 June 1985.

The first **umpire to be recognised in the honours lists** was Syd Buller, awarded the MBE in 1965. He stood in 33 Tests in England between 1956 and 1969.

SCORERS

William Ferguson, 'Fergie', acted as **scorer and baggage master for five Test playing nations** in 43 tours from 1905 when he came with the Australians to England until 1957 when he scored for West Indies in England. In addition to those three countries he also worked for New Zealand and South Africa, and in all scored in 208 Tests.

OTHER INTERNATIONAL MATCHES

TEST MATCHES THAT WERE NOT QUITE TEST MATCHES!

At the end of World War II a series of **'Victory Tests'** was played in England in 1945, between England and Australia, the latter composed of Australian servicemen in Europe. The first such match was played at Lord's on 19, 21–22 May. England 267 and 294 lost to Australia 455 and 107–4 by four wickets. Keith Miller (105) scored the first century in Australia's first innings, in which John Stephenson took 5–116, the first bowler to take five wickets in an innings in these matches. England's first century was scored by Walter Hammond (100) in the next match, won by England by 41 runs, at Bramall Lane, Shef-

field on 23, 25–26 June.

After these matches there was a marvellous game played at Lord's on 25, 27–28 Aug 1945, when the Dominions, with what might be regarded as the first **representative Commonwealth team**, captained by Learie Constantine (WI), beat England by 45 runs with eight minutes to spare. There were magnificent centuries for the Dominions by Martin Donnelly (NZ), 133 in the first innings of 307 and Keith Miller (Aus), 185 in the second, as he took his overnight 61 to 185 in just 90 minutes on the third morning. For England their captain Walter Hammond made 121 and 102, and Doug Wright 5–90 and 5–105.

The first **Commonwealth tour** was organised and managed by George Duckworth to the Indian sub-continent in 1949–50, as a 'fill-in', when a proposed MCC visit could not go ahead. The Commonwealth team was composed principally of professionals, from Australia, England and the West Indies, from the Lancashire Leagues, then featuring many top-class players. The Australian 'Jock' Livingston, who went on to have a successful career with Northamptonshire was the captain. The tour was a success and further such tours were conducted in 1950–51 and 1953–54. On each tour five unofficial 'Tests' were played against India, who treated these as 'Tests'.

The first of these 'Tests' took place at Feroze Shah Kotla ground, New Delhi on 11–15 Nov 1949, when the Indian captain was Vijay Merchant. Jock Livingston scored the first century, 123, putting on 226 for the first wicket with Buddy Oldfield of Northants, who went on to score 151 in the Commonwealth total of 608–8 dec. India replied with 291 (Dattu Phadkar 110) and 327, leaving the Commonwealth to make only 12, for the first victory in the series.

India's first win was in the third 'Test', at Calcutta on 30 Dec 1949–3 Jan 1950, with Vijay Hazare the successful captain. George Tribe took five first innings wickets for 144 in 57.2 overs, the first case of five wickets in an innings.

The first double century came in the next match when West Indian Frank Worrell scored 223 not out for the Commonwealth at Kanpur.

The first **matches played in England as**

Alan Jones, on his way to a century at Fenner's in 1982, scored more runs than any other Welshman but, when the 1970 'Tests' no longer counted, became the only player to be removed from the England Test records.

Tests, but which were subsequently ruled not to have that title officially, as they were not between two nations, were those in 1970 between England and the **Rest of the World**. These matches, sponsored by Guinness, were played after the cancellation of the scheduled tour by South Africa at the request of the British Government.

The Rest of the World team, captained by Gary Sobers, was formidably strong, comprising five South Africans, five West Indians, two from Pakistan and one from Australia, and the series was a great success with much fine cricket. The first 'Test' match was played at Lord's on 17–22 June, when the Rest of the World 546 (Eddie Barlow 119, Gary Sobers 183) beat England by an innings and 80 runs. Before his brilliant innings Sobers had taken 6–21 in 20 overs in England's first innings 127. Alan Jones, the Glamorgan opener, made 5 and 0 in this his international debut, but never again played for England—the **first Test player not to be one**! His 36 049 runs in his career (1957–83) was more than any other non-Test player. England won their first victory, by eight wickets, in the second match at Trent Bridge, 2–7 July, and the next three went to the Rest of the World.

REBEL TOURS

South Africa's isolation from Test cricket due to its Government's apartheid policies meant that its cricketers were deprived of Test matches from their last, played against Australia in 1969–70. Although steps were taken to make their domestic cricket multi-racial, including the formation of the **South African Cricket Union (SACU)** in 1977 under Rashid Varachia to represent cricketers of all colours, resumption of Test playing was clearly impossible. SACU therefore determined to provide international cricket for its players, and brought teams of players to South Africa for unofficial Tests.

The first such team was a group of English players, captained by Graham Gooch and sponsored by South African Breweries in 1982. Their first match was a 50-overs game at Port Elizabeth on 6 March, when South Africa beat the SAB English XI by seven wickets, and the first **unofficial Test** was at Johannesburg on 12–15 March, won by South Africa by eight wickets. In this match Jimmy Cook made the first century (114) and Vintcent van der Bijl took 5–25 and 5–79, the first cases of five wickets in an innings and ten wickets in a match in these series of rebel Tests.

There were subsequent tours by Sri Lankans in Oct–Dec 1982, West Indians in 1983 and 1984 and Australians 1985. The first team to inflict a defeat on South Africa in an unofficial Test was the West Indians captained by Lawrence Rowe, by 29 runs at Johannesburg, 28 Jan–1 Feb 1983.

For the rebel players there were the first **bans from Test cricket**, three years for the England players in 1982, followed by virtual life bans for the Sri Lankans and West Indians.

LIMITED-OVERS INTERNATIONAL MATCHES

MILESTONES

It is now accepted that the first **bona fide limited-overs international** match was played at Melbourne between Australia and England on 5 Jan 1971. It was a hastily arranged match on the last scheduled day of a rain ruined Test match. At no time was the match billed as 'Australia versus England' (thus the dissimilarity with the first ever match accepted as a 'Test' match in 1876–77, which was regarded as a fully blown international match by the contemporary media). It is, however, extremely doubtful whether a change will be suggested with regard to the status of the 1971 match and so one can confirm its position as the first limited-overs international.

The first **ball of the first match** was bowled by Australian pace bowler Graham McKenzie to Geoffrey Boycott of England; the first run was scored by Boycott in this over and with the score at 21 Boycott became the first batsman to be dismissed, caught off Jeffrey Thomson by Bill Lawry. The match, of 40 8-ball overs per side, was won by Australia by five wickets with 42 balls remaining. John Edrich of England scored 82—the first half century and top score of the match, and Edrich was awarded with the title 'man-of-the-match'.

The first **limited-overs international competition** was in 1972, England and Australia playing a three match tournament during August, at 55 6-ball overs per side, for the Prudential Assurance Trophy. England won the series by two matches to one to become the first holders.

Dennis Amiss, batting for England against Australia at Old Trafford on 24 Aug 1972 scored 103 in 161 minutes from 134 balls, with 9 fours, the **first century** in limited-overs internationals, and laid the basis for an England victory by six wickets. Amiss, with Keith Fletcher (60) added 125 for the second wicket, for the first **century partnership** in this form of international cricket.

THE WORLD CUP

The **Prudential Cup**, staged in England in 1975, and named after the sponsors, Prudential Assurance, was the first of four World Cup competitions held to date. The Prudential Cup was again held in England in 1979 and 1983, and in 1987, under the new sponsorship of Reliance, it took place in India and Pakistan. The first three World Cups were contested as 60-over matches, while in 1987, due to the shorter hours of daylight in the sub-continent, 50-over matches were played.

Competitions have been played in two groups of four on a league basis, with the top two teams from each league then taking part in knock-out semi-finals and final.

The **first matches** were played on 7 June 1975: England beat India at Lord's, New Zealand beat East Africa at Edgbaston, Australia beat Pakistan at Leeds and West Indies beat Sri Lanka at Old Trafford, Manchester.

On that first day Glenn Turner scored the first **century**, his 171 not out for New Zealand remaining a World Cup record until 1983. Later in the day Dennis Amiss completed a century (137), and with Keith Fletcher (68) put on the first **century partnership**, 176 for the second wicket, for England, who set two firsts in any limited-overs international: their total of 334–4 was the first **score over 300**, and their winning margin over India of 202 runs was the first **victory by 200 or more**. India's Kit Ghavri had bowling figures of 0–83 in 11 overs, the first to **concede 80 runs in a match**, and the only one for eight years. For Australia Dennis Lillee became the first bowler to take **five wickets in an innings** in a limited-overs international, 5–34 in his 12 overs to ensure his team's victory by 73 runs.

The match at The Oval on 11 June 1975 produced 604 runs for nine wickets, the first **limited-overs aggregate over 600**. Australia (328–5) beat Sri Lanka (276–4). For Australia opener Alan Turner (101) scored his runs out of 178, hitting the first **century before lunch**. At Leeds on the same day India (123–0 in 29.5 overs) achieved the first **limited-overs international** ten wicket victory, as they had dismissed East Africa for 120 in 55.3 overs.

In the semi-final on 18 June 1975 Australia's left-armed pace bowler Gary Gilmour achieved figures of 6–14 in 12 overs against England at Leeds, the first instance of a bowler taking six wickets in a match. Australia skittled England for 93 in 36.2 overs and won by four wickets.

The first winners of the World Cup were West Indies, who beat Australia by 17 runs at Lord's on 21 June 1975. Batting first West Indies scored 291 for eight wickets, with their captain Clive Lloyd making 102, reaching his hundred off just 82 balls. For Australia Gary Gilmour took 5–48, and in their reply of 274, their captain Ian Chappell was the top scorer with 62, as their innings featured five run outs, the first such instance in limited-overs internationals.

In the second Prudential World Cup, Canada, playing England at Old Trafford on 14 June 1979, were all out for 45 in 40.3 overs, the first total of less than 50 in international matches. Canada batted first, their innings lasted only 157 minutes and they were beaten by eight wickets in 215 minutes. The aggregate of 91 runs for 12 wickets was the first under 100 in a completed match.

In the third World Cup in 1983 Winston Davis became the first bowler to take seven wickets in a match, 7–51 in 10.3 overs for West Indies, who beat Australia by 101 runs at Leeds, 11–12 June, and Martin Snedden the first bowler to concede more than 100 runs, with figures of 12–1–105–2 for New Zealand v England at The Oval, 9 June. For India v Zimbabwe at Leicester,

FIRST TO CAREER MILESTONES IN LIMITED-OVERS INTERNATIONALS

1000 runs:

				No. matches
WI	Vivian Richards	WI v E	Sydney, 22 Jan 1980	22
Aus	Greg Chappell	A v NZ	Adelaide, 23 Nov 1980	27
Eng	Geoff Boycott	E v A	Lord's, 4 June 1981	32
Pak	Zaheer Abbas	P v SL	Lahore, 29 Mar 1982	26
NZ	Glenn Turner	NZ v A	Adelaide, 31 Jan 1983	25
Ind	Kapil Dev	I v WI	Jamshedpur, 7 Dec 1983	46
SL	Roy Dias	SL v WI	Sydney, 17 Jan 1985	29

2000 runs:

Aus	Greg Chappell	A v NZ	Auckland, 13 Feb 1982	55
WI	Vivian Richards	WI v I	The Oval, 15 June 1983	49
Pak	Zaheer Abbas	P v I	Jaipur, 2 Oct 1983	44
Eng	David Gower	E v NZ	Wellington, 22 Feb 1984	60
NZ	John Wright	NZ v P	Colombo, 7 Apr 1986	84
Ind	Dilip Vengsarkar	I v P	Sharjah, 18 Apr 1986	67

3000 runs:

WI	Vivian Richards	WI v E	Old Trafford, 31 May 1984	74
Aus	Allan Border	A v I	Sydney, 21 Jan 1986	120
Pak	Javed Miandad	P v E	Perth, 5 Jan 1987	101
Ind	Sunil Gavaskar	I v NZ	Nagpur, 31 Oct 1987	106

4000 runs:

WI	Vivian Richards	WI v NZ	Berbice, 14 Apr 1985	96
Pak	Javed Miandad	P v SL	Hyderabad, 8 Oct 1987	120
Aus	Allan Border	A v Zim	Madras, 13 Oct 1987	153

11 June, Syed Kirmani became the first **wicket-keeper to take five dismissals in an innings**, all caught.

The first **score over 350** came in the 1987 World Cup, when despite being limited to 50 overs, West Indies amassed 360-4 v Sri Lanka at Karachi on 13 October, with Vivian Richards contributing a record individual score of 181, hitting 16 fours and 6 sixes in his 125-ball innings.

WORLD CUP CAREER MILESTONES:
First to 500 runs: Glenn Turner, in his eighth innings, New Zealand v England at Old Trafford, 20 June 1979.

First to 1000 runs: Vivian Richards in his 21st innings in 23 matches, West Indies v Pakistan at Karachi, 30 Oct 1987.

OTHER LIMITED-OVERS INTERNATIONALS FIRSTS

The **Benson & Hedges World Series Cup** has been held annually in Australia from the 1979–80 season, when the first winners were the West Indies. Each year Australia are opposed by two other nations. In the fourth match in the opening year, Desmond Haynes (80) and Vivian Richards (153 not out) added 205 for the West Indies second wicket v Australia at Melbourne, the first **double century partnership**. It remained the record stand for any wicket for four years, and West Indies won the match by 80 runs.

On 11 Feb 1984 in the second of the three

5000 runs:

				No. matches
WI	Vivian Richards	WI v E	Melbourne, 30 Jan 1987	126

50 wickets:

Aus	Dennis Lillee	A v I	Sydney, 18 Dec 1980	24
WI	Andy Roberts	WI v P	Melbourne, 21 Nov 1981	29
Eng	Ian Botham	E v SL	Colombo, 14 Feb 1982	41
NZ	Richard Hadlee	NZ v E	Perth, 5 Feb 1983	46
Pak	Sarfraz Nawaz	P v SL	Headingley, 16 June 1983	33
Ind	Kapil Dev	I v WI	Baroda, 9 Nov 1983	44
SL	Ashantha De Mel	SL v P	Lahore, 25 Oct 1985	39

100 wickets:

Aus	Dennis Lillee	A v Zim	Trent Bridge, 9 June 1983	60
WI	Michael Holding	WI v SL	Brisbane, 17 Jan 1985	69
NZ	Richard Hadlee	NZ v WI	Port-of-Spain, 27 Mar 1985	73
Eng	Ian Botham	E v A	Lord's, 3 June 1985	75
Ind	Kapil Dev	I v E	Old Trafford, 26 May 1986	77
Pak	Mudassar Nazar	P v E	Edgbaston, 25 May 1987	105

1000 runs and 100 wickets double:

Eng	Ian Botham	E v A	Lord's, 3 June 1985	75
NZ	Richard Hadlee	NZ v A	Sydney, 14 Jan 1986	78
Ind	Kapil Dev	I v E	Old Trafford, 26 May 1986	77
Pak	Mudassar Nazar	P v E	Edgbaston, 25 May 1987	105

100 dismissals:

Aus	Rodney Marsh	A v Zim	Trent Bridge, 9 June 1983	75
WI	Jeffrey Dujon	WI v P	Peshawar, 17 Oct 1986	80

match final, West Indies scored 222–5 in their 50 overs and Australia replied with 222–9 with Carl Rackemann run out off the last ball. This was the first (and so far only) **tie in limited-overs internationals**.

The first **hat-trick** was achieved by Jalal-uddin, right-arm pace bowler for Pakistan, when he dismissed Rod Marsh, Bruce Yardley and Geoff Lawson of Australia with successive balls at the Niaz Stadium, Hyderabad on 20 Sep 1982.

The first player to **score a century and take five wickets in an innings** of a limited-overs international was Vivian Richards, 119 and 5–41 in 10 overs for the West Indies as they beat New Zealand by 95 runs at Dunedin on 18 Mar 1987.

SHARJAH

Due to large numbers of expatriate cricketers from the Indian sub-continent working in the

Opposite *Vivian Richards hits a boundary—one of 26—during his ritual slaughter of England at Lord's, 1980. He reached 1000 runs against England in his sixth Test.*

General view of Shajah—First Asian Cup, April 1984, Dubai.

United Arab Emirates, cricket has recently flourished in this part of the world. A fine stadium was built at Sharjah in 1981, and there Abdul Rahman Bukhatir pioneered limited-overs internationals, bringing over the major cricketing powers.

On 4 Mar 1983 a Pakistan XI 225-6 beat an England XI 219-9 (Graeme Fowler 108) in a 45-overs match played for the India and Pakistan Cricketers' Benefit Fund. But the first official one-day international was played on 6 Apr 1984, the first match of the inaugural **Asian Cup**, when Pakistan made 187-9 but lost to Sri Lanka 190-5, for whom Roy Dias made 57 not out, the first **half-century** in Sharjah internationals. The tournament was won by India who beat both these nations.

After that first series, Sharjah has regularly hosted limited-overs tournaments, usually two per year. The next series was a four-nations tournament, in which Australia and England played for the first time. This, like the Asian Cup, was sponsored by Rothmans. In the first match

Imran Khan of Pakistan took 6–14 in 10 overs, the first bowler to take **five wickets in an innings**, in India's 125 on 22 Mar 1985; however, Pakistan made only 87 in reply.

The first **score of over 200** was made on 17 Nov 1985, Pakistan 203-4 in 45 overs v India, but there had been a near miss two days earlier when after Pakistan had scored 196-4 in 45 overs, West Indies passed that with five balls to spare, 199-3 with Richie Richardson 99 not out. Richardson went on to become the first man to make a **century** in a 45-overs game in Sharjah, 109 on 3 Dec 1986 when West Indies (248-5) beat Sri Lanka by 193 runs as they skittled them out for 55, Courtney Walsh having the amazing bowling figures of 4.3–3–1–5.

However, the first century in a limited-overs international in Sharjah had been scored in a marvellous 50-overs match on 18 Apr 1986, the final of the Australasian Cup, when after India had scored 245-7, Pakistan needed four to win off the last ball. Javed Miandad hit it for six to achieve an epic triumph and to seal his own innings of 116 not out. Pakistan had qualified for the final with the first **ten wickets victory** on 15 April, when they dismissed New Zealand for 64 in 35.5 overs, and then Mudassar Nazar (32) and Mohsin Khan (34) passed that without loss in 22.4 overs.

ICC

The **Imperial Cricket Conference** was founded on 15 June 1909, with Australia, England and South Africa the inaugural members. India, New Zealand and the West Indies were admitted to membership in 1926, and Pakistan in 1952. South Africa ceased to be a member on that nation's withdrawal from the Commonwealth in 1961. The name of the ICC was changed to the International Cricket Conference in 1965, when the first associate members, Fiji, Sri Lanka and the USA, were admitted. Sri Lanka obtained full membership in 1981, by when a further 16 associate members had joined.

The first **ICC Trophy competition** was staged at Midlands club grounds in England in 1979. It was contested by 14 nations, who took part in three groups playing 60-overs games on a league basis, with the winners and the best runner-up qualifying for semi-finals. In the final, at Worcester on 21 June, Sri Lanka, 324, beat Canada, 264, by 60 runs. Man-of-the-Match was Duleep Mendis, Sri Lanka's top scorer with 66. Both finalists qualified for the World Cup.

Subsequent competitions have been held in England in 1982 and 1986, with the winners Zimbabwe on both occasions qualifying for the following year's World Cup.

COMPETITION FIRSTS:

Century: David Houghton 135 for Zimbabwe v USA at Moseley, and Winston Reid, 128, Bermuda v Malaysia at Wednesbury, both on 16 June 1982.

Individual innings over 150: Ronald Elferink 154 not out, Holland v Fiji at Hinckley, 28 June 1982.

200 stand: David Houghton and Kevin Curran 212, Zimbabwe v USA, Moseley, 16 June 1982.

Five wickets in an innings: L. Young 5–44 for Singapore v Argentina, Pickwick, 22 May 1979.

Seven wickets in an innings: Syed Ashraful Haq 7–23 for Bangladesh v Fiji, Water Orton, 24 May 1979.

Score over 300: Sri Lanka 318–8 v Denmark (110) in semi-final at Mitchell's & Butler's, Birmingham, 6 June 1979.

Score over 400: Bermuda 407–8 v Hong Kong (180–6), Nuneaton, 13 June 1986.

Score over 450: Papua New Guinea 455–9 v Gibraltar (86), Rugeley, 18 June 1986.

Match aggregate over 500: 588 in 1979 final (see above).

Match aggregate over 600: 623, Canada 356–5 beat Papua New Guinea 267–9 by 89 runs, Walsall, 16 June 1986.

Match aggregate under 100: Canada 48–0 in 23 balls beat Gibraltar 46 in 25.5 overs, Swindon, 20 June 1986.

WORLD YOUTH CUP

The inaugural World Youth Cup was contested by teams of players under 20 at 50 overs a side matches in Australia, February–March 1988. Eight teams took part: the seven Test playing nations plus a composite team from the ICC Associates. Australia 202–5 (Brett Williams 108) beat Pakistan 201 in the final at Adelaide Oval, 13 Mar 1988.

OLYMPIC GAMES

Cricket had been an early sporting enthusiasm of the founder of the modern Olympic Games, Baron Pierre de Coubertin, and was an intended Olympic sport from the outset. It had been in the original schedule of events for the first Games in Athens, but was not included in 1896 due to lack of entries. It was included at the Paris Games of 1900, when one match was played at Vincennes. Devon County Wanderers (117 and 145–5) beat All-Paris (78 and 26) by 158 runs on 19–20 August. For the winners the highest innings was 59 by Alfred Bowerman, while Montagu Toller skittled the French by taking seven very cheap wickets, all bowled, in the second innings.

OTHER COUNTRIES

EAST AFRICA

The first **cricket match** recorded in Kenya was played in Mombasa in 1899, the East African Protectorate v 'The Rest of the World'. The first first-class match in **East Africa** was played in Kampala, **Uganda** when a visiting MCC team, captained by Mike Smith, to Kenya, Uganda and Tanganyika beat an East African Invitational XI by an innings and 71 runs on 2–4 Nov 1963. The following year East Africa played the first first-class match in **Kenya**, at Mombasa on 18–20 July 1964 against Pakistan International Airlines. Kenya first played Tanganyika in 1951 and Uganda in 1952, and from 1966 a quadrangular tournament was contested by nations in the area.

The first **father and son to play in World Cup matches** were the Pringles. Don Pringle, who captained Kenya, played for East Africa in 1975, and his son Derek made his England debut in 1979.

DENMARK AND HOLLAND

These have been the two European continental nations to take most interest in cricket. Cricket was possibly played in **Denmark** from early in the 19th century, but the first recorded match was at Randers in Jutland in 1865. Cricket was recognised by the Danish Ball Games Union from 1890, but the Danish Cricket Association was not formed until 1953.

The first international played by Denmark, as recognised by the Danish Cricket Association, was against Sir Julien Cahn's touring team in 1932.

The first reference to cricket in the **Netherlands** was in 1845 and the Nederlandse Cricket Bond was founded on 30 Sep 1883. Leagues were started in 1891, in which year a representative Dutch team played for the first time, against a touring team, the Rambling Britons.

The first of the **continental 'Tests'**, Denmark v Holland, was played at The Hague on 20–21 Aug 1955. The match was drawn: Holland 207 and 1925 dec, Denmark 243 and 47–3. Bowling firsts in this series: **five wickets in innings**: Max Maas (Hol) 5–18 in Denmark's 85 at Amsterdam, 25 July 1959; **ten wickets in match**: Wandert Pierhagen (Hol), aged 18, 7–22 and 7–47 at Amsterdam, 20–21 July 1963. Holland dominated for several years, and Denmark's first win in the series was in 1972.

The first **victory achieved by a continental team over a Test playing nation** was Holland's three wicket victory in a one innings game over the Australians (197) at The Hague on 29 Aug 1964.

FIJI

Cricket in the Fijian islands was first recorded as being played in 1874. The game has long been popular in Fiji, and the first Fijian touring team was to New Zealand in 1895, where first-class matches were played. That team was organised by the Attorney-General John Udal, who had played for the MCC in 1871–4.

NORTH AMERICA

The first mentions of cricket in America were recorded in the diary of William Byrd the younger of Westover, Virginia on 25 Apr 1709 and subsequently. His first cricket entry noted, '. . . we played at Cricket, Mr W–l–s and John Custis against me and Mr Hawkins, but we were beaten'. Later there were references to 3- and 4-a-side cricket matches, but although the diary was continued for several years, cricket is mentioned only in 1709 and 1710, and he seems to have lost interest thereafter, although he chronicles visits to England. Byrd, although born in Westover, was educated at Felsted School in England and entered the Middle Temple. He returned to Virginia in 1705, and in 1708 was appointed to the Virginia Council of State, remaining a member until his death. Byrd was a close relative of the well known early cricketer Samuel Filmer (qv).

The first **match to be played by 'international' teams** was on 1 May 1751 when the New Yorkers (80 and 86) beat Londoners (43 and 47) by 76 runs in New York. It was played 'according to the London method', presumably referring to the Laws drawn up in 1744.

The first reference to **cricket in Canada** was at Île Ste-Hélène, Montreal in 1785, when some French Canadians were reportedly in trouble for playing on a Sunday. The first actual match was Toronto v Guelph at Hamilton, Ontario in 1834.

USA v CANADA

The first **series of international matches** anywhere in the world was that between the USA and Canada. The series originated with a match on 24–26 Sep 1844 played for a stake of 1000 dollars at the Bloomingdale Road ground, New York. The US team, actually that of St George's Club, New York, beat the Canadians; the game had occurred as a result of a challenge from Toronto CC, following a game played four years earlier when St George's had visited Toronto and beaten the Canadian team by ten wickets. The international series between the USA and Canada was played fairly regularly until 1912, was officially revived in 1963, played annually until 1980 and now biennially.

TOURS AND FIRST-CLASS MATCHES

The first **overseas tour undertaken by an English team** was that organised by William Pickering and captained by George Parr of Notts to North America in 1859. Pickering was a former Cambridge and Surrey cricketer who had emigrated to Canada, where he became secretary of the Ontario Cricket Association. The 12-man team won all their matches with fair comfort from the first match played against 22 of Lower Canada at Montreal on 24, 26 Sep 1859. They also played 22-man teams from Upper Canada, the USA and a combined USA and Canada team.

Opposite *The intrepid members of the England party which set sail for North America on 7 September 1859. Back: R. P. Carpenter, W. Caffyn, T. Lockyer. Middle: John Wisden, H. H. Stephenson, G. Parr (Capt), J. Grundy, Julius Caesar, T. Hayward, J. Jackson. Front: A. J. D. Diver, John Lillywhite.*

The second Philadelphians in England under Dan Newhall; the purely amateur team handed over its share of the gate receipts to charity.

Cricket was most popular in Canada and the USA in the second half of the 19th century, and the Philadelphians were particularly renowned. Their game on 3–5 Oct 1878 at Nicetown against the visiting Australian team under Dave Gregory was arguably the first **first-class match in the USA**. Scores: Philadelphians 196 (Francis Allan 6–27) and 53 (Fred Spofforth 5–24, Allan 5–23), Australians 150 (C. A. Newhall 5–67) and 51–4.

The first **visit by the Philadelphians to England** was in 1884, and they played first-class matches for the first time on their visit in 1897 when their great fast bowler Bart King achieved notable success, which he capped with 87 wickets av. 11.01 in first-class matches on the Philadelphians' last visit in 1908. He was the first, and only, **American to top the English first-class averages**. In the equivalent of first-class matches, the first **score of over 500 in the USA** was Philadelphia's 525 v Australian tourists at Belmont, Philadelphia on 29–30 Sep, 2 Oct 1893. The first over **600** was George Patterson's XI's 689 v A. M. Wood's XI at Elmwood, Philadelphia on 21–22 Aug 1894. Patterson himself scored 271, the first **double century** in such a match.

The first match which can be regarded as **first-class in Canada**, was when a Combined Canada/United States team played the Australian tourists at Toronto on 22–23, 25 Aug 1913. Charles Macartney scored the first first-class **century** in Canada, with 186 in 4 hours with 20 fours in Australia's 402. No match in Canada has actually been played as a first-class match, as recognition for the above was retrospective and Canada v MCC at Toronto on 8–10 Sep 1951, which MCC won by 141 runs, was ruled first-class two months later.

INDIVIDUAL FIRSTS

The first known **century** in the USA was 120 by J. Turner for Union v St Georges at Camden, New Jersey in 1844. The first in Canada was 106 by M. B. Daly in Halifax, Nova Scotia in 1858.

The first **double century** in Canada was 202 by R. Liesk for Hamilton v Montreal at Montreal

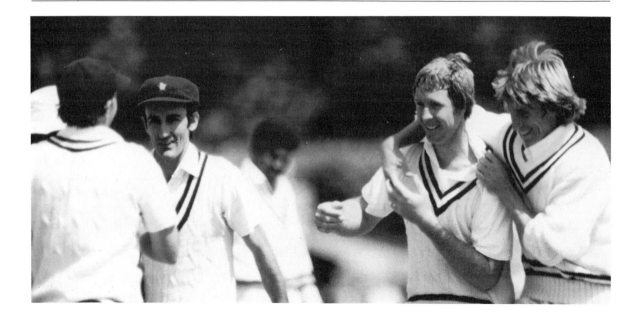

in 1877, and the first in the USA 264 not out by W. H. Massie for Orlando v the American CC in Florida in 1887.

The first **triple century** was made by Bart King, 315 for Belmont v Germantown B in Philadelphia in 1905. The following year he scored 344 v Merion B, still an American best.

The first **'all-ten'** was by H. J. Maddock, 10–16 for Toronto v the Rifle Brigade in 1848, and J. Cuddahy was the first in the USA in a club match in New York in 1888. Bart King became the first to clean bowl all ten, for Philadelphia v Irish Gentlemen in Philadelphia in 1909.

The first **'perfect tie'** anywhere occurred at Upper Brockton Point, Vancouver when both Burrard and Rowing Club made 102 all out in 169 balls and 96 minutes in 1950.

SOUTH AMERICA

Cricket was particularly popular in **Argentina**, where there is evidence of cricket being played as early as 1806.

The first **MCC team** to tour Argentina was in 1912, when Lord Hawke's team played three 'Tests', losing the first at Hurlingham on 18–20 February by four wickets, but winning the other two on a nine-match tour. These 'Tests' were the first first-class matches played in Argentina.

Argentina's first match against another country was against **Uruguay** in 1868, while the first officially recognised international between South American nations was played at Vina del Mar in December 1920, when Argentina beat **Chile** by seven wickets. Argentina then first played **Brazil** in 1921, and the first international **double century** in South America came in the 1922, 226 by James Paul for Argentina v Chile.

In 1932 a **South American** team, led by C. H. Gibson, with players from Argentina, Brazil and Chile toured England, their games including six with first-class status.

ZIMBABWE

The first recorded match in Rhodesia (now Zimbabwe) was played near Fort Victoria, at a town now known as Masvingo on 16 Aug 1890. Rhodesia's first first-class game was in the Currie Cup, v Transvaal at Johannesburg on 15–16 Mar 1905, but they did not play at home and did not re-enter the Currie Cup until 1929–30.

First-class cricket was first played in Rhodesia on 22–24 Mar 1910 when H. D. G. Leveson-Gower and three of his MCC team to South Africa 1909–10 joined forces with seven South Africans to beat Rhodesia by an innings and 120 runs at the Queen's Ground, Bulawayo. Rhodesia last competed in the Currie Cup in 1980, in which year, as Zimbabwe, they gained independence. Zimbabwe has won the ICC Trophy on both occasions that they have competed, in 1982 and 1986, without losing a match. It achieved its first **full international victory** with a win over Australia in the World Cup at Trent Bridge on 9 June 1983.

Opposite *Zimbabwe celebrate victory over Australia at Nottingham World Cup 1983.*

WORLD SERIES CRICKET

Arising out of a dispute between Kerry Packer's commercial TV company, Channel Nine, and the Australian Board of Control, World Series Cricket (WSC) was run by Mr Packer's company in Australia in 1977–78 and in 1978–79, when matches were also played in New Zealand and the West Indies.

JP Sport Pty Ltd (name changed to World Series Cricket Pty in July 1977) was formed in April 1977 and within a couple of weeks it was announced that they had signed up 35 leading cricketers, including most of the Australian Test team, to play a series of one-day matches in the Australian summer. As these would conflict with established tours the ICC initiated discussions with Mr Packer, but these failed so that the ICC issued an ultimatum stating that any player who appeared in unrecognised matches would render himself ineligible for Test cricket. This led to the first **High Court action concerning Test cricket**: the ICC and the TCCB against World Series Cricket and three leading players: Tony Greig, John Snow and Mike Procter, which started in London on 26 Sep 1977. The case lasted until 7 November, and was lost by the cricket authorities, Mr Justice Slade declaring that the proposed bans on players by the ICC from Tests, and the TCCB from English domestic cricket, were an unreasonable restraint of trade.

The first **WSC match** was a one-innings game played over two days, 16–17 Nov 1977 at Moorabbin, Victoria when Ian Chappell's XI (273–9) beat Richie Robinson's XI (271), for whom Ian Davis scored the first 'Packer' century with 124.

The first **WSC 'Super-Test'** was contested by teams from Australia and the West Indies at the VFL (Victorian Football League) Stadium, Melbourne, 2–4 Dec 1977. The West Indians 214 and 237–7 beat the Australians 256 and 192 by three wickets.

In the third match of the series, at Football Park, Adelaide on 31 Dec 1977, 2–4 Jan 1978, Ian Chappell, the Australian captain, scored the first **century**, 141, and his brother Greg, with 5–20 in the West Indians' first innings of 145, became the first to take **five wickets in an innings** in a WSC Super-Test. For West Indies Viv Richards replied with 123 in the second innings, and he scored another century (119), the first for the 'World XI', which played in a Super-Test for the first time at the Showground, Sydney v the WSC Australia XI on 14–19 Jan 1978. Their team was composed of six West Indians, three English Test players and two South Africans. In their first innings of 290 Max Walker became the first bowler to take **seven wickets in a Super-Test innings**, 7–88.

The first WSC **double century** was by Barry Richards, 207 in the first **score over 500**, 625 by WSC World XI v WSC Australian XI at Gloucester Park, Perth, 27–30 Jan 1978. The World XI's **innings victory** was also a first in this series.

The first bowler to take **ten wickets in a WSC Super-Test** was Dennis Lillee, 7–59 and 5–30 for WSC Australia v WSC World XI in their first match in New Zealand, at Auckland on 4–6 Nov 1978. The World XI's second innings score of 85 was the first **under 100**. The VFL Stadium, Melbourne staged the first important **cricket match to be played under floodlights** on 14 Dec 1977, when an Australian XI (210–4) beat a World XI (207) by six wickets in a 40 overs-a-side match. A **white ball** was used against a black sightscreen when the floodlights were switched on at 6.30 p.m. in the game which commenced at 2.30 p.m.

After much controversy and ill-feeling in the game, reconciliation was reached in May 1979 when Packer's company, PBL Sports Pty Ltd. was granted exclusive promotion rights to all matches arranged by the Australian Cricket Board in a ten-year agreement. In all 66 cricketers had played with WSC: 28 Australians, 18 West Indians, 8 from Pakistan, 6 England, 5 South Africa and 1 New Zealand.

The first player to **score over 1000 runs in WSC internationals** was Greg Chappell, who in all scored 1426 av. 54.85, and the first to take over **50 wickets** was Dennis Lillee, who had a total of 67 av. 26.86, both in 14 matches.

MISCELLANY

Cyril Washbrook drives Frank Worrell to the boundary in 1950. In 1956 the Lancashire stalwart and England selector made a dramatic and successful return to the Test scene, aged 41.

BENEFITS

The *Derby Advertiser* of 18 July 1744 announced a forthcoming fixture on Kennington Common in which the losing side's stakes were to be 'applied for the benefit of a distressed undertaker'. This was the first mention of a **benefit match**.

The first **benefit match in the County Championship** was that played for the benefit of Nottinghamshire professional Fred Wild, between Notts and Lancashire at Trent Bridge, 23–25 June 1890.

The first cricketer to receive **£2000** from his benefit was Bobby Peel of Yorkshire with exactly that in 1894, the first over **£3000** was George Hirst of Yorkshire with £3703 in 1904 (worth well into six figures nowadays), and the first to top **£10000** was Cyril Washbrook with £14000 in 1948, when his benefit match was Lancashire v Australians at Old Trafford.

Nowadays benefits are earned from fund-raising activities throughout a year, and the first to exceed **£50000** was Barry Wood (Lancashire), £62429 in 1979, **£100000:** Jack Simmons (Lancashire) £128000 in 1980, and **£150000:** Graham Gooch (Essex) with £153906 in 1985.

The first **Australian benefit** was for Richard Coulstock at Melbourne in the 1857–58 season, and the first Australian to be given a first-class match for his benefit was Jim Kelly, New South Wales v Australia at Sydney in 1905–06, which raised £1400.

BROADCASTING

The first **radio commentary** on cricket was by Lionel Watt on a testimonial match for Charles Bannerman played by New South Wales cricketers at Sydney Cricket Ground in November 1922.

Men at work stitching cricket balls at A. Reader's factory, Maidstone, Kent in 1936. They were all hand stitched.

Radio commentary in Britain on the **BBC** started in 1927 with the first commentator Pelham Warner (followed by Revd. Frank Gillingham) on the Essex v New Zealand match at Leyton on 14 May. **Ball-by-ball commentaries** in England were started in 1957.

The first **television broadcast** of cricket in England was by the BBC on 24 June 1938 of the Second Test against Australia at Lord's with commentator Teddy Wakelam.

The first cricketer to be elected **BBC Sports Personality of the Year** was Jim Laker in 1956, the year in which he took a record 46 wickets in the Test series against Australia including 19 wickets in the Test at Old Trafford. The first cricketer to win the **Australian Broadcasting Company's Sportsman of the Year** award was Richie Benaud in 1961. Interestingly, both became leading TV commentators.

EQUIPMENT AND GROUNDS

BATS AND BALLS

The **bat** was first mentioned in 1611 in *A Dictionarie of the French and English Tongues* by Randle Cotgrave, published by Adam Islip. The French word 'crosse' is defined as 'a Cricket-staffe; or, the crooked staffe wherewith boyes play at cricket'.

The term 'cricket bat' first occurred in the Easter bills of presentment of Boxgrove, Sussex when, on 5 May 1622 'a little childe had like to have her braynes beaten out with a cricket bat'. The first limitation on the width of the bat, 4¼ inches which remains to this day, was imposed in 1771, allegedly after Thomas White came to the wickets with a bat as wide as the stumps.

The **spring-handled bat**, invented by a Salisbury cutler, W. Beach, was first regularly employed by the Somerton Club in 1840, when during an extended trial it was found to be capable of driving the ball to a greater distance than usual with very little exertion on behalf of the striker, and 'entirely free from the unpleasant jar to the hand to which even the best poised bats are at some times subject'. The spring was a steel bar set into the handle. The earliest commercially produced spring-handled bats, advertised by E. & W. Page of Kennington in 1845, had whalebone springs. The first rubber-sprung handles appeared *c.* 1884.

The earliest specific reference to a **cricket ball** was in *The Mysteries of Love and Eloquence* by John Milton's nephew Edward Phillips. This was printed for N. Brooks at The Angel, Cornhill, London in 1658. A character exclaims: 'Would my eyes had been beat out of my head with a cricket-ball, the day before I saw thee!' The weight of the ball was first defined in the 1744 code: 'The ball must weigh not less than five ounces and a half, not more than five ounces and three quarters.'

The first reference to a **red cricket ball** was in

The England players of 1847 as seen by 'Felix'.
From left: W. Dennison, Wm. Clarke, W. Martingell,
F. Pilch, F. Lillywhite, G. Parr, 'Felix', J. Guy,
W. Hillyer, O. C. Pell, W. Dorrinton, A. Mynn,
T. Sewell, J. Dean.

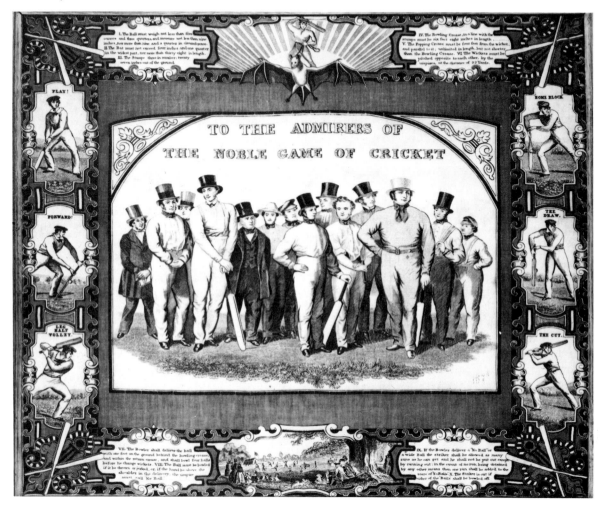

William Harrod's 1753 *Sevenoke—a Poem:* 'From nervous arm, with force impulsive, see the crimson ball attack the destin'd mark.'

Provision for the use of a **new ball** during the course of a match was first introduced into the Laws in the 1798 revision: 'At the beginning of each innings either party may call for a new ball.' The poet John Keats was hit over the eye by a **white cricket ball** while trying to bat in 1819. It was in fact merely a soft practice ball, and the first genuine white cricket balls were introduced for floodlit matches in Kerry Packer's World Series cricket (qv) in 1977.

The earliest **bowling machine** for propelling the ball to a batsman for practice was invented in 1837 by Nicholas Wanostrocht (known as Felix), the Kent, Surrey and All-England cricketer. Called the Catapulta, it was inspired by the ancient Ballista siege weapon, an arrangement of straps and springs working a rubber-headed arm which struck the ball towards the wicket from an elevated position just in front of the machine. It could be adjusted to provide balls of different speed and length. An improved version appeared in 1862 under the trade name Balista.

A **fielding machine** was marketed in 1880 as 'The Fag'. It was a mechanical contraption for returning balls to the bowler while practising in the nets, and was claimed to deal equally well with shooters and with balls striking the stumps.

Opposite below *This batsman—c. 1840—shows a nice line in modern-looking pads.*

STUMPS

Stumps were first referred to as forked sticks supporting the cross-stick, or bail, in A. Littleton's *Latine Dictionary* in 1678. In this book vibia is defined as 'a pole or stick laid across on forks, like the cricket-bar at ball-play'. In cricket the actual word **'bail'** is not documented until 1744 when James Love's *Cricket—An Heroic Poem* alluded to 'the bail, and mangled stumps', scattered across the field after being hit by a delivery from a fast bowler. This poem also made the first reference to **all-white attire** for cricket teams: the players were 'in decent white, most gracefully array'd'.

The **third stump** was introduced in the 1770s, probably simply to stop matches lasting too long. The first recorded match with a wicket of three stumps was Chertsey v Coulsdon at Laleham Burway, near Chertsey on 6 Sep 1776.

The first definite mention of a cricket **wicket** appeared in 1695 in *Parochial Antiques* by W. Kennett. This defined the word Salicetum as 'the wicket or cross stick to be thrown down by the ball at the game call'd crickets'.

PROTECTIVE CLOTHING

Batsmen commenced wearing **padded gloves** at times, especially for protection against fast bowling *c.* 1818. William Henry Caldecourt of London first marketed an 'india-rubber padded glove' in 1842. The first designed **wicket-keeping gloves** were advertised for sale in 1848 by Duke & Son of Penshurst, Kent as 'gauntlets'. Previously, wicket-keepers had sometimes worn ordinary leather gloves in an attempt to protect their hands.

The first definite use of modern-style **pads** was when they were worn by batsmen in the Sussex v England match at Brighton in 1839. They were advertised for sale—as knee-pads—by the London Toy Repository in 1843. Some 40 years earlier, however, Robert Robinson had made his own 'pads', 'two thin boards set angle-wise to guard his shin, off which the ball went with great noise, but being laughed at, he discontinued them'. Robinson, a left-handed batsman, played under the handicap of having only three good fingers on his right hand. In his early years he was engaged at Hambledon and later played for Hampshire and Surrey before finishing his career in minor matches in Norfolk shortly before his death.

The first public display of **cricketing goods** was at the Great Exhibition opened by Queen Victoria in Hyde Park, London on 1 May 1851. Bats, balls, pads, batting and wicket-keeping gloves, protectors, stumps and spiked soles were shown under class 29 in the north-east gallery. The building which housed the exhibition, the Crystal Palace, had, incidentally been designed by a cricketer, Joseph Paxton, who had captained the Gardeners XI v Chatsworth House XI in 1833! The first **protectors** were sold by Robert Dark of Lord's, and one was put on show in this exhibition. They were described as 'a newly invented body guard which can be worn under the dress without being perceived' and 'so completely protects the person from injury, that the most timid can play without fear'.

A cricket **blazer**, the 'nonpareil cricketing jacket' was advertised in 1856 by Edwin Ade of London. It was made of thin material 'cut on an entirely new and scientific principle', which could be tucked into the trousers to form a shirt, worn outside with a belt as an old-fashioned cricket jacket, or outside loose without a belt as a blazer-style jacket.

Patsy Hendren wore a **protective cap**, designed by his wife, containing extra thick padding of sponge rubber and with two extra peaks covering his ears and temples, as he claimed he needed extra protection against the persistently short-pitched bowling of the West Indians for the MCC at Lord's on 22 May 1933. In the late 1970s Mike Brearley of Middlesex and England sometimes wore a specially made padded cap, but in 1978 a properly designed hard **helmet** was introduced into first-class cricket by the Warwickshire and England batsman Dennis Amiss. Modifications of this are now used almost universally in most grades of cricket.

*The first **postage stamp** to depict a cricket scene was issued by the Cape Verde Islands on 18 Jan 1962, a 1.50 escudo value; the first by a cricket-playing nation was a 40 paisa stamp, depicting bat, ball and the Ayub trophy by Pakistan on 14 Aug 1962.*

Incidentally part of Albert Park, Suva, which is the main cricket ground in Fiji, can be seen on a Fiji 2d stamp showing government offices, issued on 19 May 1942.

*The first **cricketer to be specifically depicted on a postage stamp** was Garfield Sobers, on a 35 cent stamp issued by Barbados on 2 Dec 1966, one of a set of four stamps issued to commemorate the island's independence. The first British cricket stamps were a set of three depicting cartoons of W. G. Grace, to commemorate 100 years of county cricket 1873–1973, issued on 16 May 1973.*

*Earlier than official postage stamps, however, cricket (a batsman) was one of six sports depicted on **local labels** issued by the Fussball-Klub Nürnberg, Germany c. 1908.*

UMPIRES AND SCORERS

The first **full description of a cricket match** appeared in the Latin poem 'In Certamen Pilae' by William Goldwin in *Musae Juveniles*, published in 1706. Goldwin, educated at Eton and King's College, Cambridge, made the first reference to cricket **umpires** in this poem, describing them as the 'moderatores' who stood propped on their bats, and to scorers, sitting on a low mound where they recorded the runs by cutting notches on a stick.

The first mention of the actual word 'umpire' in cricket was in articles drawn up between the 2nd Duke of Richmond and Alan Brodrick in 1727. These authorised that there should be 'one umpire of each side' and that 'the Duke of Richmond's umpire shall pitch the wickets when they play in Sussex; and Mr Brodrick's when they play in Surrey'.

CRICKET GROUNDS

The earliest recorded **boundaries** were on Kennington Common when for London v Sevenoaks on 12 July 1731 it was announced that 'the

An engraving of a now lost painting by Francis Hayman, showing cricket in about 1743 'as played in the Artillery Ground, London'—therefore not necessarily on that ground. Contemporary references to the Artillery ground, which mention a wall confirm that it could not possibly be an accurate representation.

The GAME *at* CRICKET *as playd in the* ARTILLARY *Ground* LONDON.

ground will be roped around and all persons are desired to keep without side of the same'.

The first **ground laid out primarily for cricket** was apparently one at Deptford called 'Mr Siddle's new cricket-ground', where a combined team representing Deptford and Greenwich opposed London on 23 Aug 1748. This was probably the field behind the Fountain Inn, scene of other matches in the middle of the 18th century. The first genuine **cricket ground to be properly enclosed** was the original Lord's ground opened by Thomas Lord in May 1787.

The first recorded **attendance of more than 1000** was for Kent v a Sussex, Surrey and Hampshire Combined XI in Penshurst Park on 28 Aug 1729.

Admission was first charged, at 2d (or 0.8 of a 'new' penny), in 1744 at the Artillery Ground, near Finsbury Square, London, the training ground leased by the Honourable Artillery Company from the City of London. There the earliest known **tickets** were issued, for readmission to the ground during Kent v England on 18 June

1744. The first **stand** erected for people to watch cricket from was probably the 'very good stand with benches above one another' put up by the landlord of the White Hart Inn for Kent v Hampshire at Guildford, 23–24 July 1772.

Nets were first employed for practice at Chislehurst by the Kent amateur Charles Harenc c. 1830. He bowled at a wicket with a large net spread behind. The balls were retrieved by his groom.

Pitch covers were first introduced at Lord's and tarpaulins at Prince's in 1872, 23 years after they had originally been suggested in a letter to a newspaper in 1849.

The first **printed score-cards** were those for Hampshire v Kent at Broadhalfpenny Down, Hambledon on 3–5 July 1776, advertised in a Kentish newspaper a few days before the match as being on sale at 1d from T. Pratt, Kent scorer, at the Printing Office, Sevenoaks. They were described as 'a list of gentlemen cricketers who finished playing at Broadhalfpenny, July 5, with the state of the game'. Scorecards for the next

CRICKET.

A GRAND MATCH WILL BE PLAYED

In LORD's NEW Cricket Ground,

St. JOHN's WOOD MARY-LE-BONE,

On TUESDAY, JUNE the 20th. 1815, and the following day
between TWO SELECT ELEVENS of all ENGLAND.

For One Thousand Guineas a Side.

The WICKETS to be Pitched at ELEVEN o'Clock

PLAYERS,

LORD F. BEAUCLERK	Sir T. JONES Bart.
Hon. D. KINNAIRD	G. OSBALDESTON Efq.
T. MELLISH Efq.	E. H. BUDD Efq.
C. MITFORD Efq.	J. PAULETT Efq.
— BRAND Efq.	W. WARD Efq.
— HOWARD	J TANNER Efq.
— HAMMOND	A. SHABNER Efq.
— BELDHAM	— LAMBERT
Jas. SHERMAN	H. BENTLEY
J. WELLS Junr.	J. BENNETT
B. DARK.	— SMALL.

ADMITTANCE SIX PENCE, GOOD STABLING on the GROUND.
The Cricket Laws, BATS, BALLS, and STUMPS to be had at the Ground or at Mr. LORD's
HOUSE in Upper Glofter Street,— the nearest Carriage way is along the New Road through
Upper Baker-Street or the Road oppofite Mary le-bone Work-house NO DOGS ADMITTED.
— A MARQUEE to be Let, or SOLD. will Hold 100 PERSONS.

Craft, Printer, Welh-Street, Oxford-Street.

A handbill for a 'grand' match at Lord's new ground in 1815— the year of Waterloo.

Below *The oldest cricket score book, showing the first innings, Oxford v Cambridge 1829.*

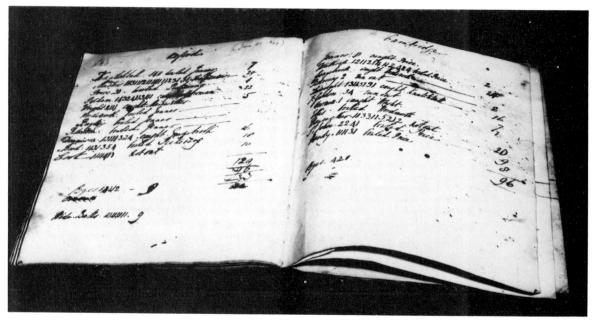

Below A hundred players of such standard would probably have lost the match for Norfolk! 'Quantity, not quality'.

A GRAND CRICKET MATCH, Play'd between Eleven Men of all ENGLAND, against Thirty-three of the County of NORFOLK,

On SWAFHAM RACE GROUND, Monday July 17th, 1797. and two following Days.

For FIVE HUNDRED GUINEAS.

c ftands for *catch't out*. b. ftands for *bowl'd out*. and s. for *ftump'd out*,

NORFOLK,	No. of Notches. First Innings.		No. of Notches. Second Innings.	
Mr. Brown,	6	b, T. Walker,	0	s, Hammond,
Sculfer,	1	run out,	2	c, H. Walker,
M. Raven,	3	c, Fennex,	1	c, ditto,
Harmer,	0	c, Hammond,	9	b, Lord Beauc
James Fuller,	7	c, Lord Beauclerk,	0	b, ditto,
Jackfon,	1	c, Freemantle,	0	b, ditto,
Stibbard.	0	s, Hammond,	9	b, Fennex,
Rev'd. Mr. Allen,	5	b, Wells,	2	b, ditto,
John Fuller,	6	c, Beldam,	1	ran out,
Archer,	9	b, Wells,	9	b, Wells,
R. Raven,	0	c, H. Walker,	2	b, Lord Beauclerk,
Cock,	1	b, Lord Beauclerk,	7	c, ditto,
James Withers,	0	c, Hammond,	0	b, Wells,
Brooks,	0	b, Wells,	0	s, Hammond,
Ruft,	1	c, Beldam,	3	b, Wells,
G. Withers.	0	c, ditto,	4	s, Hammond,
Bayfield Fuller,	0	c, Hammond.	0	c, Wells,
Rayner,	0	b, Lord Beauclerk,	0	c, H. Walker,
Curtis,	0	c. Small,	8	c, Fennex,
Rumbal,	0	c, Fennex,	0	b, ditto,
Bennet,	0	c, Hammond,	3	s, Hammond,
Ulph,	0	b, Lord Beauclerk,	0	c. ditto,
Sturley,	1	b. Wells,	0	b, Fennex,
Paul,	2	s, Hammond,	0	b, Lord Beauclerk,
Scott,	0	c, Lord Beauclerk,	0	c, H. Walker.
Watlin,	0	c, Beldam,	1	leg before wicket,
Milligan,	6	b, Lord Beauclerk,	0	b, Wells,
Mitchel,	0	b, Lord Beauclerk,	14	leg before wicket,
Ben. Fuller,	1	c, H. Walker,	0	b, Wells,
Lafcock,	0	not out	0	c, Small,
Cuthing,	0	run out	0	c, Wells,
Emerfon,	0	b, Lord Beauclerk,	0	c, Fennex,
Warner,	0	b, ditto,	1	not out.
Bye runs	0	Bye runs,	5	
	50		81	Total 131

ALL ENGLAND.				
Mr. T. Walker,	55	c, Scott,		
Fennex,	4	b, Millgan,		
Small,	2	c, Sculfer,		
Freemantle,	4	b, G. Withers,		
Robinfon,	2	c, Rayner,		
Lord Beauclerk,	39	c, Emerfon,		
Hon. T. Tufton,	19	c, Archer,		
Hammond,	10	c, J. Fuller,		
Beldam,	6	not out,		
H. Walker,	0	b, Ben. Fuller,		
Wells,	3	c, Warner		
Bye runs	0			
	144			

All England won at One Innings. by 12 runs.

The youthful Eric (left) and Alec Bedser—the best of more than a score of pairs of twins in first-class cricket. The first were probably Edward and George Ede who played for Hampshire in the 1860s.

match, between the Duke of Dorset's Kent side and Hampshire at Sevenoaks Vine on 15–17 July were on sale from the Printing Office within half an hour of the finish. Score-cards exist for matches before 1776, but although reproduced as genuine in some books they are in fact modern fakes, based on a collection of old scores published in 1862.

A **score-board**, described simply as 'the board' was first installed at Lord's for MCC v Sussex, 29–30 June 1846.

The first **score-box** was probably the one put up for Kent v England at the St Laurence ground, Canterbury on 2–4 Aug 1847: 'a stand for the scorers, who were thus out of reach of pestering'. Previously, the scorers had sat either on the ground or at a table placed near the boundary.

FAMILIES

The first **brothers to play together in a first-class match** were Richard, Adam and John Newland, all members of the England team which played Kent at the Artillery Ground, 18 June 1744. Richard was the captain of the England team, which lost the match by one wicket.

John Small, Snr, and John Small, Jnr, played their first first-class or 'great' match together for Hampshire against England at Sevenoaks Vine, 1–2 June 1784—the first instance traced of **father and son appearing together** in so important a cricket match.

Lord John Philip Sackville, who played much 'first-class' or 'great' cricket for Kent in the 1730s and 1740s was **grandfather** of the Hon. John Tufton and the Hon. Henry Tufton, who played much first-class cricket, mainly for MCC teams, from 1793 to 1801. It is interesting, though not entirely relevant, that the Hon. J. S. R. Tufton, who played for Kent and MCC 1897-9, was a great-grandson of the Hon. Henry Tufton through an illicit relationship between Henry and a French whore while Henry was imprisoned in France during the Napoleonic War. Thus from Lord J. P. Sackville to the Hon. J. S. R. Tufton we have, surely, the first case of a great-great-great grandfather and grandson playing first-class cricket, with an interval of more than 160 years.

RIOTS

The earliest notice of a **riot linked with cricket** was on 6 June 1693. According to an entry in the *Calendar of Treasury Books* Thomas Reynolds, Henry Gunter and Elenor Lansford (widow) petitioned Queen Mary to remit fines set on them for riot and battery against one Ralph Thurston in Sussex, 'they being only spectators at a game of cricket'.

The Riot Act was read on 10 Sep 1726 at a cricket match in Writtle, Essex on the authority of a magistrate 'obsessed with the idea that such games as cricket etc. were only pretences to collect a crowd of disaffected people in order to raise a rebellion'.

The first instance of **crowd trouble halting play** was during a women's match between Charlton and Westdean & Chilgrove (Sussex) at the Artillery Ground, London on 13 July 1747. 'The company broke in, so that it was impossible for the game to be played out.' Some of the women were 'very much frightened, and others hurt' and the game had to be completed the following day.

The first **'great' match postponed due to serious crowd disturbances** was that between Surrey and Dartford at the Artillery Ground on 9 Aug 1765, in front of nearly 12 000 people: 'the mob (many of whom had laid large bets), imagining foul play,' began to riot, 'and several were dangerously wounded and bruised'. The players left the field but they resumed the next day and Surrey won the match.

The first match known to have been **abandoned because of fighting between the players** was Surrey v Kent at Carshalton on 19 July 1762. 'This match ended abruptly owing to a dispute about one of the players being catched out, when Surrey was 50 a-head the first innings; from words, they came to blows, which occasioned several broken heads, as likewise a challenge between two persons of distinction; the confusion was so great that the betts were all withdrawn.'

The first **religious riot** at a cricket match occurred when the Secular Club met a scratch team on the council ground at Leicester on Sunday, 21 June 1885. The wickets were stormed by a Christian mob which threatened to throw the players into the nearby river. Wickets were then set up on the other side of the ground and while one set was captured and disposed of by the mob play was restarted and carried on 'with vigour' with the other set. Finally the crowd attacked the other set and play had to be abandoned.

Several Test matches, particularly in the West Indies, have been interrupted by rioting, but the third and final Test of the 1968–69 series between Pakistan and England at Karachi became the first **Test match to be abandoned because of rioting** by the spectators. Due to take place from 6–10 Mar 1969, the match was called off before lunch on the third day with England 502-7 in their first innings. The trouble, mainly sparked off by students, was political and had nothing to do with England or the cricket.

NO-BALLED FOR THROWING

John Willes was **no-balled for throwing** when he bowled round-arm for Kent v MCC in 1822. He was so incensed by the umpire's decision that he vowed never to play again.

The first bowler to be **no-balled for throwing in a Test match** was the Australian fast bowler Ernest Jones at Melbourne against England in the second Test, 1–5 Jan 1898, by umpire Jim Phillips. Concentrating thereafter on greater control, Jones continued to play for Australia, making 19 Test appearances in all until 1903.

The first English bowler to be no-balled in a Test match was Tony Lock, in the second innings against West Indies in the first Test at Sabina Park, Kingston, Jamaica on 19 Jan 1954, by umpire Perry Burke when he delivered his 'quick one' to Gerry Gomez, just after he had bowled the great Jamaican idol George Headley (for 1 in his last Test innings) with a similar ball. Lock had previously been no-balled for Surrey in 1952, three times in a match v Indians and was to be no-balled again in 1959 and 1960, but then remodelled his action, switching to a slower pace.

The first **sustained spell of no-balling** by an umpire of a bowler in a Test match occurred at Lord's on 24 Jun 1960 when Geoff Griffin of South Africa was 'called' eleven times by umpire Frank Lee, but went on to take the first hat-trick by a South African in Test cricket, his victims being Mike Smith, Peter Walker and Fred Trueman. After the Test, won by England by an innings and 73 runs, an exhibition game was played in which both Lee and Syd Buller again no-balled Griffin, and he never played Test cricket again. Griffin had sustained an accident which left him unable to straighten his right arm. He had twice been no-balled in South Africa in 1958–59 and on several occasions earlier on the South African tour in 1960.

David Gregory, who was to become Australia's first Test captain, was reputedly no-balled for throwing four times in a row—the first under the revised Law X concerning the straightening of the bowling arm, rather than its height—while playing for New South Wales v Victoria at the Albert Ground, Sydney, 9–13 Mar 1872.

TRAGEDIES

An inquest held at West Hoathley, Sussex on 12 Sep 1624 was told that Jasper Vinall, while playing 'crickett' at Horsted Keynes on 28 August, was attempting to take a catch when the batsman, Edward Tye, unwittingly struck Vinall on the head with his 'batt'. Vinall died on 10 September as a result of the blow, the first recorded **fatality at cricket**. The jury returned a verdict of 'misadventure'.

The first recorded **death of a player in Australia** happened when Alured Tasker Paunce, a police magistrate at Queanbeyan, collapsed and died while bending to pick up the ball, playing for Married v Single in Sydney in 1837.

George Summers died in Nottingham on 19 June 1870 from the effects of a blow to the cheek bone by a ball from John Platts, a fast bowler making his first-class debut for MCC v Nottinghamshire at Lord's, the accident occuring on the third day of the match played on 13–15 June 1870. This was the first **fatality due to an accident on the field during a first-class match**.

The first **first-class cricketer to be killed in a motor accident** was George Street, the Sussex wicket-keeper, in a motor-cycle accident in 1924. He played one Test for England v South Africa on the 1922–23 tour.

The first **player to die during a county championship match** was Maurice Nichol, found dead in his hotel room on the second morning of the Worcestershire v Essex match at Chelmsford, 21 May 1934, aged 29.

The first **Test cricketer to die while playing at Lord's** was Andy Ducat in a match between Home Guard units in 1942, 21 years after his one Test. He also played six times for England at soccer.

In the final of the 1958–59 Qaid-I-Azam competition, Karachi v Services at Karachi, 16–21 Jan 1959, wicket-keeper Abdul Aziz retired hurt after being hit over the heart by an off-spinner during Karachi's first innings. After being carried off unconscious, he died on the way to hospital; he was the first to **die in a match in Pakistan**. A heart condition was diagnosed.

OTHER SPORTS

Cricketers with other sporting distinctions:

ANGLING

Tony Pawson became the first first-class cricketer to acquire a **world angling title**, when he won the world fly-fishing title at Salamanca, Spain in 1984. He gained his county cap for Kent in his debut season of 1946, and captained Oxford University in 1948. He also won an amateur international cap for England and played for Charlton Athletic at soccer.

ARCHERY

Henry Palairet played two first-class matches for

E. M. Grace ('The coroner') was overshadowed by the towering talents of his younger brother, but continued to play enthusiastically and sometimes prolifically until his late sixties.

C. B. Fry—a Greek God indeed. Sadly, massive natural talents masked a troubled mind.

the MCC in 1868–69 and was the British national champion at archery in 1876, 1880–3.

ATHLETICS

The first Test cricketer to have been credited with a **world record at an athletics event** was Dr Edward M. Grace, with a triple jump of 12.21m at Bristol on 25 Aug 1866, 14 years before he played in the first Test held in England. His younger brother 'W.G.' achieved a unique double when, after scoring 224 not out (then the highest ever first-class score) for England v Surrey at the Oval on 30–31 Aug 1866, he missed the final day to run at the first National Olympic Association meeting at Crystal Palace on 1 August, when he won the 440 yards hurdles.

Charles Fry was the first **athletics world record holder to captain England** at cricket. He equalled the record at long jump with 7.17m at Oxford on 4 Mar 1893 for Oxford University v London AC. Fry three times won the long jump for Oxford v Cambridge. The first **AAA champion** to play first-class cricket was John Le Fleming, AAA 120 yards hurdles winner in 1887, who played for Kent, 1889–99 and who also played for England at rugby in 1887.

Alastair McCorquodale was the first first-class cricketer to reach an **Olympic final**, as he was fourth at 100m in 1948. He had just one season at the top in athletics before retiring to concentrate on business and play cricket. He made his first-class debut in 1948 and played for Middlesex in 1951.

BASEBALL

Norrie Claxton, who played for South Australia, 1883–96, also represented the state at Australian Rules football and baseball and was a champion cyclist. He donated the Claxton Shield in 1934 as the trophy for the Australian Baseball Championship.

BOXING

Thomas Faulkner, who played for Surrey v Kent at Dartford on 6 July 1750 and for Kent v England at the Artillery Ground on 20–21 May 1751 and in other less important matches, was to have fought Jack Slack for the world heavyweight boxing championship in 1753, but the match was banned by magistrates. Faulkner also twice unsuccessfully fought former champion George Taylor, but on their third meeting Taylor conceded defeat after 77 minutes (perhaps about 20 rounds), and never recovering from the beating he took, died three months later.

The first Test cricketer to have won an **Olympic gold medal** was John Douglas at middleweight in 1908, when he narrowly defeated the great all-round sportsman Reg 'Snowy' Baker of Australia on points. Douglas played in 23 Tests (captain in 18) for England, making his debut when he deputised as captain for Pelham Warner against Australia in 1911–12 when England regained the Ashes. Douglas also gained an England amateur cap at soccer.

EQUESTRIAN EVENTS

Major Peter Borwick, who played three matches for Northants in 1932, was the first first-class cricketer to **ride a horse to an Olympic medal**—a bronze for the British three-day event team in 1948.

FIVES

Peter May became the first Test cricketer to win the Kinnaird Cup, the **amateur doubles championship** at Eton Fives. Partnered by his brother John, his wins were in 1951–3, coincident with the start of his Test career. The first first-class cricketer to win this event had been Howard Fabian (Cambridge blue, 1929–31), four times between 1930 and 1948.

The first notable cricketer to win the Jesters' Club Cup, the **amateur singles championship** at Rugby Fives was Jack Davies in 1936–7 and 1939. He played for Kent, 1934–51, having won his blue at Cambridge 1933–4, and was President of the MCC in 1986.

GOLF

The first **English amateur golf champion** to play first-class cricket was Leonard Crawley, champion in 1931, who played in the Walker Cup teams of 1932, 1934, 1938 and 1947. He made his first-class debut for Worcestershire in 1922, won his blue at Cambridge, 1923–5 and played for Essex, 1926–36. He went on the MCC tour to the West Indies in 1925–26. He had been preceded as the first **international golfer** to play first-class cricket, as Charles Hooman played in the first Walker Cup match for England v USA in 1922, uniquely winning his singles match at an extra hole. He had played cricket for Oxford University and Kent, 1907–10. Eric Dalton became the first Test cricketer to win the **South African amateur golf championship** in 1950. He played in 15 Tests, 1929–39.

No Australian amateur champion has played Test cricket, but the 1932 winner, Dr Reginald Bettington, captained Oxford University and played five times for New South Wales.

HOCKEY

The first **Olympic hockey gold medallist** to have played first-class cricket was Reginald Pridmore (Great Britain, 1908) for Warwickshire in 1909–12. Cyril Wilkinson, who captained Surrey at cricket in 1914 and 1919–20, won a gold medal for Great Britain in 1920. Brian Booth played in 29 Tests for Australia, 1961–66, having played for Australia at hockey at the 1956 Olympic Games. The Australian hockey team that won the World Cup in 1987 included Dr Ric Charlesworth, who played his 201st international for

Australia in the final; he had played for Western Australia at cricket from 1972–73 to 1980.

Lynne Thomas played cricket for England from 1966 to 1978, including 13 Test matches, and also hockey for Wales from 1961 to 1979. She played in three World Cups at cricket: 1973, when she scored the first century, and 1978 for England, and in 1982 when she captained the International XI; and in World Championships at hockey in 1975 for Wales.

Jean Cummins, Rachel Heyhoe-Flint and Janette Brittin have all played both cricket and hockey for England, and Ina Lamason did so for New Zealand.

HORSE RACING

Major Jack Wilson (Yorkshire 1911–12) won the Grand National on *Double Chance* in 1925.

LACROSSE

Joy Partridge was the first **double international** for England at lacrosse (1926–30) and cricket (1930–5). Betty Snowball, in addition to her exploits for England at cricket 1934–48 (see women's cricket) played for Scotland at both lacrosse and squash. Carol Evans played cricket for England (1968–9) and lacrosse for Wales (1962–3).

RACKETS

Harry Foster was the **English amateur champion** at rackets: singles, 1894–1900 and 1904, and eight doubles between 1893 and 1903, including with his brothers Bill in 1898 and Basil in 1903 (seven brothers played first-class cricket!); and at cricket won his blue at Oxford 1894–6 and played for Worcestershire 1899–1925, captaining the county in 1901–10 and 1913. He was, however, preceded as the **amateur rackets champion** by two first-class cricketers: Cyril Buxton, the inaugural singles champion in 1888 won his blue at Cambridge all four years, 1885–8, and Walter Hedley (Somerset) won the inaugural doubles title in 1890. Hubert Doggart became the first Test cricketer to contest the final of the Amateur

Rackets Singles Championship, losing in 1950, as did Colin Cowdrey in 1952.

REAL TENNIS

Henry Crawley (Cambridge University 1886) was amateur champion in 1892–4.

RUGBY LEAGUE

There are no double internationals, but Alan Walker came closest. He played rugby league for Australia on their tour of England in 1947–48 and at cricket went with Australia to South Africa in 1949–50 but did not play in a Test. Test cricketers to play rugby league to a high standard include: Alan Wharton (one Test for England, 1949) for Salford and Broughton Park, Billy Merritt (six Tests for New Zealand, 1929–31) for Halifax, and Maurice Leyland (41 Tests, 1928–38) who played rugby league for Lancashire Schools.

RUGBY UNION

The first **double international at cricket and rugby union** was A. N. 'Monkey' Hornby. He made three Test appearances, 1879–84, his first against Australia at Melbourne on 2–4 Jan 1879, and played nine times for England at rugby, 1877–82. He was also the first man to **captain England at both sports**, both of which he did in

*The first **cricket match played on a ship** was in 1859 aboard the Great Eastern, which had been built by Isambard Kingdom Brunel, and launched in 1858. With 18914 gross tonnage, 692 ft long and a beam of 120 ft, it was the largest ship ever built at that time. The game was played while the ship was in Southampton Water, prior to its first Atlantic crossing.*

1882, at rugby against Scotland and at cricket against Australia at The Oval on 28–29 August, when Australia achieved their first win in England and as a result of which the Ashes came into being. He also captained England at cricket in the first Test in 1884. The first man to captain England to wins at both cricket and soccer was Andrew Stoddart. He played in 16 tests, 1888–99, captaining England eight times, and played ten times at rugby, 1885–8, four as captain. His first Test captaincy was in a drawn match against Australia at Lord's on 17–19 July 1893 and his first win against Australia at Sydney on 14–20 Dec 1894.

The wicket-keeper Gregor MacGregor played in eight Tests for England, 1890–3, and was the first **Test cricketer to play rugby for Scotland**, 13 caps 1890–6. The next was 'Kim' Elgie (eight caps 1954–5) who played three tests for South Africa in 1961–62. The first and only **Test cricketer who has played rugby for Wales** was the Glamorgan captain Maurice Turnbull. He appeared in nine Tests for England

in 1930–6, played twice for the Welsh rugby team in 1933 and also played hockey for Wales.

The first **rugby international to play Test cricket for Australia** was Sammy Woods. For England he played 13 internationals at rugby, 1890–5, having played in three tests for Australia at cricket in 1888 in England. He later played in three Tests for England v South Africa, 1895–96. He won his blue at Cambridge, 1888–91, and played for Somerset 1891–1910. The first to play both games for Australia was Otto Nothling, whose one Test was against England in 1928.

William Milton played rugby for England in 1874 and cricket for **South Africa** in their first three Tests (two as captain), 1889–92, but the first man to play both games for South Africa was Alfred Richards, with three rugby internationals in 1891, the last as captain. He captained South Africa in his one Test match, at Cape Town on 21, 23 Mar 1896, when he scored 6 and 0.

For **New Zealand**, George Dickinson played three Tests 1930–2, and at rugby he went on the NZ tour to Australia in 1922 but did not play in a

Opposite *The Gentlemen of 1894 who played the Players at Lord's, when F. S. Jackson and S. M. J. Woods bowled unchanged and victoriously. The group shows seven current or future Test men, and, in Woods, Stoddart and MacGregor, three football Internationals.*

Teddy Wynyard, Army officer, forthright and determined as both cricketer and personality. He played for Hampshire irregularly from 1878 to 1908 and won the F.A. Cup winners' medal for Old Carthusians in 1881.

full international. The first full double international was Eric Tindall, rugby 1936, cricket 1937–47. The first New Zealand Test cricketer to play rugby for England was Martin Donnelly, seven Tests, 1937–49, and rugby for England against Ireland in 1947.

SNOOKER

Albert Brown, who played one match for Warwickshire in 1932, is the most distinguished snooker player amongst first-class cricketers. He was beaten 5–3 by John Pulman in the final of the 1946 English amateur championship and was beaten by Walter Donaldson in the semi-finals of the world championships in 1950 and 1952.

SOCCER

The first **double international at soccer and cricket** was the Hon. Alfred Lyttelton, soccer for England 1877, cricket 1880–4. He was also the first Test cricketer to have played in the **FA Cup Final,** for Old Etonians, beaten 3–0 by Wanderers in a replay after a 0–0 draw in 1876. His elder brother Edward was also in that team and played first-class cricket for Cambridge University and Middlesex. R. E. 'Tip' Foster is the only man to have captained England at both soccer and cricket. He played in five full internationals at soccer in 1900–02 and in eight Tests, 1903–07.

The first Test cricketer to have received an **FA Cup winners medal** was Edward Wynyard, for Old Carthusians, who beat Old Etonians 3–0 in 1881. He played three Tests for England in 1896–1906.

The first man to have been an international at both cricket and soccer for England and to have been on winning sides in the major competitions at both sports was Harry Makepeace; he played four times for England at each sport, with Everton won an FA Cup winners medal in 1906, and the League title in 1915, and played for Lancashire's County Championship winning side in 1926–9.

The first, and only, man to play **first-class cricket and soccer on the same day** was Chris

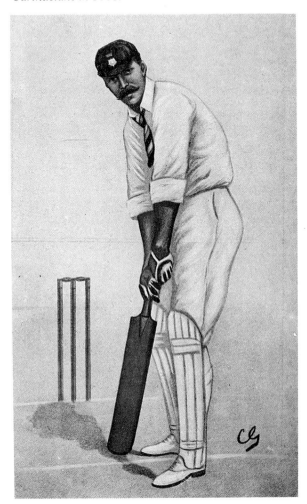

Balderstone on 15 Sep 1975. After batting for Leicestershire v Derbyshire at Chesterfield, he played an hour later, after a hectic car journey, at home for Doncaster Rovers v Brentford in a Football League Division Four match, which was a 1–1 draw; 51 not out overnight, he took his score to 116 the next day.

SQUASH

The first winner of the **British amateur championship,** 1922–3, was Tommy Jameson, who played cricket for Hampshire, 1919–32, and went on MCC tours to the West Indies, 1925–26, and South America, 1926–27.

TABLE TENNIS

Charles Bull (Kent and Worcestershire, 1929–39) won the **English Open** men's doubles table tennis title three times, 1928–30, with Fred Perry.

Louis Devereux, who played for Middlesex, Worcestershire and Glamorgan in his first-class career, 1949–60, played for England at table tennis in Prague in November 1949.

TENNIS

The first **Wimbledon champion** to have played first-class cricket was Spencer Gore, who played two matches for Surrey in 1874–5, and who won the men's singles title in 1877. His successor as Wimbledon champion, Patrick Hadow, played four matches for Middlesex, 1873–4.

Cota Ramaswami played in two **Davis Cup** ties for India at tennis in 1922. When he played in two Tests against England in 1936 at the age of 40, making 40 and 60 on his debut, he became the first such double international. Percy Sherwell had, however, prior to institution of the Davis Cup, won the **South African singles** title in 1904 and doubles titles in 1903–04 at tennis and later played against England. He participated in 13 Tests as captain and wicket-keeper, 1906–11, and on his debut at the Old Wanderers, Johannesburg, led South Africa to its first Test win against England.

Dr Les Poidevin played Davis Cup tennis for Australia, losing all three matches in 1906, while a Lancashire cricketer. He had previously played for New South Wales, and in the 1918–19 season became the first Australian to score a hundred centuries in all matches in his career.

POLITICIANS AND STATESMEN

Although it is difficult to be certain, it is thought that Sir William Gage, **Member of Parliament** for Seaford, 1727–44, was the first MP to play 'first-class' cricket, for Sussex v Kent in Penshurst Park, August 1728.

Sir Alec Douglas-Home, as Lord Dunglass, played first-class cricket for Middlesex, 1924–25, Oxford University, 1926, and went on the MCC tour to South America, 1926–27. He was the first first-class cricketer to become **Prime Minister** of England. However, Francis H. D. Bell, who had played for Wellington, 1873–7, achieved that distinction in New Zealand, where he was Prime Minister for just two weeks, 14–30 May 1925. The Duke of Wellington, great soldier and later Prime Minister, played, as the Hon. Captain Wesley (later Wellesley), for All-Ireland v The Garrison in 1792, but only scored 5 and 1 (see Ireland).

The captain of the Bombay Governor's XI which played the Commonwealth XI at Bombay, 25–27 Nov 1950, was the governor himself, Raja Maharaj Singh. He made 4 in his only innings and became the first man to play **first-class cricket over the age of 70**. Born at Kapurthala, India on 17 May 1878, he was 72 years 192 days old when he batted on the opening day of the match. Many years earlier, as Kunwar Singh, he had been educated at Harrow and Balliol College, Oxford, where he had played no cricket of any standard but had won a boxing blue.

First first-class cricketers to achieve the following notable offices:

Viceroy of India: Viscount Chelmsford, 1916–21. As the Hon. Frederic Thesiger he won his blue at Oxford University in 1888, 1890–1 and played for Middlesex. He had previously been the Governor of both Queensland and New South Wales, and in 1924 became First Lord of the Admiralty.

Governor-General of Australia: Lord Forster of Lepe, 1920–5, who had played for Hampshire and Oxford University in a career 1885–95, following 27 years as MP for Sevenoaks.

Governor-General of New Zealand: 10th Viscount Cobham, 1957–62. As the Hon. Charles Lyttelton he was a very fine cricketer, who captained Worcestershire, 1936–9. He was President of the MCC in 1954 and its Treasurer in 1963–4.

Governor-General of Canada: Lord Willingdon, 1926–31. As Thomas Freeman, later Freeman-Thomas, he played for Cambridge University and Sussex, 1886–90, reappearing in

David Sheppard of Sussex and England with Archbishop Ramsey of Canterbury, after being consecrated Bishop of Woolwich, in 1969.

first-class matches in India, 1916–9, when he was Governor of Bombay. He was Viceroy of India in 1931–6.

First first-class cricketers to fill leading British offices:

Lord Chancellor: Lord Loreburn, 1905–12. As Robert Reid he was an Oxford blue in 1866–8. He was also the first first-class cricketer to be Solicitor General and Attorney General.

Colonial Secretary: the Hon. Alfred Lyttelton, 1903–05. He played four Tests for England, 1880–4, and played for Cambridge University and Middlesex.

Home Secretary: Viscount Bridgeman, 1922. He won his Cambridge blue in 1887 and played county cricket for Shropshire and Staffordshire.

A unique double of **Lord Mayor of London** was achieved by two Studds. Sir Kynaston Studd was Lord Mayor in 1928–9, having played for Middlesex and Cambridge University, and his great-nephew, Sir Peter Studd, was Lord Mayor in 1970–1, having won his blue at Cambridge in 1937–9. Both were captain of Cambridge, Kynaston succeeding his younger brothers, George and Charles, both of whom played for England, in that office.

THE CHURCH

The first **Test cricketer to become a bishop** was David Sheppard, Bishop of Liverpool since 1975. He played in 22 Tests for England, 1950–63. Ordained in 1955, he was recalled to the England team against Australia in 1956 and made 113 at Old Trafford, the first **Test appearance and century by a serving priest**. He played only limited first-class cricket from then, and not at all in 1961, but in 1962 he made a remarkable return to score 100 in the final Gentlemen v Players match at Lord's, play in two Tests v Pakistan and tour Australia and New Zealand in 1962–63, playing in all the Tests, scoring 113 v Australia at Melbourne. That was the end of his first-class career.

Tom Killick of Middlesex and Cambridge University was ordained a year after he had made two Test appearances for England v South Africa, opening the innings with Jack Hobbs. No Reverend has played Test cricket for Australia, but E. F. 'Mick' Waddy came close; ordained in 1905, he was 12th man against England at Sydney in the fifth Test in 1907–08, at the end of a season in which he topped the Australian first-class averages (351 runs av. 70.20).

The first **professional cricketer to take holy orders** was Jack Parsons in 1929. His first-class career stretched from 1910 to 1936, and he played regularly for Warwickshire. He also won the Military Cross in a cavalry charge during World War I.

KNIGHTHOODS

The first man to be **knighted for his services to cricket** was Francis Lacey in 1926, on the conclusion of his 28 years as Secretary of the MCC. He won his blue at Cambridge in 1882 and played for Hampshire 1880–97.

The first **Test cricketer to be knighted for his services to the game** was Sir Pelham Warner in 1937. He had played 15 Tests for England, 1899–1912, ten as captain, and his influence in cricket was legion, including many stints as a Test selector between 1905 and 1938. He founded *The Cricketer* magazine in 1921 and was President of the MCC in 1950–51.

The first **Test knight from Australia** was Sir Don Bradman, 1949, and the first from the **West Indies** Sir Frank Worrell in 1964. The first **professional cricketer** to be knighted was Sir John Berry Hobbs in 1953.

MCC

The first **Test cricketer to take on the position as President and Treasurer of the MCC** was the 4th Lord Harris, the father-figure of Kent cricket for some 50 years. He captained England in four Tests in 1879–84, was President of the MCC in 1895 and was Treasurer from 1916 to his death in 1932. He was appointed Under-Secretary of State for India in 1885 and was later Under-Secretary for War and Governor of Bengal.

The first Test cricketer to become **Secretary of the MCC** was S. C. 'Billy' Griffith, 1962–74. A fine wicket-keeper, he scored his maiden first-class century on his Test debut for England v West Indies at Queen's Park Oval, Port-of-Spain, Trinidad on 11 Feb 1948.

The first **professional cricketer to be elec-**

---

*The first **cigarette cards** depicting cricket were issued in 1882. The first major set featuring cricketers was one of 50 issued by Wills in 1896.*

---

ted a member of the MCC during his playing career** was Len Hutton, who was knighted in 1956, following his retirement as England captain.

ROYALTY

Cricket was first known to have been **patronised by a member of the Royal Family** in 1702, when Charles II's illegitimate son, Charles, 1st Duke of Richmond, of Goodwood House is said to have rewarded his team with brandy after their defeat at Arundel. The Earl of Sussex, a son-in-law of Charles II, is known to have attended a 'crekitt match' on Dicker Common, Sussex in 1677.

Cricket was first known to have been **played by a member of the Royal family** in 1723 by James II's son, 'The Old Pretender', who was exiled in Rome, and who had 'a great number of batts and other utensils for cricket-playing' imported for the purpose.

The first **reigning monarchs known to have attended a game of cricket** were King George III and Queen Charlotte, who, from a tent in a nearby garden, watched the play on Richmond Green on 17 Aug 1767. Afterwards the King ordered all the players a dinner at the Feathers Inn and gave the winners a guinea each, the loser 10s 6d each. On 20 Aug 1770 King George donated a silver cup 'to be played for at cricket' on Richmond Green, 'on account of the Princes' (who included the future King George IV) 'having been much pleased with a cricket match there on Monday last'. Later the King gave another silver cup to be played for by Richmond and the Temple Mills calico-printing works 'for the amusement of the young princes' on Kew Green on 3 Sep 1770.

HRH Prince Christian-Victor of Schleswig-Holstein was the first member of the Royal Family to play **first-class cricket**, as he played for I Zingari v Gentlemen of England at Scarborough, 29–31 Aug 1887, scoring 35 and 0.

The Revd. Lord Frederick Beauclerk, who was the leading cricketer at the turn of the 19th century and a notable administrator at Lord's, was a great-grandson of Charles II and actress Nell Gwynn, Duchess of St Albans. He was the son of the 5th Duke.

THE ARTS AND LITERATURE

Cricket first featured on the **theatrical stage** when George Alexander Stevens 'in the character of a cricketeer' spoke the prologue of 'the play desir'd by the gentlemen cricketeers of Barrow' produced at the Norwich Theatre on or shortly before 15 Sep 1744.

Cricket featured in **opera** for the first time in the production of Macfarren's *She Stoops to Conquer* at Covent Garden, London in 1864. This contained 'a very characteristic cricket chorus', set against the scene of a match on the village green.

The first man to write **a poem to celebrate his first** (and only) **first-class wicket** was Sir Arthur Conan Doyle, the creator of Sherlock Holmes, who, on his first-class debut at the age of 41, playing for the MCC against London County on 25 Aug 1900, dismissed W. G. Grace, caught behind. Two years later in the same fixture he obtained his highest first-class score, 43, and was stumped off the bowling of Grace.

A game was **played on stage** at the Coliseum, London in February 1908 by four-a-side teams from Middlesex and Surrey, including Test players, such as Jack Hobbs. The pitch was 15 yards (14m) long and light bats and balls were used. Contested over a week of shows, Middlesex were the winners.

The first first-class cricketer to win a **Nobel Prize** was the Irish playwright Samuel Beckett in 1969. He had played for Dublin University in two matches against Northants in 1925 and 1926.

The first full-length **feature film** based on cricket was *The Final Test*, directed by Anthony Asquith with screenplay by Terence Rattigan in 1953. Starring Jack Warner, who played a Test cricketer in his final season, and Robert Morley, it included appearances by several England Test cricketers.

Below *Sir Arthur Conan Doyle played first-class cricket and dismissed W. G. Grace. The names of many of his fictional characters betrayed his cricket interest.*

Bottom of page *Sam Beckett played first-class cricket before he wrote* Waiting for Godot *and earned international literary recognition.*

WOMEN'S CRICKET

The first recorded **women's cricket match** was played at Gosden Common, near Guildford, Surrey, when eleven maids of Hambledon beat eleven maids of Bramley by 127 notches to 119. The *Reading Mercury* of 26 July 1745 reported of the game played 'on 26th of last month' that 'the girls bowled, batted, ran, and catched as well as most men could do at that game'.

The first **inter-county match** was in 1811, when Hampshire beat Surrey by 14 runs at Newington Green, Middlesex. The match was made by two noblemen for 500 guineas.

The first recorded **women's cricket club** was the White Heather, formed in Yorkshire in 1887 owing to 'the large amount of cricket being played at Normanhurst, Glynde and Eridge'; their first match was played in 1888. Their membership grew from eight in 1887 to 50 in 1890, and the club, whose most notable member was Lucy Ridsdale, later Mrs Stanley Baldwin, was in existence until 1950.

The first **women's touring team** was organised by the English Cricket and Athletic Association Ltd., two teams known as 'The Original English Lady Cricketers' who travelled incognito but extensively in 1890 playing exhibition games. Their first match, at Liverpool on Easter Monday, was watched by a crowd of 15 000.

The first **national association** was the Women's Cricket Association (WCA) formed in London on 4 Oct 1926; its inaugural chairman was Mrs Heron-Maxwell. Its laws were those of the MCC, except that a smaller (5oz/142g) ball was determined. The International Women's Cricket Council (IWCC) was formed in Australia on 19 Feb 1958 by Australia, England, the Netherlands, New Zealand and South Africa.

The first **women's representative match** was played at Beckenham, Kent on 17 July 1929, a draw between London & District and the Rest of England. In this match Carol Valentine took 6–32, including the first **hat-trick** in a major fixture. The first **inter-county match** was contested by Durham v Cheshire and Lancashire at Castle Eden on 12 Aug 1931.

The first woman to score a **century** was Miss Norcross, 107 for Single v Married Ladies at Cobham in 1788; the first **double century** was by Mabel Bryant, 224 not out for Visitors v Residents at Eastbourne, August 1901.

The first woman bowler to take **all ten wickets for 0 runs** was Rubina Winifred Humphries for Dalton Ladies v Woodfield SC at Huddersfield on 26 June 1931.

Women's Cricket, edited by Marjorie Pollard, was the appropriate title for the first **publication devoted exclusively to the women's game**. It first appeared in May 1930. In the previous year there had been three special cricket numbers published of *Hockey Field & Lacrosse*.

The first men's county ground to be used for a women's match was that at Worcester on 24 June 1932. On this ground, Betty Archdale, playing for The South v The West on 8 July 1933, scored the first **century in a representative match**. Women first played at The Oval on 15 June 1935, England Touring Team v Rest of England, and at Lord's for the WCA 50th Jubilee match on 4 Aug 1976, when England (162–2) beat Australia (161) by eight wickets.

The first **international tour** by women was that by England to Australia and New Zealand in 1934–5. In Australia the tourists, captained by Betty Archdale, won seven and drew seven of their 14 matches and they won all seven in New Zealand. Four Test matches were contested, England beating Australia 2–0 with one drawn and New Zealand 1–0.

TEST CRICKET

The first **women's Test match** was held at Brisbane on 28–31 Dec 1934; England beat Australia by nine wickets. Scores: Australia 47 (M. Maclagan 7–10) and 138 (E. Shevill 63*, M. Spear 5–15); England 154 (M. Maclagan 72, A. Palmer 7–18) and 34–1. Myrtle Maclagan took the first wicket, indeed the first **five wickets**, ending with marvellous figures of 7–10, before scoring the first **50**. Nell McLarty of Australia made the first **duck**. In the second Test, at Sydney on 4, 7–8 Jan 1935, Maclagan scored the first **Test century**, 119´ and with Betty Snowball (71) put on the first **century stand**, 145 for the first

This ladies' match is dated 1889 but they played the game very much earlier.

wicket, in England's score of 301–5 dec. Snow-ball also made four stumpings in an innings, still a Test record.

Against New Zealand at Christchurch on 16, 18 Feb 1935, England responded to New Zealand's 44 (Maclagan 5–22) by amassing the first **Test score of over 500**, and their total remains a test record. In their 503–5 dec. Betty Snowball scored 189 in 222 minutes (a Test record until Sandhya Aggarwal scored 190 for India against England in 1986) and Molly Hide 110. Together they put on 235 for the second wicket, the first **stand over 200** in Tests. New Zealand scored 122 in their second innings, as England won by an innings and 337 runs, the first Test match innings victory. The first **sisters to play in Tests** were the Australians Esse and Rene Shevill and Margaret and Barbara Peden who played together in the second Test at Sydney in 1935. Margaret Peden was Australia's first Test captain, and she led their first tour of England, in 1937 when the

Australians won 11, lost 1 and drew 7 of their 19 matches, including 1–1 with one drawn in the Test series. The first Australian Test victory was by 31 runs in the first Test at Northampton on 12–15 June: England 204 and 167, Australia 300 and 102.

The first woman to score **1000 runs in a Test career** was Myrtle Maclagan, whose final record was 1007 runs av. 41.95 in 14 Tests. She was also the first to take **50 wickets**, ending with 60 av. 15.60.

Rachael Heyhoe-Flint, also a hockey interna-tional, hit the first **six in a Test**, for England in 1963. She achieved the most runs in a Test career, 1814 av. 49.02 in 25 matches, 1960–79.

The first woman to achieve the **double of 1000 runs and 100 wickets for a touring team** was Enid Bakewell for England in Aus-tralia and New Zealand in 1968–9. In 20 matches she scored 1031 runs (av. 39.65) and took 118 wickets (av. 9.77). With 113 v Australia at Burton

Oval in 1968 she had been the first England player to score a century on her Test debut. She was also the first England cricketer, man or woman, to score a **century and take ten wickets in a Test match**, when v West Indies at Edgbaston on 1–3 July 1979 she scored 68 and 112 not out and took 3–14 and 7–61.

The first wicket-keeper to take **five dismissals in a Test innings** was Shirley Hodges for England v New Zealand in the second innings of both second and third Tests in 1969; in each she took a record six in the match.

WORLD CUP

The first World Cup competition was staged in England in June and July 1973. Contested by five nations at 60 overs per side matches, the winners were England, captained by Rachael Heyhoe-Flint, who beat Australia in the final at Edgbaston by 92 runs. Subsequent World Cup competitions have been held in India in 1977–8 and in New Zealand in 1982, Australia winning on both occasions.

In the first match, International XI v England, the first wicket was taken by Mary Pilling, that of Audrey Disbury (22) of England playing for the International XI, for whom New Zealand's Patricia McKelvey (54) made the first 50. In reply England's Lynne Thomas made the first **century**, 134, adding 246 (still the record partnership) for the first wicket with Enid Bakewell (101*).

The first bowler to take **five wickets in an innings** was Tina Macpherson, 5–14 for Australia v Young England in 1973.

AUSTRALIA

The first women's match in Australia was played by miners' daughters at Bendigo, Victoria on 21 Apr 1874. The *Melbourne Argus* reported that the players wore calico dresses and red and blue jackets. The first **inter-colonial match** was between Victoria and New South Wales in Sydney in 1890, but the inter-State championships did not start until 1931, when New South Wales were the inaugural winners.

The first major **association** was the Victorian Women's Cricket Association, originally formed in 1905, and it disbanded and was reformed in 1923. The Australian Women's Cricket Council was formed in 1931 by Victoria, NSW and Queensland, with South Australia and Western Australia joining in 1934.

Rosalie Deane, batting for Inter-colonial Ladies v Sydney Cricket Club on the Sydney Cricket Ground in 1891 scored 195 and 104, the first instance anywhere in the world of a woman scoring a **century in each innings**. She then scored 139 against Morpeth Ladies at West Maitland, three hundreds in successive innings. She was the first **woman cricketer recorded in Wisden**.

The first women's **score of over 500**, and still the highest ever, was 567 by Tarana v Rockley at Rockley, New South Wales in October 1896.

The first **double century** in a major match by an Australian woman was 200 retired by Pat Holmes at Basingstoke for Australians v West, 3–5 July 1937. The first **triple century** in any match was 390 not out by Dot Laughton for YWCA Golds v Wyverns on 19 Mar 1949; this remains the highest ever score by a woman.

The first Australian to score a **Test century** was Una Paisley, with 108 v New Zealand at Wellington in 1948. She put on a record 163 for the fourth wicket with Betty Wilson, who went on to score the first Test century against England, 111 at Adelaide on 15 Jan 1949. In that match Wilson became the first woman to score a **century and take five wickets in a Test innings**, with 6–23 in England's first innings 72. Wilson's 7–7, including the first, and to date only, **Test match hat-trick** against England at St Kilda's ground on 22 Feb 1958, was Australia's best ever bowling performance. On the same day Mary Duggan took 7–6 for England, as Australia were out for 38 and England for 35, the lowest totals in women's Test history. With a second innings score of exactly 100 and taking 4–9 in England's second innings Betty Wilson became the first man or woman to achieve a **Test match double of 100 runs and ten wickets**.

'A match between the Countess of Derby and some other Ladies of Quality and Fashion, at Seven Oaks, Kent, 1779.'

The first **triple century partnership** in Tests was 309 for the third wicket by Denise Annetts, who scored the Test record 193 in 381 minutes, and Lindsay Reeler (110 not out) for Australia v England at Collingham, West Yorkshire on 23–24 Aug 1987.

NEW ZEALAND

The first recorded women's match was played in Nelson in 1886. The first provincial association was that of Auckland, formed in 1928. The New Zealand Women's Cricket Council was founded in 1934, a year prior to the first tour by England, who won the first Test contested by New Zealand (see above).

The first tour by a New Zealand team was to New South Wales, to coincide with the 150th anniversary of the state, in 1938. New Zealand's first tour to England was in 1954, and their first Test victory was against Australia in 1972.

OTHER TEST PLAYING NATIONS

The first visit by a **Dutch** women's team to Britain was in 1937, three years after the formation of the Nederlandse Dames Cricket Bond.

The South African & Rhodesian Women's Cricket Association was founded in 1952.

South Africa's first Test match was against the visiting England team on their tour in 1960–1; England won one and the other three Tests were drawn.

The **Jamaican** Women's Cricket Association was formed in 1966. In 1971 they hosted a triangular series against England and Trinidad, but merged with other islands to form the West Indies team from 1973, when the Caribbean Women's Cricket Federation was founded. The **West Indies** played their first Tests against Australia in Jamaica in 1976.

The Women's Cricket Association of **India** was founded in 1973. Their first 'Tests' were against Australia under-25s in 1975, and they hosted tours by New Zealand in 1976 and by West Indies in 1977. First tours to England were conducted by the West Indies in 1979 and by India in 1986.

INDEX

CRICKETERS

SELECTED BIBLIOGRAPHY

Cricket Quarterly, 1963–70
Sports Quarterly, 1977–81
Sports History, 1982–87
Wisden Cricketers Almanack, 1864–1987
MCC Cricket Scores & Biographies: Vols 1–15
The Cricketer, 1921 to date
The Cricketer International Quarterly,
   1973 to date
Cricket News, 1977–79
The Cricket Statistician, 1973 to date
Cricket—A Weekly Record of the Game,
   1882–1913
The World of Cricket, 1914
Lillywhites Cricketers Guide, 1849–66
Lillywhites Cricketers Annual, 1872–1900
Lillywhites Cricketers Companion, 1865–85
Fresh Light on 18th Century Cricket, G. B.
   Buckley, 1935
Fresh Light on Pre-Victorian Cricket, G. B.
   Buckley, 1937
Hambledon Cricket Chronicle, F. S. Ashley
   Cooper, 1924
Hambledon's Cricket Glory, Ronald Knight,
   1975–84
The Hambledon Men, E. V. Lucas, 1907
Cricket—A History of its Growth &
   Development, Rowland Bowen, 1970

PICTURE CREDITS